Diabetes & Heart Healthy Meals for Two

Over 170 Delicious Recipes that
Help You (Both) Eat Well and Eat Right

American Heart
Association

Learn and Live

American
Diabetes
Association.

Cure • Care • Commitment®

Director, Book Publishing, Robert Anthony; *Managing Editor, Book Publishing,* Abe Ogden; *Editor,* Rebekah Renshaw; *Production Manager,* Melissa Sprott; *Composition,* Design Literate, Inc. /Jody Billert; *Cover Design,* Jennifer Sage; *Printer,* R. R. Donnelley.

Printed in the United States of America
1 3 5 7 9 10 8 6 4 2

The suggestions and information contained in this publication are generally consistent with the *Clinical Practice Recommendations* and other policies of the American Diabetes Association, but they do not represent the policy or position of the Association or any of its boards or committees. Reasonable steps have been taken to ensure the accuracy of the information presented. However, the American Diabetes Association cannot ensure the safety or efficacy of any product or service described in this publication. Individuals are advised to consult a physician or other appropriate health care professional before undertaking any diet or exercise program or taking any medication referred to in this publication. Professionals must use and apply their own professional judgment, experience, and training and should not rely solely on the information contained in this publication before prescribing any diet, exercise, or medication. The American Diabetes Association—its officers, directors, employees, volunteers, and members—assumes no responsibility or liability for personal or other injury, loss, or damage that may result from the suggestions or information in this publication.

♾ The paper in this publication meets the requirements of the ANSI Standard Z39.48-1992 (permanence of paper).

ADA titles may be purchased for business or promotional use or for special sales. To purchase more than 50 copies of this book at a discount, or for custom editions of this book with your logo, contact the American Diabetes Association at the address below, at booksales@diabetes.org, or by calling 703-299-2046.

For all other inquiries, please call 1-800-DIABETES.

American Diabetes Association
1701 North Beauregard Street
Alexandria, Virginia 22311

American Heart Association
7272 Greenville Avenue
Dallas, Texas 75231
1-800-AHA-USA1
www.americanheart.org

Library of Congress Cataloging-in-Publication Data

Diabetes and heart healthy cookbook 2 / American Diabetes Association and American Heart Association.
    p. cm.
  Includes index.
  ISBN 978-1-58040-305-4 (alk. paper)
  1. Diabetes--Diet therapy--Recipes. 2. Heart--Diseases--Diet therapy--Recipes. I. American Diabetes Association. II. American Heart Association.

  RC662.D496 2008
  641.5'6314--dc22

            2008033646

TABLE OF CONTENTS

ACKNOWLEDGEMENTS

American Heart Association Consumer Publications

Director:	Linda S. Ball
Managing Editor:	Deborah A. Renza
Senior Editor:	Janice Roth Moss
Science Editor/Writer:	Jacqueline F. Haigney
Assistant Editor:	Roberta Westcott Sullivan
Senior Marketing Manager:	Bharati Gaitonde

Recipe Developers

Ellen Boeke

Linda Drachman

Mary Ellen Evans

Nancy S. Hughes

Annie King

Kathryn Moore

Carol Ritchie

Cheryl Sternman Rule

Julie Shapero, RD, LD

Carla Fitzgerald Williams

Roxanne Wyss

MAKING HEALTHY CHOICES

When you make healthy food and lifestyle choices, you and your family can enjoy the benefits for years to come. The most important things are to develop a healthy eating pattern that includes a wide variety of nutritious foods and to be physically active.

EAT A VARIETY OF NUTRIENT-RICH FOODS

You may be eating plenty of food, but your body may not be getting the nutrients it needs to be healthy. Nutrient-rich foods provide vitamins, minerals, fiber, and other nutrients, without a lot of empty calories.

Eat a diet rich in vegetables and fruits

- Focus on eating the deeply colored vegetables and fruits, such as spinach, carrots, peaches, and berries. They tend to be higher in vitamins and minerals than others, such as white potatoes.
- Eat whole vegetables (fresh, frozen, or canned) and fruits instead of drinking juice.
- When fresh fruits are not available to you, choose frozen and canned vegetables and fruits in water without added sugar, saturated and trans fats, or salt.
- Prepare vegetables and fruits without added saturated and trans fats, sugar, and salt.

Choose whole-grain, high-fiber foods

Choose whole-grain foods, such as whole wheat, oats/oatmeal, rye, barley, and corn. Also try popcorn, brown rice, wild rice, buckwheat, bulgur (cracked wheat), millet, quinoa, and sorghum. Choose breads and other foods that list whole grains as the first item in the ingredient list.

Eat fish, preferably fish containing omega-3 fatty acids, at least twice a week

- Examples of fish that are relatively high in omega-3 fatty acids include salmon, trout, and tuna.

- Grill, bake, or poach fish. Limit commercially fried fish and don't add cream sauces.

- Prepare fish without added saturated and trans fats.

EAT LESS OF THE NUTRIENT-POOR FOODS

The Nutrition Facts label on packaged foods can help you identify the amount of carbohydrate, saturated fat, trans fat, cholesterol, sodium (salt), and other nutrients in foods. The ingredients list can also help you identify foods that have added sugars. The nutritional information in this book also includes the Exchanges/Choices for each recipe. These Exchanges/Choices are calculated from the new Choose Your Foods: Exchange Lists for Diabetes published by the American Diabetes Association and American Dietetics Association.

Limit how much saturated fat, trans fat, and cholesterol you eat

- Choose lean meats and poultry without skin and prepare them without added saturated and trans fats.

- Remove all visible fat from meat and poultry before cooking.

- Grill, bake, or broil meats and poultry.

- Cut back on processed meat that is high in saturated fat and sodium.

Nutrition Facts

Serving Size 1 cup (228g)
Servings Per Container 2

Amount Per Serving

Calories 260   **Calories from Fat** 120

	% Daily Value*
Total Fat 13 g	**20%**
Saturated Fat 5g	**25%**
Trans Fat 2g	
Cholesterol 30 mg	**10%**
Sodium 660mg	**28%**
Total Carbohydrate 31 g	**10%**
Dietary Fiber 0g	**0%**
Sugars 5g	
Protein 5g	

Vitamin A 4%	•	Vitamin C 2%
Calcium 15%	•	Iron 4%

*Percent Daily Values are based on a 2,000 calorie diet. Your Daily Values may be higher or lower depending on your calorie needs.

	Calories:	2,000	2,500
Total Fat	Less than	65g	80g
Sat Fat	Less than	20g	25g
Cholesterol	Less than	300mg	300mg
Sodium	Less than	2,400mg	2,400mg
Total Carbohydrate		300g	375g
Dietary Fiber		25g	30g

Calories per gram:
Fat 9   •   Carbohydrate 4   •   Protein 4

Select fat-free, 1% fat, and low-fat dairy products

- Reduce your intake of whole milk and other full-fat dairy products, such as yogurt and cheese.

- If you drink whole or 2% milk or use whole-fat dairy products, gradually switch to fat-free or low-fat dairy products.

Cut back on foods containing partially hydrogenated vegetable oils to reduce trans fat in your diet

- Use liquid vegetable oils and light tub margarines in place of hard margarine or shortening.

- Limit cakes, cookies, crackers, pastries, pies, muffins, doughnuts, and French fries made with partially hydrogenated or saturated fats.

Cut back on foods high in dietary cholesterol

- Try to eat less than 300 mg of cholesterol each day.

- Some commonly eaten cholesterol-containing foods include egg yolks, shellfish, organ meats, and whole milk.

Cut back on beverages and foods with added sugars

- Examples of added sugars are sucrose, glucose, fructose, maltose, dextrose, corn syrups, high-fructose corn syrup, concentrated fruit juice, and honey.

- Read the ingredients lists. Choose items that don't have added sugars in their first four listed ingredients.

Choose and prepare foods with little or no salt

- Compare the sodium content of similar products (for example, different brands of tomato sauce) and choose the products with less sodium.

- Aim to eat less than 2,300 mg of salt per day. Some people—African Americans, middle-aged and older adults, and people with high blood pressure—need less than 1,500 mg per day.

If you drink alcohol, drink in moderation

- Limit yourself to one drink per day if you are a woman and two drinks per day if you are a man.

- One drink is equal to 12 ounces of beer, 4 ounces of wine, or 1 1/2 ounces of 80-proof distilled spirits.

Follow the American Heart Association and American Diabetes Association's recommendations when dining out

- To keep portions smaller, split an entrée with your dining partner or take half home when dining alone.

- Ask for sauces and dressing on the side to control the fats, sodium, and calories you eat.

- When ordering, choose foods that have been grilled, baked, steamed, or poached instead of those fried, sautéed, or smothered, or prepared au gratin.

BE PHYSICALLY ACTIVE

- Regular physical activity helps you manage your weight, gives you energy, and strengthens your heart. It also improves the body's sensitivity to insulin and reduces blood pressure and other risk factors for heart disease.

- Aim for at least 30 minutes of moderate physical activity on 5 or more days of the week. If you prefer, you can get the same benefit by accumulating three 10-minute sessions throughout the day.

For more information on cardiovascular health and diabetes, visit www.americanheart.org or www.diabetes.org.

HOW TO USE THESE RECIPES

To help you with meal planning, we have carefully analyzed each recipe in this cookbook to provide useful nutrition information. If your health care professional has told you to follow a recommended diet, read the analyses and choose your recipes carefully. The recipes in this cookbook meet the American Diabetes Association nutrition guidelines, which have been specifically designed to support people with diabetes who strive for improved blood glucose management. They also meet the dietary recommendations of the American Heart Association. We've made every effort to provide accurate nutrition information. Because of the many variables involved in analyzing foods, however, these values should be considered approximate.

EACH ANALYSIS is based on one serving of the dish and includes all the ingredients listed. Optional ingredients and garnishes are not analyzed unless noted; neither are foods suggested as accompaniments.

WHEN A RECIPE gives ingredient options, we analyze the first one listed.

INGREDIENTS WITH A RANGE—for example, a 2 1/2- to 3-pound chicken—are analyzed using the average of the range.

VALUES FOR saturated, trans, monounsaturated, and polyunsaturated fats are rounded and may not add up to the amount listed for total fat.

WE USE OLIVE and canola oils for the analyses as specified in each recipe, but other unsaturated oils, such as corn, safflower, soybean, and sunflower, are also acceptable.

MEATS ARE ANALYZED as cooked and lean, with all visible fat discarded. Values for ground beef are based on meat that is 95% fat free.

IF MEAT, poultry, or seafood is marinated and the marinade is discarded, we calculate only the amount of marinade absorbed. For marinated vegetables and basting liquids, we include the total amount of the marinade in the analysis.

IF A RECIPE includes alcohol and is cooked, we estimate that most of the alcohol calories evaporate during the cooking time.

THE SPECIFIC INGREDIENTS listed in each recipe are analyzed. For instance, we used both fat-free and low-fat cream cheese in this collection of recipes, depending on the taste and texture desired. In each case, the type listed was used for the nutrition analysis. If a recipe calls for a fat-free product but you prefer to use low-fat, go ahead. Just know that the fat values will change with such substitutions. Other nutrient values, such as sodium, may change as well. On the other hand, if you want to substitute reconstituted lemon juice for fresh, or white onions for yellow, the substitutions won't change the ingredient analyses enough to matter.

THE SPECIFIC AMOUNT of an ingredient listed, not the amount sometimes shown in parentheses, is analyzed. The amounts in parentheses are guidelines to help you decide how much of an ingredient to buy for that recipe.

PROCESSED FOODS can be very high in sodium. To keep the level of sodium in our recipes low, we call for unprocessed foods or low-sodium products when possible and add table salt sparingly for flavor. For instance, a recipe may use a can of no-salt-added tomatoes and a quarter-teaspoon of table salt. The amount of sodium in the finished dish will be less than if we called for a regular can of tomatoes and no table salt.

PRODUCTS IN THE marketplace come and go quickly, and the labeling changes as well. To avoid confusion, we use the generic terms "fat-free" for products that may be labeled either "fat-free" or "nonfat" and "low-fat" for products that may be labeled "low-fat" or "reduced-fat." The important thing is to read labels and purchase the lowest-fat, lowest-sodium products available that will provide good results.

WE USE THE abbreviations "g" for gram and "mg" for milligram.

EVERY RECIPE ALSO includes a preparation time, the amount of time we think the average person will need to remove the ingredients from the pantry, refrigerator, or freezer and do any *mise en place* steps (getting the ingredients ready for combining), such as rinsing, peeling, slicing, and measuring. In almost every instance, we rounded up to the nearest five-minute increment.

APPETIZERS, SNACKS, AND BEVERAGES

AVOCADO-CUCUMBER DIP

Serves 2; 1/4 cup per serving
Preparation time: 5 minutes

For an elegant appetizer, dip thick slices of cucumber or slender leaves of Belgian endive into this refreshing mixture.

1/2 small avocado
1 pickling cucumber (such as Kirby), or 1/3 small cucumber
2 tablespoons fat-free sour cream
1 teaspoon chopped fresh mint or 1/4 teaspoon dried mint, crumbled
1 teaspoon fresh lime juice
1/8 teaspoon salt
1/8 teaspoon celery seeds
1/8 teaspoon pepper

1. In a medium bowl, mash the avocado with a fork until the desired consistency (slightly chunky or smooth).

2. Finely chop the pickling cucumber or peel, seed, and finely chop the regular cucumber. (You should get about 1/3 cup.) Stir the cucumber and remaining ingredients into the avocado. Serve immediately or cover and refrigerate for up to 8 hours.

COOK'S TIP: *To store the remaining avocado half, leave the peel on and either rinse the cut surface with cold water or sprinkle it with fresh lemon juice, lime juice, or white vinegar. Cover with plastic wrap or place in an airtight container and refrigerate. The avocado will keep for one to two days (discard any discolored flesh).*

Exchanges/Choices
1 Fat

Calories	55	
Calories from Fat	30	
Total Fat	3.5	g
Saturated Fat	0.5	g
Trans Fat	0.0	g
Polyunsaturated Fat	0.5	g
Monounsaturated Fat	2.4	g
Cholesterol	0	mg
Sodium	160	mg
Total Carbohydrate	3	g
Dietary Fiber	2	g
Sugars	1	g
Protein	2	g

GOAT CHEESE AND GARLIC SPREAD

Serves 2; 2 tablespoons per serving
Preparation time: 5 minutes

This four-ingredient appetizer is so easy to make you'll want to serve it often. Enjoy this spread on a variety of raw vegetables, such as cucumbers and bell peppers, or on low-sodium whole-wheat crackers without trans fat.

3/4 ounce low-fat soft goat cheese
2 tablespoons fat-free sour cream
1/2 medium garlic clove, minced
1 tablespoon snipped fresh parsley

1. In a small bowl, stir together the goat cheese, sour cream, and garlic until well combined. Sprinkle with the parsley.

COOK'S TIP: *To soften the goat cheese quickly, put it on a microwaveable plate. Microwave on 100% power (high) for 10 seconds.*

Exchanges/Choices		
1 Lean Meat		
Calories	35	
Calories from Fat	15	
Total Fat	1.5	**g**
Saturated Fat	1.1	g
Trans Fat	0.0	g
Polyunsaturated Fat	0.0	g
Monounsaturated Fat	0.4	g
Cholesterol	10	**mg**
Sodium	60	**mg**
Total Carbohydrate	1	**g**
Dietary Fiber	0	g
Sugars	1	g
Protein	3	**g**

CHERRY TOMATO TOPPERS

Serves 2; 8 tomato halves and 1 1/2 tablespoons topping mixture per serving
Preparation time: 5 minutes

If you're in the mood for a satisfying and attractive appetizer, this recipe will fill the bill.

2 tablespoons fat-free sour cream
1 tablespoon light tub cream cheese
1 1/4 teaspoons Dijon mustard (country-style preferred)
1/2 small garlic clove, minced
8 cherry tomatoes, halved crosswise
1 tablespoon chopped fresh basil

1. In a small bowl, stir together the sour cream, cream cheese, mustard, and garlic. Spoon onto each tomato half. Sprinkle with the basil.

Exchanges/Choices
1 Vegetable
1/2 Fat

Calories	45	
Calories from Fat	15	
Total Fat	1.5	**g**
Saturated Fat	0.8	g
Trans Fat	0.0	g
Polyunsaturated Fat	0.2	g
Monounsaturated Fat	0.5	g
Cholesterol	5	**mg**
Sodium	115	**mg**
Total Carbohydrate	5	**g**
Dietary Fiber	1	g
Sugars	3	g
Protein	2	**g**

COOK'S TIP: *Be sure to use regular cherry tomatoes, not grape tomatoes. Grape tomatoes may be too sweet to balance with the flavors and too small for the amount of topping.*

Portobello Party Bites

PORTOBELLO PARTY BITES

Serves 2; 2 mushrooms per serving
Preparation time: 10 minutes

These fun tidbits will help create a festive atmosphere perfect for any celebration.

Cooking spray
4 baby portobello mushrooms (about 4 ounces total), stems discarded
1/4 cup fat-free ricotta cheese
1/4 teaspoon dried basil, crumbled
1/4 teaspoon dried oregano, crumbled
1/4 teaspoon garlic powder
1/8 teaspoon pepper
8 fresh baby spinach leaves, coarsely chopped
2 teaspoons shredded or grated Parmesan cheese
1/8 teaspoon paprika

1. Preheat the oven to 400°F. Lightly spray an 8-inch square baking pan with cooking spray.

2. Lightly spray the rounded side of the mushroom caps with cooking spray. Place with the sprayed side down in the baking pan.

3. In a small bowl, stir together the ricotta, basil, oregano, garlic powder, and pepper. Stir in the spinach. Spoon into the mushrooms. Sprinkle with the Parmesan and paprika.

4. Bake for 14 to 15 minutes, or until the mushrooms are tender and the filling is heated through.

Exchanges/Choices
1 Vegetable
1 Lean Meat

Calories	45	
Calories from Fat	10	
Total Fat	1.0	g
Saturated Fat	0.4	g
Trans Fat	0.0	g
Polyunsaturated Fat	0.1	g
Monounsaturated Fat	0.2	g
Cholesterol	10	mg
Sodium	45	mg
Total Carbohydrate	5	g
Dietary Fiber	1	g
Sugars	2	g
Protein	6	g

Pita Nachos

Pita Nachos

PITA NACHOS

Serves 2; 2 wedges per serving
Preparation time: 10 minutes

Piled high with typical nacho ingredients, these tempting bites are perfect for an afternoon snack.

Cooking spray
1 (6-inch) whole-wheat pita bread (only half is used)
1/4 cup no-salt-added canned black beans, rinsed and drained
1 tablespoon salsa (lowest sodium available)
1/8 teaspoon chili powder
1/8 teaspoon ground cumin
2 tablespoons shredded low-fat cheddar cheese
2 cherry tomatoes, thinly sliced
2 tablespoons diced yellow or green bell pepper
1 tablespoon snipped fresh cilantro

1. Preheat the oven to 350°F. Lightly spray a small baking sheet with cooking spray.

2. Cut the pita bread in half. Save one pocket for another use. Cut the remaining pocket into 4 wedges. Do not separate the tops from the bottoms. Transfer to the baking sheet.

3. Bake for 5 minutes, or until toasted.

4. Meanwhile, in a small bowl, mash the beans with a fork or small potato masher until slightly chunky or smooth. Stir in the salsa, chili powder, and cumin. Spoon onto the toasted pita wedges. Sprinkle with the cheddar. Top with the tomato slices, bell pepper, and cilantro.

5. Bake for 5 minutes, or until the cheddar is melted and the toppings are heated through.

Exchanges/Choices
1 Starch
1/2 Fat

Calories	100	
Calories from Fat	20	
Total Fat	2.0	g
Saturated Fat	1.0	g
Trans Fat	0.0	g
Polyunsaturated Fat	0.3	g
Monounsaturated Fat	0.5	g
Cholesterol	5	mg
Sodium	195	mg
Total Carbohydrate	16	g
Dietary Fiber	3	g
Sugars	2	g
Protein	6	g

Chicken Lettuce Wraps

Serves 2; 2 wraps per serving
Preparation time: 15 minutes

To turn this dish into an entrée, omit the lettuce leaves and serve the chicken over steamed brown rice. Try the leftover sweet chili sauce in Thai dishes or add a bit to dipping sauces.

1 teaspoon toasted sesame oil
3 ounces chicken tenders, all visible fat discarded, finely diced
2 medium green onions, finely chopped
1/2 small red bell pepper, finely chopped
2 medium button mushrooms, finely chopped
1/2 cup packaged shredded cabbage and carrot coleslaw mix
1 teaspoon grated peeled gingerroot
1 medium garlic clove, minced
1 teaspoon sweet chili sauce or 1/4 teaspoon crushed red pepper flakes
1 teaspoon soy sauce (lowest sodium available)
1 teaspoon plain rice vinegar
4 large lettuce leaves, such as romaine, Boston, or iceberg, carefully removed and
    kept whole

1. In a small nonstick skillet, heat the oil over medium-high heat, swirling to coat the bottom. Cook the chicken for 3 to 4 minutes, or until golden on the outside and no longer pink on the inside, stirring frequently. Transfer to a plate.

2. In the same skillet, cook the green onions, bell pepper, mushrooms, and coleslaw mix for about 4 minutes, or until the bell pepper is tender, stirring occasionally. Stir in the gingerroot, garlic, and chili sauce. Cook for 1 minute, stirring frequently. Stir in the cooked chicken. Add the soy sauce and rice vinegar. Cook for 45 seconds to 1 minute, stirring frequently. Remove from heat.

3. Put the lettuce leaves on a flat surface. Spoon about 1/4 cup mixture down the center of each leaf. Roll up tightly, jelly-roll style.

Exchanges/Choices
1 Vegetable
1 Lean Meat
1/2 Fat

Calories	100	
Calories from Fat	30	
Total Fat	3.5	g
Saturated Fat	0.6	g
Trans Fat	0.0	g
Polyunsaturated Fat	1.3	g
Monounsaturated Fat	1.3	g
Cholesterol	25	mg
Sodium	170	mg
Total Carbohydrate	6	g
Dietary Fiber	2	g
Sugars	3	g
Protein	11	g

Roasted Chick-Peas

Roasted Moroccan Chick-peas

Serves 2; 1/4 cup plus 2 tablespoons per serving
Preparation time: 5 minutes

Chick-peas, also known as garbanzo beans, are a common ingredient in Moroccan cooking. Here they are roasted with an enticing blend of spices to use as an appetizer or snack.

1/2 (15-ounce) can no-salt-added chick-peas, rinsed, drained, and patted dry
1/2 teaspoon canola or corn oil
1 teaspoon and 1/2 teaspoon ground cumin, divided use
1/2 teaspoon ground coriander
1/4 teaspoon ground cinnamon
1/8 teaspoon salt
Pinch of cayenne
1/4 teaspoon ground ginger

1. Preheat the oven to 375°F.

2. Put the chick-peas in a shallow 9-inch baking dish (a cake pan or pie pan works well). Drizzle the oil over the chick-peas, rolling to coat.

3. In a small dish, stir together 1 teaspoon cumin, coriander, cinnamon, salt, and cayenne. Sprinkle over the chick-peas, rolling to coat.

4. Bake for 40 to 45 minutes, or until crisp on the outside.

5. Meanwhile, in the same small dish, stir together the remaining 1/2 teaspoon cumin and ginger.

6. Remove the roasted chick-peas from the oven. Sprinkle with the cumin mixture. Shake the dish to coat the chick-peas. Let cool in the baking dish for about 10 minutes or serve at room temperature.

Exchanges/Choices
1 Starch
1 Lean Meat

Calories	135	
Calories from Fat	30	
Total Fat	3.5	g
Saturated Fat	0.3	g
Trans Fat	0.0	g
Polyunsaturated Fat	1.2	g
Monounsaturated Fat	1.3	g
Cholesterol	0	mg
Sodium	155	mg
Total Carbohydrate	20	g
Dietary Fiber	6	g
Sugars	3	g
Protein	7	g

POMEGRANATE PUNCH

Serves 2; 6 ounces per serving
Preparation time: 5 minutes

Depending on the season, serve this spiced beverage warm with a cinnamon stick garnish or over ice with a slice of orange or lemon.

2 tablespoons frozen orange juice concentrate
1 teaspoon honey
1 teaspoon fresh lemon juice
1/8 teaspoon ground allspice
1/8 teaspoon ground cinnamon
1/2 cup pomegranate juice
3/4 cup plus 2 tablespoons unsweetened orange-flavored sparkling water, divided use
2 cinnamon sticks (each about 3 inches long) for hot punch (optional)
2 slices orange or lemon for cold punch (optional)

1. In a small saucepan, whisk together the orange juice concentrate, honey, lemon juice, allspice, and cinnamon. Bring to a simmer over medium-high heat, whisking occasionally. Simmer for 1 to 2 minutes, or until the flavors have blended.

2. To serve warm, pour the pomegranate juice and sparkling water into the orange juice mixture. Bring to a simmer over medium-high heat. Simmer for 2 to 3 minutes, or until heated through, stirring occasionally. Pour into cups. Add the cinnamon sticks.

3. To serve over ice, remove the pan from the heat. Let the orange juice mixture cool for 5 minutes. Pour into glasses. Put 1/2 cup ice in each glass. Stir in the pomegranate juice and sparkling water. Garnish with the orange or lemon.

Exchanges/Choices		
1 Fruit		
Calories	**80**	
Calories from Fat	0	
Total Fat	**0.0**	**g**
Saturated Fat	0.0	g
Trans Fat	0.0	g
Polyunsaturated Fat	0.0	g
Monounsaturated Fat	0.0	g
Cholesterol	**0**	**mg**
Sodium	**10**	**mg**
Total Carbohydrate	**20**	**g**
Dietary Fiber	0	g
Sugars	18	g
Protein	**0**	**g**

GREEN TEA SPRITZER
WITH RASPBERRIES

Serves 2; 8 ounces per serving
Preparation time: 5 minutes

Here's a fizzy, refreshing drink with a bold raspberry flavor. Unlike many commercial iced teas, it isn't excessively sweet. You can prepare the tea ahead of time and refrigerate it until needed.

1 cup water
1 bag green tea
2 teaspoons honey
1/4 teaspoon fresh lemon juice
1/2 cup frozen unsweetened raspberries
3/4 cup chilled sparkling water

1. In a small saucepan, bring the water to a boil over high heat. Pour into a glass measuring cup. Add the tea bag and steep for 3 minutes. Discard the tea bag. Stir in the honey and lemon juice.

2. Meanwhile, fill a medium metal bowl halfway with ice water. Set the measuring cup with the steeped tea mixture in the bowl. Stir the tea until it reaches room temperature, about 3 minutes.

3. In a blender, process the tea and raspberries until smooth. Pour into a strainer and strain into the measuring cup. Discard the seeds.

4. Pour the sparkling water into the tea mixture. Pour into tall, ice-filled glasses. Serve immediately.

Exchanges/Choices		
1 Fruit		
Calories	**45**	
Calories from Fat	0	
Total Fat	**0.0**	**g**
Saturated Fat	0.0	g
Trans Fat	0.0	g
Polyunsaturated Fat	0.1	g
Monounsaturated Fat	0.0	g
Cholesterol	**0**	**mg**
Sodium	**10**	**mg**
Total Carbohydrate	**12**	**g**
Dietary Fiber	0	g
Sugars	11	g
Protein	**0**	**g**

CHERRY-VANILLA SMOOTHIE

Serves 2; 8 ounces per serving
Preparation time: 5 minutes

For a sweet, creamy breakfast drink or mid-day energy booster, whip up a smoothie in almost no time. Keep a stash of peeled bananas in the freezer to make preparation go even faster.

1/2 medium banana, cut into 1/2-inch slices
1 (6-ounce) container fat-free vanilla yogurt
4 ounces frozen unsweetened pitted dark cherries (about 2/3 cup)
1/2 cup fat-free milk
1/4 teaspoon vanilla extract

1. Put the banana slices on a freezer-safe plate. Put in the freezer for 20 minutes, or until firm and very cold.

2. In a blender, process all the ingredients for 30 seconds, or until thick and smooth. (You can also use an immersion, or handheld, blender.)

Exchanges/Choices
1 Fruit
1 Fat-Free Milk

Calories	135	
Calories from Fat	0	
Total Fat	0.0	g
Saturated Fat	0.2	g
Trans Fat	0.0	g
Polyunsaturated Fat	0.1	g
Monounsaturated Fat	0.1	g
Cholesterol	5	mg
Sodium	90	mg
Total Carbohydrate	27	g
Dietary Fiber	2	g
Sugars	20	g
Protein	7	g

SOUPS

SOUPS

Herb-Tomato Soup

Quick Herb-Tomato Soup

Serves 2; 1 cup per serving
Preparation time: 5 minutes

Crushed rosemary and roasted garlic hummus give this recipe flavor and body. Best of all, it comes together in a snap.

> 1 (14.5-ounce) can no-salt-added diced tomatoes, undrained
> 1/4 cup roasted garlic hummus
> 1 teaspoon crushed dried rosemary
> 1/2 teaspoon Italian seasoning blend, crumbled
> 1/2 teaspoon pepper (coarsely ground preferred)
> 1 tablespoon snipped fresh parsley (optional)

1. In a small saucepan, stir together all the ingredients except the parsley. Bring to a simmer over medium-low heat. Reduce the heat and simmer for 5 minutes. Carefully pour into a blender and process until smooth (or remove from the heat and use an immersion, or handheld, blender).

2. Return to the pan. Heat over medium-low heat for 2 to 3 minutes, or until just simmering. Ladle into bowls. Garnish with the parsley.

COOK'S TIP: *Use the remaining hummus as a spread on sandwiches or as a dip with crisp vegetables.*

Exchanges/Choices
1/2 Starch
2 Vegetable
1 Fat

Calories	125	
Calories from Fat	55	
Total Fat	6.0	g
Saturated Fat	1.1	g
Trans Fat	0.0	g
Polyunsaturated Fat	2.4	g
Monounsaturated Fat	2.7	g
Cholesterol	0	mg
Sodium	200	mg
Total Carbohydrate	16	g
Dietary Fiber	5	g
Sugars	7	g
Protein	4	g

GARDEN HARVEST SOUP

Garden Harvest Soup

Serves 2; 1 1/4 cups per serving
Preparation time: 10 minutes

Tailor this versatile soup to suit your preferences by using your favorite fresh or frozen vegetables.

1 teaspoon olive oil
2 cups chopped uncooked vegetables (such as any combination of bell peppers, carrots, corn, green beans, peas, yellow summer squash, or zucchini)
1/4 cup finely chopped onion
1 teaspoon Italian seasoning blend, crumbled
2 cups low-sodium vegetable broth or fat-free, low-sodium chicken broth
1 cup loosely packed fresh spinach leaves, coarsely chopped
1 tablespoon shredded or grated Parmesan cheese

1. In a medium saucepan, heat the oil over medium heat, swirling to coat the bottom. Cook the 2 cups chopped vegetables, onion, and seasoning blend for 8 to 10 minutes, or until tender-crisp, stirring occasionally. (If the vegetables get dry or start to scorch, add a little water to the saucepan.)

2. Stir in the broth. Increase the heat to medium high and bring to a boil. Reduce the heat and simmer for 15 minutes so the flavors blend, stirring occasionally. Stir in the spinach. Sprinkle each serving with Parmesan cheese.

> **COOK'S TIP:** *Chop firmer vegetables, such as carrots, into smaller pieces than tenderer vegetables, such as zucchini, so all the vegetables will cook at the same rate.*

Exchanges/Choices
3 Vegetable
1/2 Fat

Calories	95	
Calories from Fat	30	
Total Fat	3.5	g
Saturated Fat	0.9	g
Trans Fat	0.0	g
Polyunsaturated Fat	0.4	g
Monounsaturated Fat	2.0	g
Cholesterol	5	mg
Sodium	200	mg
Total Carbohydrate	13	g
Dietary Fiber	4	g
Sugars	6	g
Protein	3	g

BROCCOLI-CHEDDAR SOUP

Serves 2; 1 cup per serving
Preparation time: 15 minutes

On a cool day, fit some veggies in with this smooth, broccoli-packed soup.

1/4 teaspoon cumin seeds
1 tablespoon olive oil
1/2 large onion, chopped
1/3 cup chopped celery
1 1/2 cups finely chopped broccoli florets
1/4 cup frozen edamame (shelled green soybeans)
1/8 teaspoon pepper
1 cup water
1/2 cup low-sodium vegetable broth
2 tablespoons snipped fresh parsley
2 tablespoons and 2 teaspoons shredded fat-free cheddar cheese, divided use

2 tablespoons fat-free half-and-half
1 teaspoon white wine vinegar
1/2 teaspoon fresh lemon juice

Exchanges/Choices

3 Vegetable
1 1/2 Fat

Calories	155	
Calories from Fat	70	
Total Fat	8.0	g
Saturated Fat	1.2	g
Trans Fat	0.0	g
Polyunsaturated Fat	1.4	g
Monounsaturated Fat	5.3	g
Cholesterol	0	mg
Sodium	180	mg
Total Carbohydrate	14	g
Dietary Fiber	4	g
Sugars	5	g
Protein	8	g

1. In a small skillet, dry-roast the cumin seeds over medium heat for about 2 minutes, or until very fragrant, stirring occasionally. Pulverize in a spice grinder or crush with a mortar and pestle until powdery. Set aside.

2. In a medium saucepan, heat the oil over medium heat, swirling to coat the bottom. Cook the onion and celery for about 5 minutes, or until they begin to brown, stirring occasionally.

3. Stir in the broccoli, edamame, pepper, and cumin. Cook for about 3 minutes, or until the broccoli is bright green, stirring constantly. Stir in the water and broth. Increase the heat to medium high and bring to a boil. Reduce the heat and simmer, partially covered, for about 10 minutes, or until tender. Stir in the parsley.

4. Carefully transfer the soup to a blender. Process until smooth. (The soup will be very hot, so use extreme caution. You may want to hold a tea towel over the blender lid.) Return the soup to the pan. Add 2 tablespoons cheddar cheese, half-and-half, vinegar, and lemon juice, stirring until the cheese has melted. Ladle into bowls. Garnish with the remaining 2 teaspoons cheddar.

BEANS AND GREENS SOUP

Serves 2; 1 1/2 cups per serving
Preparation time: 15 minutes

Crusty whole-grain rolls and fresh fruit salad pair especially well with this
hearty soup.

  2 teaspoons olive oil
  3 small green onions, finely sliced
  1/2 medium rib of celery, finely chopped
  10 ounces frozen chopped spinach, thawed and squeezed dry
  1 (14.5-ounce) can no-salt-added diced tomatoes, undrained
  1 cup fat-free, low-sodium chicken broth
  2 tablespoons snipped fresh parsley
  1/4 teaspoon dried marjoram, crumbled
  1/8 teaspoon cayenne
  1/8 teaspoon ground nutmeg
  2/3 cup canned no-salt-added white beans, such as navy beans, drained and rinsed

1. In a medium nonstick saucepan, heat the oil over medium heat, swirling
   to coat the bottom. Cook the green onions and celery for 4 to 5 minutes,
   or until the celery is tender-crisp, stirring occasionally. Stir in the
   spinach. Cook for 2 to 3 minutes, or until any liquid has evaporated and
   the mixture comes away from the side of the skillet, stirring frequently.

2. Stir in the remaining ingredients except the beans. Increase the heat to
   medium high and bring to a boil, covered. Reduce the heat and simmer,
   covered, for 10 minutes, or until the flavors blend and the vegetables are
   tender.

3. Stir in the beans. Cook, uncovered, for 1 minute, or until the beans are
   hot. For a thicker broth, increase the heat to medium when you add the
   beans. Cook, partially covered, until some of the liquid evaporates and
   the soup is the desired consistency.

Exchanges/Choices		
1 Starch		
3 Vegetable		
1 Lean Meat		
1/2 Fat		
Calories	220	
Calories from Fat	55	
Total Fat	**6.0**	**g**
Saturated Fat	0.9	g
Trans Fat	0.0	g
Polyunsaturated Fat	1.2	g
Monounsaturated Fat	3.5	g
Cholesterol	**0**	**mg**
Sodium	**235**	**mg**
Total Carbohydrate	**32**	**g**
Dietary Fiber	12	g
Sugars	8	g
Protein	**14**	**g**

Onion-Sage Soup

Onion-Sage Soup

Serves 2; 1 cup per serving
Preparation time: 10 minutes

The key to rich flavor in this soup is to be patient and let the onion develop a deep color. Don't be tempted to increase the temperature to cook it faster, or it may burn and become bitter.

1 teaspoon olive oil

1/2 large sweet onion, such as Vidalia or OsoSweet, thinly sliced

1 medium garlic clove, chopped

2 tablespoons dry sherry or low-sodium vegetable broth

1 tablespoon all-purpose flour

2 1/2 cups low-sodium vegetable broth or fat-free, no-salt-added beef broth

1 large or 2 small sage leaves

1/8 teaspoon pepper

1 tablespoon chopped green onions (green part only) or snipped fresh parsley (optional)

1. In a medium saucepan, heat the oil over medium heat, swirling to coat the bottom. Cook the onion, covered, for 15 minutes, stirring occasionally. Stir in the garlic. Reduce the heat to medium low. Cook, uncovered, for 15 to 20 minutes, or until the onion is a deep golden brown, stirring occasionally.

2. Increase the heat to medium. Stir in the sherry. Simmer until almost all the liquid is evaporated. Stir in the flour. Gradually stir in the broth. Increase the heat to medium high and bring to a boil. Reduce the heat and simmer for 10 minutes.

3. Meanwhile, chop the sage. Stir the sage and pepper into the simmered soup. Simmer for 5 minutes. Ladle into bowls and garnish with the green onions.

Exchanges/Choices		
2 Vegetable		
1/2 Fat		
Calories	85	
Calories from Fat	20	
Total Fat	2.5	g
Saturated Fat	0.3	g
Trans Fat	0.0	g
Polyunsaturated Fat	0.2	g
Monounsaturated Fat	1.7	g
Cholesterol	0	mg
Sodium	180	mg
Total Carbohydrate	12	g
Dietary Fiber	2	g
Sugars	4	g
Protein	1	g

Noodle Bowls

Serves 2; 1 cup per serving
Preparation time: 10 minutes

You'll have soup with tender-crisp vegetables in just a few minutes when you try this unique approach to soup making: Quickly soak rice noodles, add them to bowls of vegetables, then pour in boiling stock.

1 ounce uncooked thin rice noodles
2 cups boiling water
6 fresh snow peas, trimmed and cut crosswise into 1/4-inch pieces
1/2 medium carrot, shredded
1 medium green onion, thinly sliced
1 teaspoon soy sauce (lowest sodium available)
1 teaspoon toasted sesame oil
1 1/2 cups fat-free, low-sodium chicken broth

1. Put the rice noodles in a shallow bowl. Pour in the boiling water. Cover with plastic wrap. Let stand at room temperature for 10 minutes. Drain in a colander.

2. Meanwhile, put the snow peas, carrot, and green onion in soup bowls. Drizzle the soy sauce and sesame oil over the vegetables.

3. When the noodles are almost ready, in a small saucepan, bring the broth to a rolling boil over high heat.

4. Using tongs, transfer the noodles to the soup bowls. Pour the boiling broth into the bowls, stirring to combine. Let stand for 2 minutes, or until the vegetables are tender-crisp.

COOK'S TIP: *Delicate yet firm, dried rice noodles are available in the Asian section of the grocery store. Make cleanup easy by holding the package over a large bowl when you open it and separate the amount of noodles you need. Kitchen scissors are very helpful for this. Add any noodle fragments from the bowl to the dish you are preparing.*

Exchanges/Choices		
1/2 Starch		
1 Vegetable		
1/2 Fat		
Calories	105	
Calories from Fat	20	
Total Fat	2.5	g
Saturated Fat	0.5	g
Trans Fat	0.0	g
Polyunsaturated Fat	1.0	g
Monounsaturated Fat	0.9	g
Cholesterol	5	mg
Sodium	200	mg
Total Carbohydrate	16	g
Dietary Fiber	1	g
Sugars	2	g
Protein	3	g

Pumpkin Soup

Serves 2; 1 1/4 cups per serving
Preparation time: 5 minutes

Using canned pumpkin makes it easy to quickly prepare this elegant soup, which is delicately laced with spice.

1 teaspoon canola or corn oil
2 tablespoons finely chopped onion
1 cup canned solid-pack pumpkin (not pie filling)
1 cup low-sodium vegetable broth or fat-free, low-sodium chicken broth
1/8 teaspoon ground cinnamon
1/8 teaspoon ground nutmeg
1/4 cup fat-free half-and-half
Dash of cayenne
2 teaspoons thinly sliced green onions (green part only)

1. In a medium saucepan, heat the oil over medium heat, swirling to coat the bottom. Cook the onion for 3 to 4 minutes, or until soft, stirring occasionally.

2. Add the pumpkin, broth, cinnamon, and nutmeg, whisking to combine. Cook for about 4 minutes, or until heated through, whisking occasionally.

3. Whisk in the half-and-half and cayenne. Cook for about 1 minute, or until heated through. Sprinkle each serving with the green onions.

Exchanges/Choices		
1 Starch		
1/2 Fat		
Calories	95	
Calories from Fat	25	
Total Fat	3.0	g
Saturated Fat	0.6	g
Trans Fat	0.0	g
Polyunsaturated Fat	0.7	g
Monounsaturated Fat	1.5	g
Cholesterol	0	mg
Sodium	105	mg
Total Carbohydrate	15	g
Dietary Fiber	4	g
Sugars	7	g
Protein	2	g

Cuban Black Bean Soup

Serves 2; 1 1/4 cups per serving
Preparation time: 10 minutes

A meal in a bowl in less than 30 minutes, this satisfying soup has a hint of smokiness that's perfect for a chilly day.

1 teaspoon canola or corn oil
5 medium green onions, white and pale green parts chopped and 1 tablespoon dark green part, thinly sliced
1 slice turkey bacon, cut into 1/2-inch pieces
1 large garlic clove, minced
1 (15-ounce) can no-salt-added black beans, rinsed and drained
1 (14.5-ounce) can no-salt-added diced tomatoes, undrained
2 teaspoons ground cumin
1 teaspoon red wine vinegar
1/8 teaspoon cayenne
2 tablespoons fat-free plain yogurt

1. In a small saucepan, heat the oil over medium-low heat, swirling to coat the bottom. Cook the white and pale green parts of the green onions and the turkey bacon for 4 to 5 minutes, or until the green onions are soft and the turkey bacon is just beginning to brown. Stir in the garlic. Cook for 30 seconds to 1 minute, or until fragrant.

2. Increase the heat to medium high. Stir in the black beans, tomatoes with liquid, cumin, vinegar, and cayenne. Bring to a simmer. Reduce the heat and simmer for 5 minutes.

3. Carefully pour into a blender and process until slightly chunky (or remove from the heat and use an immersion, or handheld, blender). Return to the pan. Heat over medium heat for 2 to 3 minutes, or until simmering. Ladle into bowls. Spoon 1 tablespoon yogurt onto each serving. Garnish with the dark green part of the green onions.

Exchanges/Choices		
2 Starch		
3 Vegetable		
1 Lean Meat		
Calories	280	
Calories from Fat	45	
Total Fat	5.0	g
Saturated Fat	0.7	g
Trans Fat	0.0	g
Polyunsaturated Fat	1.4	g
Monounsaturated Fat	2.2	g
Cholesterol	5	mg
Sodium	195	mg
Total Carbohydrate	48	g
Dietary Fiber	12	g
Sugars	11	g
Protein	16	g

Chilled Cucumber Gazpacho

Serves 2; 3/4 cup per serving
Preparation time: 10 minutes

This soup is cool and refreshing—perfect for a hot summer day. The dramatic contrast of the soup and the vibrant tomato and carrot garnish is very appealing.

1 small garlic clove
1 large cucumber, peeled, seeded, and chopped (about 1 1/4 cups)
1 medium yellow bell pepper, chopped
1 medium green onion, sliced crosswise
2 teaspoons snipped fresh dillweed or 1/4 teaspoon dried dillweed, crumbled
1/8 teaspoon salt
1/8 teaspoon pepper (white preferred)
2 tablespoons shredded carrots
2 tablespoons diced tomatoes

1. In a food processor, process the garlic for 5 to 10 seconds, or until minced. Add the cucumber, bell pepper, green onion, dillweed, salt, and pepper. Pulse 5 or 6 times. Process for 1 to 1 1/2 minutes, or until the desired texture.

2. Pour into bowls or martini glasses. Top with the carrots and tomatoes.

Exchanges/Choices
2 Vegetable

Calories	40	
Calories from Fat	0	
Total Fat	0.0	g
Saturated Fat	0.0	g
Trans Fat	0.0	g
Polyunsaturated Fat	0.1	g
Monounsaturated Fat	0.1	g
Cholesterol	0	mg
Sodium	160	mg
Total Carbohydrate	9	g
Dietary Fiber	2	g
Sugars	4	g
Protein	2	g

CHILLED FRUIT SOUP

Serves 2; 1 cup per serving
Preparation time: 5 minutes

When it's hot outside, grab some fruit from your freezer and make this refreshing soup to enjoy with your favorite sandwich or salad. It's also a great starter for brunch.

3/4 cup frozen unsweetened strawberries, partially thawed
3/4 cup frozen unsweetened peach slices, partially thawed
1 (6-ounce) container fat-free vanilla yogurt
1 (6-ounce) can pineapple juice
1/2 teaspoon ground ginger

1. In a food processor or blender, process all the ingredients until smooth. Ladle into bowls.

COOK'S TIP: *Each time you have some leftover fruit, drop it into a resealable plastic freezer bag and store it in your freezer. You'll always have fruit on hand for soups or smoothies, and small amounts of fruit won't be wasted.*

Exchanges/Choices		
1 1/2 Fruit		
1/2 Fat-Free Milk		
Calories	125	
Calories from Fat	0	
Total Fat	0.0	g
Saturated Fat	0.0	g
Trans Fat	0.0	g
Polyunsaturated Fat	0.1	g
Monounsaturated Fat	0.0	g
Cholesterol	0	mg
Sodium	40	mg
Total Carbohydrate	29	g
Dietary Fiber	2	g
Sugars	22	g
Protein	4	g

FISH CHOWDER

Serves 2; heaping 1 1/2 cups per serving
Preparation time: 20 minutes

The combination of mild fish and traditional chowder vegetables is so satisfying, especially on a rainy or snowy day.

1 1/2 cups and 1/4 cup cold water, divided use
1 small red potato (about 4 ounces), cut into 1/2-inch cubes
1/2 small onion (yellow preferred), finely chopped
1 medium carrot, cut into 1/2-inch slices
1/2 medium rib of celery, cut into 1/2-inch slices
2 flounder or other thin, mild fish fillets (about 4 ounces each), rinsed and patted dry, cut into bite-sized pieces
1 (5-ounce) can fat-free evaporated milk
1 tablespoon snipped fresh parsley
1/2 teaspoon dried thyme, crumbled
1/8 teaspoon cayenne
1/8 teaspoon salt
2 teaspoons cornstarch

1. In a medium saucepan, bring 1 1/2 cups water, potato, onion, carrot, and celery to a boil, covered, over medium-high heat. Lower the heat and simmer, covered, for 8 to 10 minutes, or until the vegetables are tender-crisp. Add the fish and cook, covered, for 3 to 4 minutes, or until the fish flakes easily when tested with a fork.

2. Stir in the evaporated milk, parsley, thyme, cayenne, and salt. Increase the heat to medium low and cook for 1 to 2 minutes, or until the milk is hot.

3. Meanwhile, in a small bowl, whisk together the cornstarch and remaining 1/4 cup cold water until smooth. Stir into the hot soup and cook for about 1 minute, or until the soup has thickened slightly, stirring frequently.

Exchanges/Choices		
1 Starch		
1/2 Fat-Free Milk		
2 Vegetable		
2 Lean Meat		
Calories	265	
Calories from Fat	20	
Total Fat	2.0	g
Saturated Fat	0.5	g
Trans Fat	0.0	g
Polyunsaturated Fat	0.7	g
Monounsaturated Fat	0.3	g
Cholesterol	65	mg
Sodium	385	mg
Total Carbohydrate	32	g
Dietary Fiber	3	g
Sugars	13	g
Protein	29	g

Fish Chowder

CHICKEN SOUP PRIMAVERA

Serves 2; 1 1/4 cups per serving
Preparation time: 15 minutes

Vegetables play a starring role in this chunky entrée soup. There's so much chicken in here that you'll get several hearty bites in each spoonful.

1 cup water
1 cup fat-free, low-sodium chicken broth
1 (8-ounce) boneless, skinless chicken breast, all visible fat discarded, butterflied
1 small leek (white and light green parts) sliced (about 1/2 cup)
1/4 medium carrot, diced
1 medium garlic clove, minced
4 medium asparagus spears, trimmed, tips left intact, stalks sliced diagonally into
    1/2-inch pieces
1 cup loosely packed fresh spinach leaves
1/4 cup frozen peas
1 teaspoon fresh lemon juice
1/8 teaspoon pepper, or to taste

1. In a medium saucepan, bring the water, broth, and chicken to a boil over medium heat. Reduce the heat to a simmer, turning the chicken once and skimming off any foam that rises to the surface.

2. Stir in the leek, carrot, and garlic. Simmer, covered, for 15 to 20 minutes, or until the chicken is cooked through. Transfer the chicken to a cutting board. Stir the asparagus into the soup. Cook for 3 minutes, or until tender-crisp. Stir in the spinach and peas. Cook for 2 minutes.

3. Meanwhile, using a fork, shred the chicken into irregular, bite-sized pieces. Return the chicken to the saucepan. Stir in the lemon juice and pepper.

COOK'S TIP: *To butterfly, put the chicken on a cutting board so the smaller ends are at the top and bottom. Holding a sharp knife parallel to the board, begin slicing the chicken in half, but do not cut all the way through. Open the chicken like a book.*

Exchanges/Choices		
2 Vegetable		
3 Lean Meat		
Calories	180	
Calories from Fat	25	
Total Fat	3.0	g
Saturated Fat	0.9	g
Trans Fat	0.0	g
Polyunsaturated Fat	0.7	g
Monounsaturated Fat	1.0	g
Cholesterol	70	mg
Sodium	155	mg
Total Carbohydrate	10	g
Dietary Fiber	2	g
Sugars	3	g
Protein	28	g

Turkey Tortilla Soup

Turkey Tortilla Soup

Serves 2; 1 1/2 cups per serving
Preparation time: 15 minutes

This tomato-based soup is an excellent way to use leftovers from roasted turkey or grilled chicken.

1 teaspoon canola or corn oil
1/2 small onion, thinly sliced
1 small garlic clove, halved
1 (14.5-ounce) can no-salt-added whole tomatoes, undrained
1 (6-inch) corn tortilla, chopped
1 tablespoon tomato paste
1 tablespoon chopped fresh jalapeño, seeds and ribs discarded
1/4 teaspoon ground cumin
1 cup fat-free, no-salt-added chicken broth
1 cup chopped cooked skinless turkey breast or chicken breast, cooked without salt
1 ounce queso fresco, crumbled, or farmer cheese, shredded (about 1/4 cup)
2 tablespoons chopped avocado

1. In a medium saucepan, heat the oil over medium heat, swirling to coat the bottom. Cook the onion and garlic for 3 to 4 minutes or until soft, stirring occasionally. Stir in the tomatoes with liquid, tortilla, tomato paste, jalapeño, and cumin. Cook for 2 minutes, stirring constantly.

2. In a blender, process the mixture until smooth. Return to the saucepan. Stir in the broth and turkey. Bring to a boil over medium-high heat. Reduce the heat and simmer for 15 minutes. Ladle into bowls. Sprinkle with the queso fresco and avocado.

COOK'S TIP: *Queso fresco* (KAY-soh FRAY-skoh) *literally translates to "fresh cheese." It is a mild white Mexican cheese that crumbles nicely. You can use farmer cheese, another mild white cheese (similar to Monterey Jack), if queso fresco isn't available.*

Exchanges/Choices		
1/2 Starch		
2 Vegetable		
3 Lean Meat		
1 Fat		
Calories	285	
Calories from Fat	90	
Total Fat	**10.0**	**g**
Saturated Fat	3.3	g
Trans Fat	0.0	g
Polyunsaturated Fat	1.6	g
Monounsaturated Fat	4.2	g
Cholesterol	**70**	**mg**
Sodium	**295**	**mg**
Total Carbohydrate	**23**	**g**
Dietary Fiber	6	g
Sugars	9	g
Protein	**29**	**g**

ASIAN PORK SOUP

Serves 2; 1 heaping cup per serving
Preparation time: 10 minutes

Complex flavors from fresh and dried ingredients form an ideal combination in this main dish soup.

1 cup water
3/4 cup fat-free, low-sodium chicken broth
1/2 cup dried shiitake mushrooms
1 teaspoon minced peeled gingerroot
1/2 ounce Chinese noodles, broken into pieces (about 1/8 cup)
1 (5-ounce) boneless pork chop, all visible fat discarded, cut into 1/8-inch strips
1 baby bok choy, cut crosswise into 1/4-inch slices (about 1/2 cup), or 1/2 cup sliced
    bok choy or napa cabbage

1. In a small saucepan, bring the water and chicken broth to a boil over medium heat. Remove from heat. Stir in the mushrooms. Let soak for 20 to 30 minutes, or until rehydrated. Strain through a coffee filter or paper towel into a liquid measuring cup to remove any dirt or grit. Chop the mushrooms, discarding any stems that are still hard. Return the broth and mushrooms to the pan.

2. Stir in the gingerroot. Bring the soup to a gentle boil over medium-low heat. Stir in the noodles. Cook for 2 minutes. Stir in the pork and bok choy. Cook for 2 to 3 minutes, or until the pork is no longer pink.

Exchanges/Choices		
1/2 Starch		
1 Vegetable		
2 Lean Meat		
Calories	150	
Calories from Fat	40	
Total Fat	4.5	g
Saturated Fat	1.7	g
Trans Fat	0.0	g
Polyunsaturated Fat	0.4	g
Monounsaturated Fat	2.1	g
Cholesterol	35	mg
Sodium	80	mg
Total Carbohydrate	12	g
Dietary Fiber	1	g
Sugars	2	g
Protein	16	g

SALADS

Watercress and Apple Salad with Citrus Vinaigrette

Serves 2; 1 cup (packed) per serving
Preparation time: 10 minutes

A citrus dressing tempers the peppery bite of the watercress. Sweet apples and crunchy almonds add to the salad's irresistible contrast of flavors and textures.

Citrus Vinaigrette

2 teaspoons olive oil (extra-virgin preferred)
1/2 tablespoon fresh orange juice
1/2 tablespoon fresh lemon juice
1/4 teaspoon honey

Salad

2 ounces watercress, coarse stems discarded (about 1 1/4 cups, firmly packed)
1/2 medium Fuji apple with peel, sliced
2 tablespoons slivered almonds, dry-roasted

1. In a medium serving bowl, whisk together the vinaigrette ingredients. Add the watercress, apple, and almonds. Toss to combine. Serve immediately.

COOK'S TIP: *If Fuji apples aren't readily available, any red "eating" apple, such as Gala, Jonathan, Cortland, or Pink Lady, substitutes well.*

Exchanges/Choices		
1/2 Fruit		
2 Fat		
Calories	115	
Calories from Fat	80	
Total Fat	**9.0**	**g**
Saturated Fat	0.9	g
Trans Fat	0.0	g
Polyunsaturated Fat	1.5	g
Monounsaturated Fat	6.0	g
Cholesterol	**0**	**mg**
Sodium	**10**	**mg**
Total Carbohydrate	**9**	**g**
Dietary Fiber	2	g
Sugars	6	g
Protein	**2**	**g**

SPINACH AND ORANGE SALAD WITH PUMPKIN SEEDS

Serves 2; 1 cup salad and 2 tablespoons dressing per serving
Preparation time: 15 minutes

This fresh salad will taste perfect any time of the year but may be especially welcome in the fall or winter, when citrus is more plentiful and other produce is in short supply.

1 cup loosely packed baby spinach leaves
2 tablespoons sliced celery
2 small button mushrooms, sliced
1 thin slice red onion, halved and separated into rings
1/2 medium orange, peeled and sectioned
2 tablespoons fresh orange juice
1 tablespoon fresh lemon juice
1 teaspoon olive oil (extra-virgin preferred)
1 teaspoon soy sauce (lowest sodium available)
1 teaspoon honey
1/8 teaspoon ground ginger
1/8 teaspoon pepper (coarsely ground preferred)
1 tablespoon shelled roasted unsalted pumpkin seeds (pepitas)

1. In a medium salad bowl, toss together the spinach, celery, mushrooms, onion, and orange sections.

2. In a small bowl, whisk together the remaining ingredients except the pumpkin seeds. Drizzle over the salad. Toss to combine. Garnish with the pumpkin seeds.

Exchanges/Choices		
1/2 Fruit		
1 Vegetable		
1 Fat		
Calories	105	
Calories from Fat	45	
Total Fat	5.0	g
Saturated Fat	0.9	g
Trans Fat	0.0	g
Polyunsaturated Fat	1.7	g
Monounsaturated Fat	2.6	g
Cholesterol	0	mg
Sodium	115	mg
Total Carbohydrate	13	g
Dietary Fiber	2	g
Sugars	9	g
Protein	4	g

Salad Greens
with Hoisin-Plum Dressing

Serves 2; 1 1/2 cups greens and 2 tablespoons dressing per serving
Preparation time: 5 minutes

Add an Asian flair to your next meal with this lovely green salad. Toasted sesame seeds complement the tangy-sweet dressing.

Hoisin-Plum Dressing
2 tablespoons plum sauce
1 tablespoon orange juice
1 tablespoon hoisin sauce
1 teaspoon olive oil (extra-virgin preferred)
1/4 teaspoon ground ginger

Salad
2 cups mixed salad greens
1 cup fresh snow peas, trimmed
2 tablespoons sesame seeds, dry-roasted

1. In a small bowl, whisk together the dressing ingredients.

2. Mound the salad greens in salad bowls. Arrange the snow peas on top. Drizzle with the dressing. Sprinkle with the sesame seeds.

COOK'S TIP: *You should be able to find plum sauce and hoisin sauce in the Asian section of your grocery store. If, however, you can find only one of them, use it for the total amount (3 tablespoons).*

Exchanges/Choices		
1 Carbohydrate		
1 Vegetable		
1 Fat		
Calories	145	
Calories from Fat	65	
Total Fat	7.0	g
Saturated Fat	1.0	g
Trans Fat	0.0	g
Polyunsaturated Fat	2.5	g
Monounsaturated Fat	3.5	g
Cholesterol	0	mg
Sodium	215	mg
Total Carbohydrate	17	g
Dietary Fiber	3	g
Sugars	5	g
Protein	4	g

CHOPPED SALAD WITH ITALIAN DRESSING

Chopped Salad

Serves 2; 1 1/2 cups salad and 2 tablespoons dressing per serving
Preparation time: 15 minutes

Homemade apple-tinged Italian dressing is an excellent match for this crunchy multi-vegetable salad.

Italian Dressing

2 tablespoons apple juice concentrate

2 teaspoons cider vinegar

1 teaspoon fresh lemon juice

1 teaspoon olive oil (extra-virgin preferred)

1/4 teaspoon dried oregano, crumbled

1/4 teaspoon salt

1/8 teaspoon garlic powder

1/8 teaspoon paprika

1/8 teaspoon dry mustard

1/8 teaspoon pepper

Salad

2 cups green-leaf lettuce, torn into bite-sized pieces

1/4 cup chopped broccoli florets

1/4 cup chopped cauliflower florets

2 tablespoons chopped carrot

2 tablespoons chopped radishes

2 tablespoons chopped cucumber

2 medium cherry tomatoes, halved

1. In a small bowl, whisk together the dressing ingredients.

2. Put the lettuce in shallow salad bowls. Arrange the remaining ingredients on the lettuce. Pour the dressing over the salad.

> **COOK'S TIP:** *You can find bagged vegetable blends near the bagged lettuce in the produce section of the grocery store. A common blend is broccoli florets, cauliflower florets, and baby carrots. If you don't want to purchase a head of cauliflower or a bunch of broccoli, bagged vegetables are a handy alternative.*

Exchanges/Choices		
1/2 Fruit		
1 Vegetable		
1/2 Fat		
Calories	75	
Calories from Fat	20	
Total Fat	2.5	g
Saturated Fat	0.3	g
Trans Fat	0.0	g
Polyunsaturated Fat	0.4	g
Monounsaturated Fat	1.7	g
Cholesterol	0	mg
Sodium	320	mg
Total Carbohydrate	12	g
Dietary Fiber	2	g
Sugars	9	g
Protein	2	g

SPICY MARINATED BROCCOLI SALAD

Serves 2; 1/2 cup per serving
Preparation time: 15 minutes

This salad gets a thumbs up for its visual appeal and its sweet and spicy tang.

1 cup fresh broccoli florets, cut into bite-sized pieces
1/2 medium carrot, grated
1/4 cup chopped red onion
1/4 cup diced roasted red bell pepper, rinsed and drained if bottled
2 tablespoons plain rice vinegar
1 tablespoon water
1/2 tablespoon olive oil (extra-virgin preferred)
1 teaspoon honey
1 small garlic clove, minced
1/4 teaspoon crushed red pepper flakes
1/4 teaspoon dried basil, crumbled
1 teaspoon shredded or grated Parmesan cheese

1. In a medium bowl, stir together the broccoli, carrot, onion, and bell pepper.

2. In a small bowl, whisk together the remaining ingredients except the Parmesan. Pour over the broccoli mixture. Stir gently to coat. Cover and refrigerate for 1 to 2 hours, stirring occasionally. Before serving, sprinkle with the Parmesan.

Exchanges/Choices		
2 Vegetable		
1/2 Fat		
Calories	80	
Calories from Fat	35	
Total Fat	4.0	g
Saturated Fat	0.7	g
Trans Fat	0.0	g
Polyunsaturated Fat	0.5	g
Monounsaturated Fat	2.6	g
Cholesterol	0	mg
Sodium	70	mg
Total Carbohydrate	11	g
Dietary Fiber	2	g
Sugars	7	g
Protein	2	g

Cucumber and Blue Cheese Chopped Salad

Serves 2; 1/2 cup per serving
Preparation time: 10 minutes

A small amount of sharp blue cheese provides an interesting complement to this slightly sweetened salad.

1/2 large cucumber, peeled and diced
2 tablespoons finely chopped red onion
2 tablespoons snipped fresh parsley
1 tablespoon cider vinegar
2 teaspoons sugar
2 tablespoons crumbled low-fat blue cheese
1 medium tomato, cut into 4 slices

1. In a small bowl, stir together the cucumber, onion, parsley, vinegar, and sugar. Stir in the blue cheese. Let stand for 5 minutes so the flavors blend.

2. Place 2 tomato slices on each plate. Spoon the cucumber mixture on top.

COOK'S TIP: *If you slice tomatoes lengthwise instead of the usual crosswise, they retain their shape and are less messy.*

Exchanges/Choices		
1/2 Carbohydrate		
1 Vegetable		
Calories	65	
Calories from Fat	15	
Total Fat	1.5	g
Saturated Fat	1.0	g
Trans Fat	0.0	g
Polyunsaturated Fat	0.1	g
Monounsaturated Fat	0.4	g
Cholesterol	5	mg
Sodium	105	mg
Total Carbohydrate	10	g
Dietary Fiber	2	g
Sugars	7	g
Protein	3	g

Marinated Mushrooms

MARINATED MUSHROOMS WITH TARRAGON

Serves 2; 1/2 cup per serving
Preparation time: 10 minutes

Tarragon adds its distinctively mild sweetness to this simple mushroom salad, which should be served the same day it is made.

1 tablespoon vinegar
1 tablespoon water
1 teaspoon dehydrated minced onion
1 teaspoon sugar
1 teaspoon olive oil (extra-virgin preferred)
3/4 teaspoon Dijon mustard
1/2 teaspoon dried tarragon, crumbled
4 ounces button mushrooms, sliced
1/4 cup grape tomatoes, halved

1. In a medium bowl, whisk together the vinegar, water, onion, sugar, oil, mustard, and tarragon. Stir in the mushrooms and tomatoes to coat. Cover and refrigerate for 1 hour, stirring occasionally.

Exchanges/Choices
1 Vegetable
1/2 Fat

Calories	50	
Calories from Fat	20	
Total Fat	2.5	g
Saturated Fat	0.3	g
Trans Fat	0.0	g
Polyunsaturated Fat	0.3	g
Monounsaturated Fat	1.7	g
Cholesterol	0	mg
Sodium	50	mg
Total Carbohydrate	6	g
Dietary Fiber	1	g
Sugars	4	g
Protein	2	g

Zucchini-Tomato Salad

Serves 2; 1/2 cup per serving
Preparation time: 10 minutes

Crisp and refreshing, this salad requires almost no effort to put together. Serve it soon after preparation for maximum texture and eye appeal.

1/2 small zucchini (about 2 ounces), cut into 1/2-inch dice

1 medium tomato, cut into 1/2-inch pieces

2 tablespoons chopped fresh basil

2 tablespoons snipped fresh cilantro

1 tablespoon chopped red onion, rinsed under cold water and patted dry

2 teaspoons fresh lemon juice

2 teaspoons olive oil (extra-virgin preferred)

1. In a small bowl, toss together all the ingredients.

COOK'S TIP: *Rinsing the red onion in this recipe helps mellow some of its raw taste.*

Exchanges/Choices		
1 Vegetable		
1 Fat		
Calories	60	
Calories from Fat	40	
Total Fat	4.5	g
Saturated Fat	0.6	g
Trans Fat	0.0	g
Polyunsaturated Fat	0.6	g
Monounsaturated Fat	3.4	g
Cholesterol	0	mg
Sodium	10	mg
Total Carbohydrate	4	g
Dietary Fiber	1	g
Sugars	2	g
Protein	1	g

ROASTED ASPARAGUS SALAD

Serves 2; 4 spears per serving
Preparation time: 5 minutes

Dress up even simple dinners with this dramatic-looking salad.

Cooking spray
8 medium asparagus spears, trimmed and patted very dry
1 tablespoon chopped walnuts
2 teaspoons light balsamic vinaigrette
Pepper, to taste (coarsely ground preferred)

1. Preheat the oven to 425°F. Line a baking sheet with aluminum foil. Lightly spray with cooking spray.

2. Arrange the asparagus in a single layer on the baking sheet. Sprinkle the walnuts around the asparagus. Lightly spray the asparagus with cooking spray. Roll back and forth to coat.

3. Roast for 5 minutes. Using tongs, turn the asparagus over gently. Roast for 4 minutes, or until the walnuts begin to brown. Transfer to a plate.

4. Spoon the vinaigrette over the asparagus and walnuts. Roll back and forth to coat. Sprinkle with the pepper. Let stand for 10 minutes so the flavors blend.

COOK'S TIP: *Be sure to dry the asparagus thoroughly before cooking or it will not brown properly.*

Exchanges/Choices		
1 Vegetable		
1/2 Fat		
Calories	45	
Calories from Fat	30	
Total Fat	**3.5**	**g**
Saturated Fat	0.3	g
Trans Fat	0.0	g
Polyunsaturated Fat	2.2	g
Monounsaturated Fat	0.5	g
Cholesterol	**0**	**mg**
Sodium	**85**	**mg**
Total Carbohydrate	**3**	**g**
Dietary Fiber	1	g
Sugars	1	g
Protein	**2**	**g**

Beet and Arugula Salad with Feta

Serves 2; 1 cup (packed) per serving
Preparation time: 10 minutes

Sweet roasted beets, tangy feta, and peppery arugula combine to create a mouth-tingling medley.

2 medium beets, trimmed, peeled, each cut into eighths
1 teaspoon and 2 teaspoons olive oil, divided use
1/8 teaspoon pepper
1/2 teaspoon white wine vinegar
1/4 teaspoon Dijon mustard
1 1/2 ounces baby arugula, packed (about 1 1/2 cups)
3 tablespoons crumbled fat-free feta cheese

1. Preheat the oven to 400°F.

2. Put the beets in a single layer on a rimmed baking sheet. Drizzle the beets with 1 teaspoon oil. Sprinkle the pepper over the beets.

3. Roast for 20 to 25 minutes, or until tender when tested with a fork. Let cool on the baking sheet for 10 minutes.

4. Meanwhile, in a large bowl, whisk together the remaining 2 teaspoons oil, vinegar, and mustard. Add the arugula, swirling the leaves in the dressing (tongs work well for this). Add the cooled beets. Sprinkle with the feta. Toss to combine.

> **COOK'S TIP:** *Most recipes advise roasting beets whole, then peeling them once cooked. To cut cooking time considerably, peel them raw (a vegetable peeler works well) and cut them into quarters or eighths before roasting. Beets can stain clothes, so consider donning an apron and a pair of disposable plastic gloves before handling the beets.*

Exchanges/Choices		
2 Vegetable		
1 1/2 Fat		
Calories	105	
Calories from Fat	65	
Total Fat	7.0	g
Saturated Fat	0.9	g
Trans Fat	0.0	g
Polyunsaturated Fat	0.8	g
Monounsaturated Fat	5.0	g
Cholesterol	0	mg
Sodium	280	mg
Total Carbohydrate	8	g
Dietary Fiber	2	g
Sugars	5	g
Protein	4	g

JEWELED CARROT SLAW

Serves 2; 1/2 cup (packed) per serving
Preparation time: 10 minutes

With its garnet-colored cranberries and emerald green pistachios, this light and fruity carrot slaw is a welcome change from the traditional mayonnaise-based coleslaw.

2 teaspoons canola or corn oil
1 teaspoon finely snipped fresh cilantro
1 teaspoon fresh orange juice
1/8 teaspoon pepper
1/2 small Granny Smith apple, shredded
1/3 medium carrot, shredded
2 tablespoons dried sweetened cranberries
2 tablespoons dry-roasted unsalted pistachios

1. In a medium serving bowl, whisk together the oil, cilantro, orange juice, and pepper.

2. Add the apple and carrot to the dressing. Toss to coat. Add the cranberries and pistachios. Toss.

Exchanges/Choices		
1 Fruit		
1 1/2 Fat		
Calories	130	
Calories from Fat	70	
Total Fat	8.0	g
Saturated Fat	0.8	g
Trans Fat	0.0	g
Polyunsaturated Fat	2.5	g
Monounsaturated Fat	4.6	g
Cholesterol	0	mg
Sodium	10	mg
Total Carbohydrate	13	g
Dietary Fiber	2	g
Sugars	9	g
Protein	2	g

Fresh Citrus and Ginger Coleslaw

Serves 2; 2/3 cup per serving
Preparation time: 7 minutes

Orange, lemon, and ginger combine to make this slaw pop with freshness.

1/4 teaspoon grated orange zest
3 tablespoons fresh orange juice
1 tablespoon fresh lemon juice
2 1/2 teaspoons sugar
1 teaspoon canola or corn oil
1/2 teaspoon grated peeled gingerroot
1 1/2 cups packaged shredded cabbage and carrot coleslaw mix
2 tablespoons finely chopped red onion

1. In a medium bowl, whisk together the orange zest, orange juice, lemon juice, sugar, oil, and gingerroot.

2. Add the coleslaw mix and onion. Toss thoroughly. Let stand for 5 minutes before serving so the flavors blend.

Exchanges/Choices		
1 Carbohydrate		
Calories	70	
Calories from Fat	20	
Total Fat	2.5	g
Saturated Fat	0.2	g
Trans Fat	0.0	g
Polyunsaturated Fat	0.7	g
Monounsaturated Fat	1.3	g
Cholesterol	0	mg
Sodium	15	mg
Total Carbohydrate	12	g
Dietary Fiber	1	g
Sugars	9	g
Protein	0	g

Corn and Couscous Salad

CORN AND COUSCOUS SALAD
WITH GREEN ONION VINAIGRETTE

Serves 2; 1/2 cup per serving
Preparation time: 5 minutes

You can prepare this salad, a pleasing blend of delicately textured couscous and plump corn kernels dressed with zesty green onion vinaigrette, up to two days in advance. The flavor just gets better and better.

Salad

3 tablespoons uncooked couscous

3 tablespoons water

1/2 cup frozen whole-kernel corn, thawed

1 (2-ounce) jar diced pimientos, drained

Green Onion Vinaigrette

1 medium green onion, cut crosswise into 4 to 6 pieces

3 tablespoons fat-free, low-sodium chicken broth

1 tablespoon white wine vinegar

1 teaspoon olive oil (extra-virgin preferred)

1/2 teaspoon light brown sugar

1/2 medium garlic clove, minced

1/8 teaspoon pepper

Exchanges/Choices		
1 1/2 Starch		
1/2 Fat		
Calories	125	
Calories from Fat	20	
Total Fat	2.5	g
Saturated Fat	0.4	g
Trans Fat	0.0	g
Polyunsaturated Fat	0.4	g
Monounsaturated Fat	1.7	g
Cholesterol	0	mg
Sodium	15	mg
Total Carbohydrate	23	g
Dietary Fiber	2	g
Sugars	3	g
Protein	4	g

1. Prepare the couscous using the package directions, but with 3 tablespoons water and no salt or oil. Transfer to a medium bowl. Cover and refrigerate for 5 minutes to cool slightly.

2. In a food processor or blender, process the dressing ingredients for 15 to 20 seconds, or until the green onion is very finely chopped.

3. Pour the dressing over the couscous. Stir in the corn and pimientos. Serve immediately, or cover and refrigerate for up to two days.

CANTALOUPE-BLUEBERRY SALAD WITH MINT AND LIME

Serves 2; 2 cantaloupe wedges and 1/4 cup blueberries per serving
Preparation time: 10 minutes

Specks of dark green mint and vibrant lime zest further enhance the lovely color contrast of orange cantaloupe with bold blueberries.

1/2 medium cantaloupe, seeded, rind discarded, and cut into 4 wedges
1/2 cup fresh or frozen blueberries, thawed if frozen and patted dry
1 tablespoon chopped fresh mint
1/4 teaspoon grated lime zest
1 tablespoon fresh lime juice

1. Place two cantaloupe wedges on each salad plate. Spoon half the berries over each serving. Sprinkle with the mint and lime zest. Pour the lime juice over all.

COOK'S TIP: *Look for a halved cantaloupe in your supermarket's produce section if you don't have room in your refrigerator for leftovers.*

Exchanges/Choices		
1 Fruit		
Calories	70	
Calories from Fat	5	
Total Fat	0.5	g
Saturated Fat	0.1	g
Trans Fat	0.0	g
Polyunsaturated Fat	0.2	g
Monounsaturated Fat	0.0	g
Cholesterol	0	mg
Sodium	15	mg
Total Carbohydrate	17	g
Dietary Fiber	2	g
Sugars	14	g
Protein	2	g

Red and Green Apple Salad

Red and Green Apple Salad with Raspberry Vinaigrette

Serves 2; 1/2 cup salad and 2 tablespoons dressing per serving
Preparation time: 10 minutes

Apples and celery provide the crunch, dried cherries provide the sweetness, and raspberry vinegar adds a bit of tartness to this easy-to-assemble salad.

Raspberry Vinaigrette

1/4 cup fresh or frozen unsweetened raspberries, thawed and patted dry if frozen
1 1/2 tablespoons raspberry vinegar, red wine vinegar, or cider vinegar
2 teaspoons canola or corn oil
1 teaspoon chopped fresh mint
1 teaspoon minced shallot
1 teaspoon honey
1/2 teaspoon Dijon mustard

Salad

1/2 small red apple, such as Red Delicious, sliced
1/2 small green apple, such as Granny Smith, sliced
1/2 medium rib of celery, cut into 1/4-inch slices
1 tablespoon plus 1 teaspoon sweetened dried cherries or sweetened dried cranberries

1. In a small bowl, mash the raspberries with a fork. Add the vinegar, oil, mint, shallot, honey, and mustard, whisking until well blended.

2. Arrange the remaining ingredients on salad plates. Drizzle 2 tablespoons dressing over each salad. Serve immediately.

COOK'S TIP: *Slicing apples right before you need them helps keep them from turning brown. If you want to do this step earlier, sprinkle the apples with any kind of citrus juice, then toss to coat.*

Exchanges/Choices		
1 Fruit		
1 Fat		
Calories	100	
Calories from Fat	40	
Total Fat	4.5	g
Saturated Fat	0.3	g
Trans Fat	0.0	g
Polyunsaturated Fat	1.4	g
Monounsaturated Fat	2.7	g
Cholesterol	0	mg
Sodium	45	mg
Total Carbohydrate	15	g
Dietary Fiber	2	g
Sugars	11	g
Protein	0	g

TUNA-STUFFED TOMATOES

Serves 2; 1/2 cup tuna and 1 tomato per serving
Preparation time: 5 minutes

For a welcome change from tuna sandwiches, try tomatoes stuffed with a nontraditional tuna salad.

3 ounces low-sodium chunk white albacore tuna, packed in water, drained
1/2 cup packaged shredded cabbage and carrot coleslaw mix, finely chopped
1 medium green onion, thinly sliced
2 tablespoons fat-free plain yogurt
2 tablespoons light ranch dressing
2 teaspoons capers, drained
2 medium tomatoes

1. Put the tuna in a medium bowl. Flake using a fork. Stir in the coleslaw mix and green onion. Gently stir in the yogurt, ranch dressing, and capers.

2. Cut and discard a 1/4-inch crosswise slice from the stem end of each tomato. Core the tomatoes, discarding the pulp and seeds. Spoon the tuna mixture into each tomato.

Exchanges/Choices
2 Vegetable
1 Lean Meat
1/2 Fat

Calories	120	
Calories from Fat	40	
Total Fat	4.5	**g**
Saturated Fat	0.7	g
Trans Fat	0.0	g
Polyunsaturated Fat	0.4	g
Monounsaturated Fat	0.2	g
Cholesterol	20	**mg**
Sodium	440	**mg**
Total Carbohydrate	9	**g**
Dietary Fiber	2	g
Sugars	5	g
Protein	12	**g**

QUINOA AND SHRIMP SALAD

Serves 2; 1 cup per serving
Preparation time: 15 minutes

Cucumber and green onions add crunch to this herb-enhanced salad of shrimp and quinoa (KEEN-wah), a high-protein grain. Quinoa has a bitter coating called saponin, which needs to be rinsed off.

1/3 cup quinoa, rinsed well under cool water and drained
2/3 cup and 3 cups water, divided use
8 jumbo raw shrimp in shells (21 to 25 count), rinsed
1/2 cup diced seeded cucumber (English preferred)
2 medium green onions, diced
1/4 cup firmly packed minced mixed fresh herbs (such as any combination of
　　　Italian [flat-leaf] parsley, cilantro, mint, tarragon, chervil, or dillweed)
1/2 teaspoon firmly packed grated lemon zest
1 tablespoon olive oil (extra-virgin preferred)
2 teaspoons fresh lemon juice
1/8 teaspoon salt
1/8 teaspoon pepper

1. In a small saucepan, bring the quinoa and 2/3 cup water to a boil over high heat. Reduce the heat and simmer for 10 to 12 minutes, or until all the water is absorbed. Transfer to a medium serving bowl. Set aside to cool.

2. Rinse the pan. Pour in the remaining 3 cups water. Bring to a boil over high heat. Add the shrimp. Reduce the heat and simmer for 3 to 5 minutes, or until they turn pink and are cooked through. Drain in a colander. Plunge the shrimp into a bowl of ice water to stop the cooking. Peel the shrimp, rinse, and pat dry.

3. Stir the shrimp into the quinoa. Stir in the cucumber, green onions, herbs, and lemon zest.

4. In a small bowl, stir together the remaining ingredients. Drizzle over the salad. Stir to moisten all the ingredients. Serve immediately.

Exchanges/Choices		
1 1/2 Starch		
2 Lean Meat		
1/2 Fat		
Calories	225	
Calories from Fat	80	
Total Fat	9.0	g
Saturated Fat	1.2	g
Trans Fat	0.0	g
Polyunsaturated Fat	1.6	g
Monounsaturated Fat	5.5	g
Cholesterol	90	mg
Sodium	270	mg
Total Carbohydrate	23	g
Dietary Fiber	3	g
Sugars	1	g
Protein	14	g

Spicy Chicken, Peanut, and Cucumber Salad

Serves 2; 3 1/2 cups per serving
Preparation time: 15 minutes

This mildly spicy salad is a sure palate-pleaser. Vinegar-based Thai chili-garlic sauce is an excellent condiment to keep on hand, perking up everything from pizza to seafood. It makes a great dipping sauce for vegetables or sushi.

1/2 tablespoon and 1/8 teaspoon chili-garlic sauce, divided use
1 boneless, skinless chicken breast (about 8 ounces), all visible fat discarded
3 tablespoons raspberry vinegar
1 tablespoon canola or corn oil
1/2 teaspoon soy sauce (lowest sodium available)
4 cups mixed greens
3 tablespoons thinly sliced fresh basil
3 tablespoons thinly sliced fresh mint
1/2 medium red bell pepper and 1/2 medium yellow bell pepper, or 1 medium red bell pepper, cut into rings
1/2 medium cucumber, peeled and sliced
2 tablespoons dry-roasted unsalted peanuts

1. Preheat the grill on medium high.

2. Rub 1/2 tablespoon chili-garlic sauce over both sides of the chicken. Grill, covered, for 5 to 7 minutes on each side, or until the internal temperature registers 165°F on an instant-read thermometer. Cut into strips 3/4 inch wide.

3. Meanwhile, in a medium bowl, stir together the vinegar, oil, soy sauce, and remaining 1/8 teaspoon chili-garlic sauce.

4. When the chicken is cooked, add the greens, basil, and mint to the vinegar mixture. Toss. Arrange on a platter. Place the bell pepper rings and cucumber slices on the greens. Top with the chicken strips. Sprinkle with the peanuts. Serve immediately.

Exchanges/Choices		
3 Vegetable		
3 Lean Meat		
2 Fat		
Calories	295	
Calories from Fat	135	
Total Fat	15.0	g
Saturated Fat	1.9	g
Trans Fat	0.0	g
Polyunsaturated Fat	4.3	g
Monounsaturated Fat	7.4	g
Cholesterol	65	mg
Sodium	210	mg
Total Carbohydrate	14	g
Dietary Fiber	4	g
Sugars	7	g
Protein	29	g

Grilled Chicken Couscous Salad

Serves 2; 3 ounces chicken, 1 cup lettuce, 1/2 cup couscous, and 1/2 cup vegetables per serving
Preparation time: 10 minutes

Spicy lime and Dijon vinaigrette dresses this nice combination of colorful grilled vegetables, grilled chicken, and couscous.

3 tablespoons fresh lime juice
1 tablespoon red wine vinegar
1 tablespoon olive oil
1 tablespoon Dijon mustard
1/4 teaspoon salt-free hot and spicy seasoning blend
2 boneless, skinless chicken breast halves (about 4 ounces each), all visible fat discarded
Cooking spray
3/4 cup water
1/4 cup dry-packed sun-dried tomatoes, cut into 1/2-inch pieces
1/3 cup uncooked couscous
1/2 small yellow summer squash (about 2 ounces), cut lengthwise in thirds
1/2 medium red bell pepper, cut lengthwise in thirds
2 medium green onions, chopped
2 romaine leaves, torn into bite-sized pieces
2 tablespoons sliced almonds, dry-roasted

1. In a small bowl, whisk together the lime juice, vinegar, oil, mustard, and seasoning blend.

2. Put the chicken in a medium nonmetallic bowl. Pour 2 tablespoons lime juice mixture over the chicken. Set the remaining mixture aside to use as dressing. Cover the chicken and refrigerate for 20 minutes.

3. Meanwhile, lightly spray a grill rack with cooking spray. Preheat the grill on medium high.

4. In a medium saucepan, bring the water and tomatoes to a boil over medium-high heat. Remove from heat. Stir in the couscous. Cover and let stand for 5 minutes.

5. Place the chicken in the center of the grill rack. Place the squash and bell pepper around the chicken. Grill the vegetables for 5 to 6 minutes, or until tender. Transfer to a cutting board. Turn the chicken over and grill for 4 to 5 minutes, or until no longer pink in the center. Transfer to the cutting board.

6. Cut the squash and bell pepper into bite-sized pieces. Stir with the green onions into the couscous. Slice the chicken.

7. Place the romaine on plates. Spoon the couscous mixture on top. Arrange the chicken slices down the center. Drizzle the dressing over all. Sprinkle with the almonds.

COOK'S TIP: *Although couscous looks like a grain, it is a very mild flavored pasta. It takes very little time to prepare couscous: Simply pour boiling liquid—usually water or low-sodium broth— over it and let it stand, covered, for 5 to 10 minutes to absorb the liquid. Fluff the couscous with a fork before serving. Because it has little flavor of its own, couscous makes an excellent bed for dishes such as stews and combines well with vegetables, fruits, and nuts.*

Exchanges/Choices
1 1/2 Starch
2 Vegetable
3 Lean Meat
1 1/2 Fat

Calories	360	
Calories from Fat	110	
Total Fat	12.0	g
Saturated Fat	1.8	g
Trans Fat	0.0	g
Polyunsaturated Fat	2.3	g
Monounsaturated Fat	7.0	g
Cholesterol	65	mg
Sodium	220	mg
Total Carbohydrate	33	g
Dietary Fiber	5	g
Sugars	6	g
Protein	32	g

VIETNAMESE STEAK SALAD

Serves 2; 3 ounces beef, 1 cup salad, and 2 tablespoons dressing per serving
Preparation time: 15 minutes

Warm grilled steak nestled on cool, crisp greens and topped with a touch of Asian dressing creates a memorable main dish salad.

3 tablespoons fresh lime juice

1 tablespoon white balsamic vinegar, regular balsamic vinegar, or white wine vinegar

1 tablespoon soy sauce (lowest sodium available)

1 teaspoon sugar

1 teaspoon minced fresh lemongrass, tough outer layer discarded (optional but preferred)

2 medium garlic cloves, minced

8 ounces boneless sirloin, about 3/4 inch thick, all visible fat discarded

3 ounces bite-sized pieces salad greens (about 1 1/2 cups)

1/4 cup thinly sliced cucumber

2 tablespoons shredded carrot

2 tablespoons minced green onions

2 tablespoons minced fresh cilantro

1. In a medium nonmetallic bowl, whisk together the lime juice, vinegar, soy sauce, sugar, lemongrass, and garlic. Cover and refrigerate 1/4 cup mixture to use for the dressing. Add the beef to the remaining mixture in the bowl, turning to coat. Cover and refrigerate for about 30 minutes.

2. Preheat the grill on medium high. Drain the steak, discarding the marinade. Grill the steak for about 5 minutes on each side, or until the desired doneness. Transfer to a cutting board. Cover and let stand for about 5 minutes. Thinly slice the steak across the grain.

3. In a medium bowl, toss together the salad greens, cucumber, carrot, green onions, and cilantro. Add 2 tablespoons reserved dressing. Toss to combine. Transfer to plates. Arrange the steak slices on top. Drizzle each salad with 1 tablespoon dressing.

Exchanges/Choices		
1 Vegetable		
3 Lean Meat		
Calories	170	
Calories from Fat	40	
Total Fat	**4.5**	**g**
Saturated Fat	1.6	g
Trans Fat	0.1	g
Polyunsaturated Fat	0.2	g
Monounsaturated Fat	1.7	g
Cholesterol	**40**	**mg**
Sodium	**300**	**mg**
Total Carbohydrate	**8**	**g**
Dietary Fiber	1	g
Sugars	5	g
Protein	**24**	**g**

Chopped Salad
with Green Chile Dressing

Serves 2; 2 cups lettuce and 1 1/2 cups vegetables per serving
Preparation time: 15 minutes

Bright in color and vibrant with taste, this vegetarian main dish salad features the classic complete protein combination of corn and beans.

Salad

- 2/3 cup frozen whole-kernel corn
- 1/2 (15-ounce) can no-salt-added black beans, rinsed and drained
- 1 small tomato, chopped
- 1/2 medium orange bell pepper, chopped
- 4 cups torn romaine

Green Chile Dressing

- Zest of a medium orange
- 1/4 cup fresh orange juice
- 3 tablespoons chopped green chiles
- 1 tablespoon olive oil (extra-virgin preferred)
- 2 teaspoons white wine vinegar
- 1/2 teaspoon dry mustard
- 1/2 teaspoon ground cumin
- 1/4 teaspoon pepper

1. Prepare the corn using the package directions, omitting the salt and margarine. Drain well in a colander. Set aside to cool.

2. Meanwhile, in a mini food processor or a blender, process the dressing ingredients until smooth.

3. Place the cooked corn, beans, tomato, and bell pepper in separate small bowls. Top each with 1 tablespoon dressing. Toss to coat.

4. In a large bowl, toss the romaine with the remaining dressing. Turn out onto a serving platter. Arrange each vegetable in a separate row on the romaine. Serve immediately.

Exchanges/Choices
- 1 1/2 Starch
- 2 Vegetable
- 1 1/2 Fat

Calories	255	
Calories from Fat	70	
Total Fat	8.0	g
Saturated Fat	1.1	g
Trans Fat	0.0	g
Polyunsaturated Fat	1.2	g
Monounsaturated Fat	5.2	g
Cholesterol	0	mg
Sodium	20	mg
Total Carbohydrate	40	g
Dietary Fiber	8	g
Sugars	10	g
Protein	10	g

SEAFOOD

Blackened Catfish

Serves 2; 3 ounces fish per serving
Preparation time: 10 minutes

A quick blend of everyday spices and a hot skillet let you put this dine-out-quality dish on your table in almost no time.

1 teaspoon fresh lemon juice
1 teaspoon fresh lime juice
1 teaspoon paprika
1 teaspoon garlic powder
1 teaspoon onion powder
1/4 teaspoon pepper
1/4 teaspoon dried oregano, crumbled

1/4 teaspoon dried thyme, crumbled
1/4 teaspoon cayenne
1/8 teaspoon salt
2 catfish fillets (about 4 ounces each), rinsed and patted dry
1 teaspoon canola or corn oil

1. In a small bowl, stir together the lemon and lime juices. Set aside.

2. In another small bowl, stir together the paprika, garlic powder, onion powder, pepper, oregano, thyme, cayenne, and salt. Spread on a plate. Add the fish, turning to coat, including the edge. Using your fingertips, gently press the mixture so it adheres to the fish.

3. Heat a small nonstick skillet over high heat for 2 minutes. Add the oil and swirl to coat the bottom. Cook the fish with the flat side up for 1 minute. Reduce the heat to medium. Cook the same side for 3 minutes, or until the fish looks charred but not burned, using a spatula to gently press the ends of the fish so they make contact with the skillet. Gently turn the fish over. Cook for 2 to 4 minutes, or until the second side is charred and the fish flakes easily when tested with a fork. Serve the reserved juice mixture on the fish.

COOK'S TIP: *You might want to turn on the stove-top fan or crack the kitchen window since these spices can become quite smoky, a sure sign of proper blackening!*

Exchanges/Choices		
3 Lean Meat		
1 Fat		
Calories	190	
Calories from Fat	100	
Total Fat	11.0	g
Saturated Fat	2.0	g
Trans Fat	0.0	g
Polyunsaturated Fat	2.2	g
Monounsaturated Fat	5.6	g
Cholesterol	65	mg
Sodium	235	mg
Total Carbohydrate	3	g
Dietary Fiber	1	g
Sugars	1	g
Protein	20	g

Baked Cod and Vegetables

Serves 2; 3 ounces fish and 1/2 cup vegetables per serving
Preparation time: 20 minutes

Firm-textured and mild, cod stars in this lemony dish. Substitute other colorful vegetables if you prefer.

Cooking spray
8 ounces cod fillets, rinsed and patted dry
1 slice light whole-wheat bread, processed into coarse crumbs
1 small carrot, cut into matchstick-sized pieces
1/2 medium rib of celery, thinly sliced
1/2 small red or green bell pepper, or a combination, thinly sliced
1/4 cup chopped onion
1/4 to 1/2 teaspoon grated lemon zest
2 teaspoons fresh lemon juice
1/4 teaspoon (scant) dried thyme, crumbled
1/4 teaspoon (scant) dried marjoram, crumbled
1/8 teaspoon salt
Dash of pepper
1/2 cup fat-free, low-sodium chicken broth
2 tablespoons no-salt-added canned black beans, rinsed and drained (optional)
Fresh cilantro leaves (optional)

1. Preheat the oven to 375°F.

2. Lightly spray a medium glass baking dish with cooking spray. Put the fish in the baking dish.

3. In a medium bowl, stir together the bread crumbs, carrot, celery, bell pepper, onion, lemon zest, lemon juice, thyme, marjoram, salt, and pepper. Spread over the fish. Pour the broth over all.

4. Bake, covered, for 20 minutes. Bake, uncovered, for 5 minutes, or until the fish flakes easily when tested with a fork. Serve garnished with the beans and cilantro.

Exchanges/Choices		
1/2 Starch		
1 Vegetable		
2 Lean Meat		
Calories	160	
Calories from Fat	15	
Total Fat	1.5	g
Saturated Fat	0.3	g
Trans Fat	0.0	g
Polyunsaturated Fat	0.4	g
Monounsaturated Fat	0.3	g
Cholesterol	50	mg
Sodium	340	mg
Total Carbohydrate	13	g
Dietary Fiber	3	g
Sugars	4	g
Protein	23	g

Thai-Style Halibut
with Coconut and Lime

Serves 2; 3 ounces fish and 2 scant tablespoons sauce per serving
Preparation time: 15 minutes

Coconut and lime are perfect complements for mild halibut. If you prefer more heat, simply increase the amount of crushed red pepper to your taste.

1/2 teaspoon olive oil
2 teaspoons minced shallot
1 medium garlic clove, minced
1/2 teaspoon minced peeled gingerroot
3 1/2 tablespoons light coconut milk
3 tablespoons water
1/2 teaspoon and 1/2 teaspoon firmly packed lime zest, divided use
1 tablespoon plus 1 teaspoon fresh lime juice
1/2 teaspoon dark brown sugar
1/4 teaspoon salt
1/8 teaspoon crushed red pepper flakes, or to taste
8 ounces boneless, skinless halibut, rinsed and patted dry, cut into 1 1/4-inch cubes

1. In a medium nonstick saucepan, heat the oil over medium-low heat, swirling to coat the bottom. Add the shallot, garlic, and gingerroot. Cook until soft and very fragrant, about 2 minutes, stirring constantly. Stir in the coconut milk, water, 1/2 teaspoon lime zest, lime juice, brown sugar, salt, and red pepper flakes. Bring to a simmer, still on medium low, and simmer for 5 minutes.

2. Sir in the fish. Increase the heat to medium and bring to a simmer. Reduce the heat and simmer, covered, for 5 to 7 minutes, or until the fish flakes easily when tested with a fork. Transfer to plates. Sprinkle with the remaining 1/2 teaspoon lime zest.

Exchanges/Choices		
3 Lean Meat		
1/2 Fat		
Calories	160	
Calories from Fat	45	
Total Fat	5.0	g
Saturated Fat	1.4	g
Trans Fat	0.0	g
Polyunsaturated Fat	1.0	g
Monounsaturated Fat	1.9	g
Cholesterol	35	mg
Sodium	365	mg
Total Carbohydrate	4	g
Dietary Fiber	0	g
Sugars	2	g
Protein	24	g

CREOLE SNAPPER

Serves 2; 3 ounces fish and 1 1/2 cups sauce per serving
Preparation time: 23 minutes

You'll get plenty of vegetables with this zesty dish. Round out the meal with corn on the cob.

Cooking spray
2 teaspoons canola or corn oil
1 medium rib of celery, chopped
4 ounces button mushrooms, chopped
3 ounces baby portobello mushrooms, chopped
1/2 small onion, chopped
1 cup canned no-salt-added diced tomatoes, drained
2 red snapper or other mild fish fillets with skin (about 5 ounces each),
    rinsed and patted dry
1/4 teaspoon chili powder
1/4 teaspoon onion powder
1/4 teaspoon garlic powder
1/4 teaspoon dried thyme, crumbled
1/4 teaspoon paprika
1/4 teaspoon ground cumin

1. Preheat the oven to 375°F. Lightly spray an 11 × 7 × 2-inch glass baking dish with cooking spray.

2. In a small skillet, heat the oil over medium heat, swirling to coat the bottom. Cook the celery, mushrooms, and onion for 5 to 6 minutes, or until the celery is tender-crisp, stirring frequently. Stir in the tomatoes. Cook for 1 minute, or until the tomatoes are hot. Spread the mixture in the baking dish. Place the fish with the skin side down on the vegetables.

3. In a small bowl, stir together the remaining ingredients. Sprinkle the mixture over the fish. Bake, covered, for 15 to 18 minutes, or until the fish flakes easily when tested with a fork.

Exchanges/Choices		
3 Vegetable		
3 Lean Meat		
Calories	220	
Calories from Fat	65	
Total Fat	7.0	g
Saturated Fat	0.7	g
Trans Fat	0.0	g
Polyunsaturated Fat	2.2	g
Monounsaturated Fat	3.0	g
Cholesterol	40	mg
Sodium	130	mg
Total Carbohydrate	14	g
Dietary Fiber	4	g
Sugars	7	g
Protein	28	g

Herb-Roasted Red Snapper

HERB-ROASTED RED SNAPPER

Serves: 2; 3 ounces fish per serving
Preparation time: 5 minutes

Using mayonnaise in the coating helps keep this fish moist and delicious.

Cooking spray
1/3 cup panko or plain dried bread crumbs
1 tablespoon finely snipped fresh parsley
1/2 tablespoon minced fresh dillweed or 1/2 teaspoon dried dillweed, crumbled
1 teaspoon grated lemon zest
1 red snapper fillet (about 8 ounces), rinsed and patted dry
1/2 tablespoon light mayonnaise

1. Preheat the oven to 450°F. Lightly spray a baking sheet with cooking spray.

2. In a shallow dish, stir together the panko, parsley, dillweed, and lemon zest.

3. Brush both sides of the fish with the mayonnaise. Add the fish to the panko mixture, turning to coat. Using your fingertips, gently press the crumbs so they adhere to the fish. Transfer the fish to the baking sheet.

4. Bake for 7 to 8 minutes or until the fish flakes easily when tested with a fork. Cut the fish in half.

Exchanges/Choices		
1/2 Starch		
3 Lean Meat		
Calories	155	
Calories from Fat	25	
Total Fat	3.0	g
Saturated Fat	0.5	g
Trans Fat	0.0	g
Polyunsaturated Fat	1.2	g
Monounsaturated Fat	0.6	g
Cholesterol	40	mg
Sodium	90	mg
Total Carbohydrate	7	g
Dietary Fiber	0	g
Sugars	1	g
Protein	24	g

ASIAN CITRUS SALMON

Serves 2; 3 ounces fish and 1 1/2 tablespoons sauce per serving
Preparation time: 10 minutes

Orange marmalade is the unexpected ingredient in this grilled salmon dish with Asian flair.

1/4 cup all-fruit orange marmalade
1 teaspoon grated onion (sweet preferred)
1 teaspoon toasted sesame oil
1 teaspoon soy sauce (lowest sodium available)
1 teaspoon plain rice vinegar
1 small garlic clove, minced
1/4 teaspoon grated peeled gingerroot
1/8 teaspoon cayenne
2 salmon fillets (about 4 ounces each), rinsed and patted dry

1. In a small bowl, whisk together all the ingredients except the fish. Transfer 2 tablespoons sauce to a small cup to use as the glaze. Set aside the remaining sauce to use as the topping.

2. Heat a large nonstick skillet over medium-high heat.

3. Brush 1/2 tablespoon glaze on one side of each fillet. Place the fish with the brushed side down in the skillet. Brush the top side with the remaining glaze. Cook for 3 minutes. Reduce the heat to medium. Turn the fish over. Cook for 3 to 4 minutes, or until it flakes easily when tested with a fork. Spoon the reserved topping over the fish.

COOK'S TIP: *Toasted sesame oil is usually found in small bottles in the Asian food section of the supermarket. High in polyunsaturated fats, this darker sesame oil is used as a flavor accent in cooking. A little goes a long way.*

Exchanges/Choices		
1 1/2 Carbohydrate		
3 Lean Meat		
1 Fat		
Calories	295	
Calories from Fat	110	
Total Fat	12.0	g
Saturated Fat	2.0	g
Trans Fat	0.0	g
Polyunsaturated Fat	3.1	g
Monounsaturated Fat	5.6	g
Cholesterol	75	mg
Sodium	165	mg
Total Carbohydrate	21	g
Dietary Fiber	1	g
Sugars	16	g
Protein	25	g

Salmon and Asparagus Gremolata in Parchment

Serves 2; 3 ounces fish, 4 asparagus spears, and 2 teaspoons gremolata per serving
Preparation time: 15 minutes

Gremolata, an Italian seasoning blend of parsley, lemon, and garlic, is a natural for this elegant presentation of salmon and asparagus baked in parchment. Try the gremolata as a topping for vegetables, other types of fish, and chicken, too.

Cooking spray
1 salmon fillet with skin (about 8 ounces), rinsed, patted dry, and halved
1 medium shallot, thinly sliced
Pinch of pepper
8 medium asparagus spears, trimmed and halved
1/4 cup loosely packed fresh parsley
1/2 medium garlic clove, minced
3/4 teaspoon grated fresh lemon zest

1. Preheat the oven to 425°F.

2. Cut off a 15 × 10-inch sheet of cooking parchment and fold in half to form a 7 1/2 × 10-inch rectangle. Starting at the bottom of the fold, cut into a half heart. Open and spray with cooking spray. Repeat with a second sheet. Place one fillet with the skin side down along the fold and centered on one sheet. Repeat with the second fillet and second sheet. Sprinkle the shallots and pepper over the fish. Place half the asparagus on each piece of fish.

3. Fold the other heart halves over the fish and asparagus. Seal each packet by forming a small pleat at the top of the heart and continuing to pleat the edges until reaching the bottom. Twist the point to shut tightly. Place on a baking sheet.

4. Bake for 10 minutes.

5. Meanwhile, to make the gremolata, finely chop the parsley and garlic together. Add the lemon zest. Chop until well blended.

6. Remove the parchment packets from the oven. Let stand for 3 minutes. Being careful to prevent steam burns, cut an X in the center of each packet. Test to be sure the salmon flakes easily when tested with a fork. If necessary, return the packets to the oven for 1 to 2 minutes to finish cooking. Transfer to plates.

7. Open the parchment, leaving the salmon and asparagus inside. Sprinkle with the gremolata.

COOK'S TIP: *No parchment? For an equally delicious but more casual presentation, bake the salmon and asparagus in rectangular aluminum foil packets. Remove from the packets before serving.*

Exchanges/Choices
  1 Vegetable
  3 Lean Meat

Calories	165	
Calories from Fat	55	
Total Fat	6.0	g
Saturated Fat	1.2	g
Trans Fat	0.0	g
Polyunsaturated Fat	1.9	g
Monounsaturated Fat	2.0	g
Cholesterol	40	mg
Sodium	50	mg
Total Carbohydrate	5	g
Dietary Fiber	2	g
Sugars	1	g
Protein	22	g

Salmon with Blueberry

SALMON WITH BLUEBERRY SAUCE

Serves 2; 3 ounces fish and 1/4 cup sauce per serving
Preparation time: 10 minutes

Blueberry sauce with a splash of balsamic vinegar and a hint of orange is an ideal topping for baked salmon.

Cooking spray
2 salmon fillets with skin (about 5 ounces each), rinsed and patted dry
1/4 teaspoon garlic powder
1/8 teaspoon salt
1/8 teaspoon pepper
1/4 cup low-sodium vegetable broth
1/2 tablespoon cornstarch
1/2 cup frozen blueberries
1 tablespoon fresh orange juice
2 teaspoons balsamic vinegar
1/2 teaspoon honey
2 teaspoons sliced green onion

1. Preheat the oven to 350°F. Line a baking sheet with aluminum foil. Lightly spray with cooking spray.

2. Put the fish with the skin side down on the baking sheet. Sprinkle the garlic powder, salt, and pepper over the fish.

3. Bake for 20 minutes, or until the fish flakes easily when tested with a fork.

4. Meanwhile, in a small saucepan, whisk together the broth and cornstarch until smooth. Whisk in the remaining ingredients except the green onion. Cook over medium-high heat for 5 to 6 minutes, or until the mixture comes to a boil and thickens, stirring frequently. Reduce the heat and simmer for 2 to 3 minutes, stirring often. Remove from the heat. Stir in the green onion. Spoon over the fish. Remove the skin before eating the fish.

Exchanges/Choices
1/2 Carbohydrate
3 Lean Meat
1 Fat

Calories	235	
Calories from Fat	90	
Total Fat	10.0	g
Saturated Fat	1.7	g
Trans Fat	0.0	g
Polyunsaturated Fat	2.3	g
Monounsaturated Fat	4.7	g
Cholesterol	75	mg
Sodium	230	mg
Total Carbohydrate	11	g
Dietary Fiber	1	g
Sugars	6	g
Protein	25	g

SALMON TACOS *Salmon Tacos*

Serves 2; 2 tacos per serving
Preparation time: 10 minutes

With this no-cooking-required filling and tortillas heated in the microwave, you'll have a satisfying lunch or dinner entrée in minutes.

1 (3-ounce) pouch skinless, boneless pink salmon, flaked
1/2 cup no-salt-added canned black beans, rinsed and drained
1 teaspoon fresh lemon juice
1/4 teaspoon ground cumin
1/4 teaspoon chili powder
8 cherry tomatoes, halved
1/2 small avocado, diced
2 tablespoons coarsely snipped fresh cilantro
4 (6-inch) corn tortillas
1/2 cup thinly sliced napa cabbage, baby spinach, or iceberg lettuce

1. In a small bowl, gently stir together the salmon, beans, lemon juice, cumin, and chili powder, being careful to not mash the beans.

2. In a separate small bowl, gently stir together the cherry tomatoes, avocado, and cilantro, being careful to not mash the tomatoes and avocado.

3. Wrap the tortillas in damp paper towels. Microwave on 100% power (high) for 30 to 45 seconds, or until heated through.

4. To assemble, place the tortillas on a flat surface. Spoon the salmon mixture down the center of each tortilla. Spoon the tomato mixture over each. Sprinkle with the cabbage. Roll up jelly-roll style and secure each with a toothpick, or fold the sides of each tortilla so they overlap in the center, taco style.

Exchanges/Choices		
2 Starch		
1 Vegetable		
1 Lean Meat		
1 Fat		
Calories	265	
Calories from Fat	65	
Total Fat	**7.0**	**g**
Saturated Fat	1.3	g
Trans Fat	0.0	g
Polyunsaturated Fat	1.7	g
Monounsaturated Fat	3.2	g
Cholesterol	**15**	**mg**
Sodium	**245**	**mg**
Total Carbohydrate	**38**	**g**
Dietary Fiber	8	g
Sugars	4	g
Protein	**15**	**g**

CRUMB-COATED SOLE
WITH TOMATO-BASIL SAUCE

Serves 2; 3 ounces fish and 2 tablespoons sauce per serving
Preparation time: 10 minutes

Forget traditional crumb coatings. Whole-wheat pita bread is the primary
ingredient of the crisp coating in this recipe.

Olive oil cooking spray
1/2 (6-inch) whole-wheat pita bread, torn into pieces
2 tablespoons shredded or grated reduced-fat Parmesan cheese
1/2 teaspoon grated lemon zest
1/8 teaspoon garlic powder
2 sole fillets (about 4 ounces each), rinsed and patted dry
1 teaspoon olive oil
1/2 medium garlic clove, minced
1/4 cup no-salt-added tomato sauce
1 tablespoon chopped fresh basil or 1/4 teaspoon dried basil, crumbled
1/8 teaspoon salt
1/8 teaspoon pepper

1. Preheat the oven to 400°F. Lightly spray a medium baking sheet with olive oil spray.

2. In a food processor, process the pita bread for 15 to 20 seconds to make soft bread crumbs. Add the Parmesan, lemon zest, and garlic powder. Process for 5 seconds.

3. Place the fish on the baking sheet. Lightly spray the tops with olive oil spray. Sprinkle half the crumb mixture over the fish. Using your fingertips, gently press the crumbs so they will adhere. Turn the fish over and repeat. Lightly spray the second side again with cooking spray. Bake for 8 minutes, or until the fish flakes easily when tested with a fork.

4. Meanwhile, in a small saucepan over medium heat, heat the oil, swirling to coat the bottom. Cook the garlic for 5 seconds, watching carefully so it doesn't burn. Add the remaining ingredients. Cook for 2 to 3 minutes, or until the sauce is warmed through and the basil is wilted, stirring occasionally. Pour over the cooked fish.

Exchanges/Choices		
1/2 Starch		
1/2 Carbohydrate		
3 Lean Meat		
Calories	210	
Calories from Fat	55	
Total Fat	6.0	g
Saturated Fat	1.4	g
Trans Fat	0.0	g
Polyunsaturated Fat	1.0	g
Monounsaturated Fat	2.4	g
Cholesterol	65	mg
Sodium	455	mg
Total Carbohydrate	14	g
Dietary Fiber	2	g
Sugars	2	g
Protein	25	g

TILAPIA WITH TOMATOES AND CAPERS

Serves 2; 3 ounces fish and 1/4 cup topping per serving
Preparation time: 5 minutes

Baking the topping for only a few minutes is the key to retaining its fresh taste.

- 1 teaspoon olive oil
- 1 tilapia fillet (about 8 ounces), rinsed and patted dry
- 1 medium Italian plum tomato, seeded and chopped
- 1 tablespoon finely snipped fresh parsley
- 1 teaspoon capers, drained
- 1/2 teaspoon dried basil, crumbled
- 1/4 teaspoon garlic powder

1. Preheat the oven to 400°F.

2. Pour the oil into a 10 × 6 × 2-inch baking dish. Add the fish, turning to lightly coat. If the ends of the fillet are quite thin, fold them under so baking is more even.

3. Bake for 8 minutes.

4. Meanwhile, in a small bowl, stir together the remaining ingredients. Spoon over the cooked fish.

5. Bake for 3 to 5 minutes, or until the fish flakes easily when tested with a fork.

Exchanges/Choices		
3 Lean Meat		
Calories	140	
Calories from Fat	45	
Total Fat	5.0	g
Saturated Fat	1.3	g
Trans Fat	0.0	g
Polyunsaturated Fat	1.0	g
Monounsaturated Fat	2.4	g
Cholesterol	75	mg
Sodium	75	mg
Total Carbohydrate	2	g
Dietary Fiber	1	g
Sugars	1	g
Protein	23	g

TILAPIA WITH PICANTE-PIMIENTO TOPPING

Serves 2; 3 ounces fish and 2 tablespoons topping per serving
Preparation time: 5 minutes

This entrée could hardly be any easier to make, yet it's attractive and tastes great, too.

Cooking spray
2 tilapia or other mild, thin fish fillets (about 4 ounces each), rinsed and patted dry
1/4 cup picante sauce (lowest sodium available)
1 (2-ounce) jar diced pimientos, undrained
1/2 small lemon, cut into wedges (optional)

1. Preheat the oven to 350°F. Lightly spray an 8-inch square glass baking dish with cooking spray. Place the fish in the dish.

2. In a small bowl, stir together the picante sauce and pimientos with liquid. Spoon over the fish. Cover with aluminum foil.

3. Bake for 12 minutes, or until the fish flakes easily when tested with a fork. Serve with the lemon wedges for squeezing over all.

COOK'S TIP: *Adding pimientos to the picante sauce not only gives the topping more texture but also "stretches" the flavors of the picante sauce without adding sodium.*

Exchanges/Choices		
3 Lean Meat		
Calories	130	
Calories from Fat	20	
Total Fat	2.5	g
Saturated Fat	1.0	g
Trans Fat	0.0	g
Polyunsaturated Fat	0.8	g
Monounsaturated Fat	0.7	g
Cholesterol	75	mg
Sodium	285	mg
Total Carbohydrate	3	g
Dietary Fiber	1	g
Sugars	1	g
Protein	23	g

CRISP PECAN TILAPIA

Serves 2; 3 ounces fish per serving
Preparation time: 10 minutes

Combining panko with cornmeal makes a crisp topping, and toasted pecans add a nice crunch to the tender fish.

Cooking spray
2 tablespoons yellow cornmeal
2 tablespoons panko or plain dried bread crumbs
1 teaspoon cornstarch
1/2 teaspoon salt-free lemon pepper
2 tilapia fillets (about 4 ounces each), rinsed and patted dry
2 teaspoons fresh lemon juice
2 tablespoons coarsely chopped pecans, dry-roasted
1 tablespoon snipped fresh Italian (flat-leaf) parsley

1. Preheat the broiler. Lightly spray an 11 × 7 × 2-inch baking pan with cooking spray.

2. In a shallow dish, stir together the cornmeal, panko, cornstarch, and lemon pepper. Add the fish, turning to coat, shaking off any excess. Transfer to the baking pan. Lightly spray both sides of the fish with cooking spray.

3. Broil for 3 to 4 minutes on each side, or until the fish flakes easily when tested with a fork. Transfer to plates. Drizzle with the lemon juice. Sprinkle with the pecans and parsley.

Exchanges/Choices		
1/2 Starch		
3 Lean Meat		
1/2 Fat		
Calories	**190**	
Calories from Fat	70	
Total Fat	**8.0**	**g**
Saturated Fat	1.5	g
Trans Fat	0.0	g
Polyunsaturated Fat	2.1	g
Monounsaturated Fat	3.7	g
Cholesterol	**75**	**mg**
Sodium	**35**	**mg**
Total Carbohydrate	**7**	**g**
Dietary Fiber	1	g
Sugars	1	g
Protein	**24**	**g**

Orange Tilapia

Serves 2; 3 ounces fish per serving
Preparation time: 5 minutes

Add a green salad and quick-cooking barley for an easy busy-night dinner.

Cooking spray
1/2 teaspoon ground cumin
1/2 teaspoon dried oregano, crumbled
1/2 teaspoon garlic powder
1/4 teaspoon salt
1/8 teaspoon pepper
2 tilapia fillets (about 4 ounces each), rinsed and patted dry
1 teaspoon orange zest
1 tablespoon and 1 tablespoon fresh orange juice, divided use

1. Preheat the broiler. Lightly spray a broiler pan and rack with cooking spray.

2. In a small bowl, stir together the cumin, oregano, garlic powder, salt, and pepper.

3. Put the fish on the broiler pan. Sprinkle each side with the cumin mixture, then the orange zest. Drizzle 1 tablespoon orange juice over the top side of the fillets. Lightly spray with cooking spray.

4. Broil the fish about 4 inches from the heat for 3 to 4 minutes, or until light golden brown. Turn over. Drizzle with the remaining 1 tablespoon orange juice. Lightly spray with cooking spray. Broil for 3 to 4 minutes, or until the fish flakes easily when tested with a fork.

COOK'S TIP: *Because of its mild flavor and nicely portioned fillets, tilapia is good to have on hand so you can enjoy a heart-healthy serving of fish without fuss. Buy a bag of individually wrapped frozen tilapia fillets, remove just the amount you need, and thaw in the refrigerator the night before or in a bowl of cool water shortly before starting dinner.*

Exchanges/Choices
3 Lean Meat

Calories	125	
Calories from Fat	20	
Total Fat	2.5	g
Saturated Fat	1.0	g
Trans Fat	0.0	g
Polyunsaturated Fat	0.7	g
Monounsaturated Fat	0.8	g
Cholesterol	75	mg
Sodium	320	mg
Total Carbohydrate	3	g
Dietary Fiber	0	g
Sugars	2	g
Protein	23	g

Sesame-Crusted Trout with Spinach

Sesame-Crusted Trout

Serves 2; 3 ounces fish and 1/3 cup spinach per serving
Preparation time: 10 minutes

Toasted sesame seeds and fresh ginger turn ordinary trout into something special.

1 large egg white
2 1/2 tablespoons sesame seeds, dry-roasted
1 teaspoon firmly packed grated lemon zest
1/4 teaspoon pepper
2 trout fillets (about 4 ounces each), rinsed and patted dry
1 teaspoon canola or corn oil
6 ounces fresh baby spinach
2 medium green onions, chopped
1/2 teaspoon minced peeled gingerroot
1/2 teaspoon soy sauce (lowest sodium available)
1/2 medium lemon, halved (optional)

1. In a wide, shallow bowl, whisk the egg white until frothy. In a separate wide, shallow bowl, stir together the sesame seeds, lemon zest, and pepper. Set the bowls side by side.

2. Set a large nonstick skillet over medium-high heat.

3. While the skillet heats, dip one piece of fish in the egg white, turning to coat, letting any excess drip off. Dip in the sesame seed mixture, turning to coat. Using your fingertips, gently press the sesame seed mixture so it adheres to the fish. Repeat with the second piece of fish.

4. When the skillet is very hot, add the oil, swirling to coat the bottom. Cook the fish for 2 to 3 minutes on each side, or until the sesame seeds have browned and the fish flakes easily when tested with a fork. Transfer to a plate and tent loosely with aluminum foil to keep warm.

5. Reduce the heat to medium. Stir in the spinach, green onions, gingerroot, and soy sauce. Using tongs, toss for 2 minutes, or until the spinach is wilted. Spread on plates. Place the fish on the spinach. Serve with the lemon wedges for squeezing over all.

Exchanges/Choices		
1 Vegetable		
4 Lean Meat		
2 Fat		
Calories	285	
Calories from Fat	145	
Total Fat	16.0	g
Saturated Fat	2.3	g
Trans Fat	0.0	g
Polyunsaturated Fat	5.0	g
Monounsaturated Fat	7.2	g
Cholesterol	65	mg
Sodium	200	mg
Total Carbohydrate	8	g
Dietary Fiber	4	g
Sugars	1	g
Protein	30	g

FISH FILLETS WITH FRESH ROSEMARY

Serves 2; 3 ounces fish per serving
Preparation time: 5 minutes

Fresh sprigs of rosemary act as a roasting rack under the fish as it bakes, infusing it with fragrance and flavor.

4 to 6 fresh rosemary sprigs
8 ounces trout or sole fillets, about 1/4 inch thick, rinsed and patted dry
1/2 teaspoon olive oil
1 teaspoon fresh lemon juice
1/8 teaspoon salt
1/8 teaspoon pepper

1. Preheat the oven to 350°F. Place the rosemary in a single row in a small baking pan, such as an 8-inch square pan. Top with the fish. Brush the fish with the oil. Sprinkle with the lemon juice, salt, and pepper.

2. Bake for 7 to 8 minutes or until the fish flakes easily when tested with a fork.

Exchanges/Choices
3 Lean Meat
1 Fat

Calories	**180**	
Calories from Fat	80	
Total Fat	**9.0**	**g**
Saturated Fat	1.5	g
Trans Fat	0.0	g
Polyunsaturated Fat	1.8	g
Monounsaturated Fat	4.5	g
Cholesterol	**65**	**mg**
Sodium	**210**	**mg**
Total Carbohydrate	**0**	**g**
Dietary Fiber	0	g
Sugars	0	g
Protein	**24**	**g**

Grilled Tuna

with Charmoula Marinade

Serves 2; 3 ounces fish and 1 tablespoon charmoula per serving
Preparation time: 10 minutes

A wonderful Moroccan marinade for fish, charmoula is a sprightly mix of herbs and spices.

Charmoula

3/4 teaspoon minced garlic
1/8 teaspoon salt
2 tablespoons snipped fresh cilantro
2 tablespoons snipped fresh parsley
1/2 teaspoon ground cumin
1/2 teaspoon paprika
1/4 teaspoon ground ginger
2 teaspoons olive oil
2 teaspoons fresh lemon juice
3 to 4 drops red hot-pepper sauce, or to taste
✱✱✱✱✱✱✱
1 tuna steak (about 8 ounces), 1 inch thick, rinsed, patted dry, and halved

1. On a cutting board, using the tines of a fork, mash the garlic with the salt to make a paste. Sprinkle with the cilantro and parsley. Very finely chop the mixture, occasionally scraping it together with the knife blade, until the mixture is almost a paste. Transfer to a small bowl. Stir in the cumin, paprika, and ginger. Stir in the oil, lemon juice, and hot sauce.

2. Put the tuna on a plate. Spread half the charmoula over each side of the tuna. Cover and refrigerate for 20 minutes.

3. Meanwhile, preheat the grill on medium high or preheat the broiler.

4. Grill the coated tuna, covered, or broil 4 to 6 inches from the heat for 3 to 5 minutes on each side for medium, or until the desired doneness, turning only once.

Exchanges/Choices		
3 Lean Meat		
1 Fat		
Calories	**185**	
Calories from Fat	70	
Total Fat	**8.0**	**g**
Saturated Fat	1.8	g
Trans Fat	0.0	g
Polyunsaturated Fat	1.9	g
Monounsaturated Fat	3.9	g
Cholesterol	**40**	**mg**
Sodium	**140**	**mg**
Total Carbohydrate	**1**	**g**
Dietary Fiber	0	g
Sugars	0	g
Protein	**26**	**g**

Spaghetti with Tuna

SPAGHETTI WITH TUNA AND BROCCOLI

Serves 2; heaping 1 1/2 cups per serving
Preparation time: 10 minutes

As colorful as it is flavorful, this quick entrée is ideal for busy nights. Choose light tuna for this dish. The flavor of white tuna or albacore is too mild.

3 ounces uncooked whole-grain spaghetti
4 ounces broccoli florets, broken into bite-sized pieces
2 teaspoons olive oil
2 medium garlic cloves, minced
1 teaspoon crushed red pepper flakes
2 (3-ounce) pouches chunk light tuna in water, flaked
2 teaspoons shredded or grated Parmesan cheese
1 medium lemon, halved

1. Prepare the spaghetti using package directions, omitting the salt and oil. Three minutes before the end of the cooking time, stir in the broccoli. Cook for 3 minutes. Drain well in a colander. Return the spaghetti and broccoli to the pot (the heat should be turned off). Cover to keep warm.

2. In a small nonstick skillet, stir together the oil, garlic, and red pepper flakes. Cook over medium heat for 2 minutes, stirring constantly. Add the tuna. Cook for 3 minutes, stirring frequently but being careful to not break the tuna into small pieces.

3. Spoon the spaghetti and broccoli onto plates. Spoon the tuna sauce on top. Sprinkle with the Parmesan. Squeeze a generous amount of lemon juice over all.

Exchanges/Choices		
2 Starch		
1 Vegetable		
3 Lean Meat		
Calories	320	
Calories from Fat	65	
Total Fat	7.0	g
Saturated Fat	1.3	g
Trans Fat	0.0	g
Polyunsaturated Fat	1.1	g
Monounsaturated Fat	3.7	g
Cholesterol	45	mg
Sodium	415	mg
Total Carbohydrate	36	g
Dietary Fiber	6	g
Sugars	2	g
Protein	29	g

GINGER TUNA PATTIES

Ginger Tuna Patties

Serves 2; 1 patty per serving
Preparation time: 10 minutes

Although the mixture for these patties seems loose, the egg whites will bind the ingredients together. You'll want to be careful when turning them over.

2 large egg whites
2 tablespoons thinly sliced green onions
2 teaspoons finely chopped peeled gingerroot
1 teaspoon soy sauce (lowest sodium available)
1/2 teaspoon toasted sesame oil
Dash of cayenne
9 ounces low-sodium chunk light tuna in water, drained and broken into small to
    medium pieces
1 teaspoon canola or corn oil

1. In a medium bowl, whisk together the egg whites, green onions, gingerroot, soy sauce, sesame oil, and cayenne. Add the tuna, stirring gently to combine.

2. In a large nonstick skillet, heat the oil over medium heat, swirling to coat the bottom. Divide the tuna mixture in half, making sure to get an equal amount of liquid in each so the egg white will hold each patty together. Pack one of the halves into a 1/2-cup measuring cup. Invert onto the skillet and slightly flatten the mound. Repeat with the remaining mixture. Cook for 4 minutes on one side. Gently turn over and cook for 3 to 4 minutes, or until set.

Exchanges/Choices		
4 Lean Meat		
Calories	175	
Calories from Fat	40	
Total Fat	4.5	g
Saturated Fat	0.6	g
Trans Fat	0.0	g
Polyunsaturated Fat	1.5	g
Monounsaturated Fat	2.0	g
Cholesterol	50	mg
Sodium	330	mg
Total Carbohydrate	1	g
Dietary Fiber	0	g
Sugars	1	g
Protein	31	g

Crab Cakes with Salsa

CRAB CAKES
WITH TROPICAL FRUIT SALSA

Serves 2; 2 crab cakes and 1/4 cup plus 2 tablespoons salsa per serving
Preparation time: 15 minutes

These crab cakes, topped with a salsa of tropical fruit and cilantro, are sure to become a regular addition to your meals. Serve with a delicate salad of Bibb lettuce and citrus vinaigrette.

Cooking spray
2 tablespoons diced red bell pepper
2 tablespoons finely chopped celery
2 tablespoons shredded carrots
1 medium green onion, thinly sliced
1 large egg white
1 tablespoon light mayonnaise
1/2 teaspoon salt-free lemon pepper
1 (6-ounce) can lump crabmeat, drained
1/4 cup finely crushed low-sodium thin whole-grain crackers
1 (4-ounce) can tropical mixed fruit, drained
1 medium kiwifruit, peeled and diced
1 tablespoon snipped fresh cilantro

1. Preheat the oven to 400°F. Lightly spray a medium baking sheet with cooking spray.

2. In a medium bowl, stir together the bell pepper, celery, carrot, green onion, egg white, mayonnaise, and lemon pepper. Carefully stir in the crabmeat so it stays in fairly large pieces.

3. Line a 1/4-cup measuring cup with plastic wrap. Spoon one-quarter of the crab mixture into the measuring cup, pressing lightly with the spoon to compress the mixture. Sprinkle a scant teaspoon cracker crumbs over the crab cake. Invert the measuring cup onto the baking sheet (the crumb side will be down). Remove the plastic wrap from the crab cake. Sprinkle about 2 teaspoons cracker crumbs over the top of the crab cake, carefully patting the excess onto the side of the crab cake. Repeat for the remaining three crab cakes. Lightly spray the tops and sides of the crab cakes with cooking spray.

4. Bake for 10 minutes. Turn the crab cakes over. Bake for 5 minutes, or until golden brown and heated through.

5. Meanwhile, in a small bowl, stir together the mixed fruit, kiwifruit, and cilantro. Serve with the crab cakes.

COOK'S TIP: *To crush crackers without mess, put them in a resealable plastic bag, seal the bag, and gently pound the crackers with the flat side of a meat mallet or a rolling pin. You can also break the crackers into smaller pieces, put them in a food processor, then process for 20 to 30 seconds, or until finely crushed.*

Exchanges/Choices		
1 Starch		
1 Fruit		
1 Lean Meat		
1 1/2 Fat		
Calories	185	
Calories from Fat	55	
Total Fat	6.0	g
Saturated Fat	1.0	g
Trans Fat	0.0	g
Polyunsaturated Fat	2.9	g
Monounsaturated Fat	1.2	g
Cholesterol	55	mg
Sodium	390	mg
Total Carbohydrate	24	g
Dietary Fiber	3	g
Sugars	12	g
Protein	11	g

SHRIMP AND SNOW PEA SAUTÉ

Serves 2; 1 2/3 cups per serving
Preparation time: 10 minutes

Plump pink shrimp and tender-crisp green snow peas add color and crunch to this creamy noodle dish.

3 ounces dried no-yolk noodles
2 teaspoons cornstarch
3/4 cup fat-free evaporated milk
8 ounces peeled raw medium shrimp (41 to 50 count)
4 medium garlic cloves, minced
1 teaspoon olive oil
4 ounces snow peas, trimmed, halved crosswise
1/4 cup shredded or grated Parmesan cheese

1. Prepare the pasta using the package directions, omitting the salt and oil. Drain well in a colander. Set aside.

2. Meanwhile, put the cornstarch in a small bowl. Pour in the milk, whisking to dissolve.

3. In another small bowl, stir together the shrimp and garlic.

4. In a medium nonstick skillet, heat the oil over medium heat, swirling to coat the bottom. Cook the shrimp for 30 seconds on each side. Stir in the milk mixture and snow peas. Cook for 2 minutes, or until the mixture has thickened and comes to a simmer, stirring once or twice.

5. Pour the pasta into a shallow bowl. Stir in the shrimp mixture. Sprinkle with the Parmesan cheese. Stir.

Exchanges/Choices

2 Starch
1 Fat-Free Milk
1 Vegetable
3 Lean Meat

Calories	425	
Calories from Fat	65	
Total Fat	7.0	g
Saturated Fat	2.7	g
Trans Fat	0.0	g
Polyunsaturated Fat	0.9	g
Monounsaturated Fat	3.2	g
Cholesterol	175	mg
Sodium	410	mg
Total Carbohydrate	50	g
Dietary Fiber	4	g
Sugars	16	g
Protein	37	g

GRILLED SHRIMP WITH MINT SALSA VERDE

Serves 2; 6 shrimp and 1 1/2 tablespoons salsa per serving
Preparation time: 15 minutes

A tiny dollop of yogurt gives a pleasant, unexpected creaminess to the piquant salsa that is drizzled over grilled shrimp in this attractive entrée.

1/2 tablespoon plus 1 teaspoon and 1/2 tablespoon fresh lemon juice, divided use
1 teaspoon and 1 tablespoon olive oil, divided use
1 medium garlic clove, minced
12 jumbo raw shrimp in shells (21 to 25 count), peeled, rinsed, and patted dry
2 medium green onions, chopped
3 tablespoons chopped fresh mint
1 tablespoon snipped fresh cilantro
1/2 tablespoon capers, drained
1/2 tablespoon minced fresh jalapeño, seeds and ribs discarded, or to taste
2 teaspoons fat-free plain yogurt
1 teaspoon water
1/8 teaspoon salt
1/8 teaspoon pepper
Cooking spray

1. In a small glass baking dish, whisk together 1/2 tablespoon plus 1 teaspoon lemon juice, 1 teaspoon oil, and garlic. Add the shrimp, turning to coat. Cover and refrigerate for 10 minutes, turning once.

2. Meanwhile, in a mini food processor, process the green onions, mint, cilantro, capers, jalapeño, yogurt, water, salt, pepper, remaining 1/2 tablespoon lemon juice, and remaining 1 tablespoon oil for 30 seconds, or until smooth and creamy. Scrape the side once or twice during this process.

3. Preheat a grill pan on medium-high heat. Lightly spray with cooking spray. Remove the shrimp from the marinade. Discard the marinade. Grill the shrimp for 2 to 3 minutes on each side, or until pink and cooked through. Serve with the salsa verde drizzled on top.

Exchanges/Choices		
2 Lean Meat		
1 1/2 Fat		
Calories	150	
Calories from Fat	80	
Total Fat	9.0	g
Saturated Fat	1.3	g
Trans Fat	0.0	g
Polyunsaturated Fat	1.2	g
Monounsaturated Fat	6.4	g
Cholesterol	125	mg
Sodium	365	mg
Total Carbohydrate	3	g
Dietary Fiber	1	g
Sugars	1	g
Protein	14	g

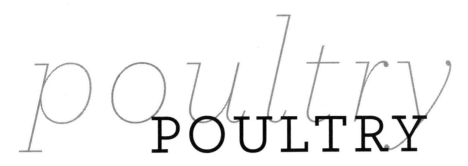

POULTRY

CREMINI-STUFFED CHICKEN BREASTS

Serves 2; 1 stuffed chicken breast and 1 heaping tablespoon sauce per serving
Preparation time: 15 minutes

Earthy cremini mushrooms and a sherry-based pan sauce combine in an entrée that's sophisticated enough for a special occasion.

2 teaspoons and 2 teaspoons olive oil, divided use
2 tablespoons and 1 teaspoon minced shallot, divided use
2 medium garlic cloves, chopped
4 ounces cremini mushrooms (about 8), finely chopped
1/8 teaspoon and 1/8 teaspoon salt, divided use
1/8 teaspoon and 1/8 teaspoon pepper, divided use
2 boneless, skinless chicken breast halves (about 4 ounces each), all visible fat discarded, butterflied and pounded to 1/4-inch thickness
1/4 cup cream sherry
1/2 cup fat-free, low-sodium chicken broth
2 teaspoons fat-free half-and-half
2 teaspoons minced chives (optional)

1. Preheat the oven to 425°F. Line a small baking sheet with aluminum foil and set aside.

2. In a medium skillet, heat 2 teaspoons oil over medium heat. Cook 2 tablespoons shallot and the garlic for about 2 minutes, or until the shallot begins to turn translucent. Add the mushrooms, 1/8 teaspoon salt, and 1/8 teaspoon pepper. Reduce the heat slightly and cook, stirring constantly, for about 4 minutes, or until the mushrooms release their liquid and the vegetables are tender. Transfer to a plate and let stand until cool enough to handle.

3. Coat both sides with the remaining 1/8 teaspoon salt and 1/8 teaspoon pepper. Spoon half the mushroom filling onto each breast, spreading lightly with the back of a spoon and leaving a 1/4-inch border. Carefully roll the chicken from top to bottom, pressing in the sides so the filling doesn't escape. Secure with kitchen twine.

4. Wipe the skillet with paper towels. Add the remaining 2 teaspoons oil, swirling to coat the bottom. Brown the chicken over medium-high heat for about 3 minutes on each side. Transfer to the baking sheet.

5. Bake for about 15 minutes, or until cooked through (the chicken should still be juicy).

6. Meanwhile, in the same skillet set over medium heat, stir together the sherry and remaining 1 teaspoon shallot, scraping with a wooden spoon to dislodge any browned bits. Pour in the broth. Increase the heat to medium high and bring to a simmer. Reduce the heat and simmer for about 3 minutes, or until reduced to 2 tablespoons. Remove from the heat and stir in the half-and-half. Cover.

7. When the chicken is ready, discard the twine and cut each breast in half on the diagonal, revealing the filling. Drizzle with the sauce and garnish with the chives.

COOK'S TIP: *Do not use sherry labeled "cooking sherry." It's generally of low quality and contains added sodium.*

Exchanges/Choices		
1 Vegetable		
4 Lean Meat		
1 Fat		
Calories	**265**	
Calories from Fat	110	
Total Fat	**12.0**	**g**
Saturated Fat	2.1	g
Trans Fat	0.0	g
Polyunsaturated Fat	1.5	g
Monounsaturated Fat	7.6	g
Cholesterol	**65**	**mg**
Sodium	**380**	**mg**
Total Carbohydrate	**8**	**g**
Dietary Fiber	1	g
Sugars	3	g
Protein	**27**	**g**

CRISP CHICKEN
WITH RASPBERRY DIPPING SAUCE

Serves 2; 3 ounces chicken and 1 heaping tablespoon sauce per serving
Preparation time: 15 minutes

Served with a sweet and tangy dipping sauce, this chicken entrée gets its crisp coating from Japanese-style bread crumbs called panko.

3 tablespoons panko
1 teaspoon garlic powder
1 teaspoon very finely snipped fresh parsley
1/2 teaspoon firmly packed grated lemon zest
1/4 teaspoon dry mustard
1/4 teaspoon salt
1/4 teaspoon pepper
2 boneless, skinless chicken breast halves (about 4 ounces each), all visible fat discarded, pounded to 1/4-inch thickness
2 teaspoons and 1/2 teaspoon olive oil, divided use
2 teaspoons minced shallot
1/2 cup fat-free, low-sodium chicken broth
2 teaspoons raspberry vinegar
2 1/2 teaspoons all-fruit raspberry spread (seedless preferred)

1. In a shallow dish, combine the panko, garlic powder, parsley, lemon zest, mustard, salt, and pepper, lightly stirring together with a fork. Put one piece of chicken in the crumbs. Using your fingertips, firmly press the crumbs so they adhere to the chicken. Turn over and repeat. Repeat with the remaining chicken. Discard any crumb mixture remaining.

2. In a large nonstick skillet, heat 2 teaspoons oil over medium-high heat, swirling to coat the bottom. Cook the chicken for about 4 minutes on each side, or until it is cooked through and the crumbs are golden brown. Transfer to a plate. Cover to keep warm.

3. To make the sauce, put the remaining 1/2 teaspoon oil in the skillet, swirling to coat the bottom. Cook the shallot over medium heat for about 1 minute, stirring constantly and scraping to dislodge the browned bits (a wooden spoon or heatproof scraper works well). Slowly pour in the broth and vinegar. (The mixture will bubble vigorously.)

4. Increase the heat to medium high and cook for about 2 minutes, or until the sauce reduces slightly. Remove from the heat. Add the raspberry spread, stirring until melted.

5. Slice the chicken diagonally into strips. Serve with the sauce on the side.

COOK'S TIP: *Japanese bread crumbs, known as panko, make a delicious, crunchy coating. Panko is coarser than the usual dried bread crumbs and contains far less sodium. Look for panko near the other packaged bread crumbs or in the Asian section of the store.*

Exchanges/Choices		
1/2 Carbohydrate		
3 Lean Meat		
1 Fat		
Calories	225	
Calories from Fat	80	
Total Fat	9.0	g
Saturated Fat	1.6	g
Trans Fat	0.0	g
Polyunsaturated Fat	1.2	g
Monounsaturated Fat	5.1	g
Cholesterol	65	mg
Sodium	310	mg
Total Carbohydrate	9	g
Dietary Fiber	1	g
Sugars	4	g
Protein	25	g

Panko Chicken
Panko Chicken
in Mustard Cream Sauce

Panko Chicken

Serves 2; 3 ounces chicken and 2 tablespoons sauce per serving
Preparation time: 10 minutes

A decadent-tasting cream sauce adds pizzazz to crisp, panko-coated chicken.

1/3 cup low-fat buttermilk
1/2 cup panko
Cooking spray
2 boneless, skinless chicken breast halves (about 4 ounces each), all visible fat discarded
1/4 cup fat-free, low-sodium chicken broth
2 tablespoons fat-free sour cream
1 tablespoon Dijon mustard
1/4 teaspoon dried tarragon, crumbled

1. Preheat the oven to 400°F.

2. Pour the buttermilk into a shallow dish. Put the panko in another shallow dish. Lightly spray an 11 × 7 × 2-inch baking pan with cooking spray. Set the dishes and baking pan in a row, assembly-line style.

3. Dip the chicken in the buttermilk, turning to coat. Roll each piece in the panko, lightly shaking off any excess. Arrange the chicken in a single layer in the baking pan. Lightly spray the top of the chicken with cooking spray.

4. Bake for 20 to 25 minutes, or until the chicken is no longer pink in the center.

5. Meanwhile, pour the broth into a small saucepan. Heat to a simmer over medium-high heat. Reduce the heat to medium low. Whisk in the sour cream, mustard, and tarragon. Cook for 1 to 2 minutes, or until smooth and heated through, whisking constantly. Pour the sauce over the cooked chicken.

Exchanges/Choices
1 Starch
3 Lean Meat

Calories	195	
Calories from Fat	30	
Total Fat	3.5	g
Saturated Fat	0.9	g
Trans Fat	0.0	g
Polyunsaturated Fat	0.7	g
Monounsaturated Fat	1.2	g
Cholesterol	70	mg
Sodium	280	mg
Total Carbohydrate	11	g
Dietary Fiber	1	g
Sugars	2	g
Protein	27	g

GRILLED TUSCAN CHICKEN

Serves 2: 3 ounces chicken per serving
Preparation time: 5 minutes

The flavors of Tuscany—lemon, garlic, oregano, and sage—brighten this marinated chicken dish.

2 tablespoons fresh lemon juice
1 tablespoon white balsamic vinegar or white wine vinegar
1 medium garlic clove, minced
1/4 teaspoon dried oregano, crumbled
1/4 teaspoon dried sage
1/8 teaspoon pepper (coarsely ground preferred)
2 boneless, skinless chicken breast halves (about 4 ounces each), all visible fat discarded, pounded to 1/2-inch thickness
Cooking spray

1. In a medium nonmetallic bowl, stir together the lemon juice, vinegar, garlic, oregano, sage, and pepper. Add the chicken, turning to coat. Cover and refrigerate for 30 minutes, turning once. Transfer the chicken to a plate and discard the marinade.

2. Meanwhile, lightly spray the grill rack with cooking spray. Preheat the grill on medium high. Grill the chicken for 4 to 5 minutes on each side, or until no longer pink in the center.

Exchanges/Choices		
3 Lean Meat		
Calories	130	
Calories from Fat	25	
Total Fat	3.0	g
Saturated Fat	0.8	g
Trans Fat	0.0	g
Polyunsaturated Fat	0.6	g
Monounsaturated Fat	1.0	g
Cholesterol	65	mg
Sodium	60	mg
Total Carbohydrate	1	g
Dietary Fiber	0	g
Sugars	0	g
Protein	24	g

TOMATO AND CAPER CHICKEN

Serves 2; 3 ounces chicken and 1/4 cup tomato-caper mixture per serving
Preparation time: 10 minutes

Each bite of this delectable dish is full of Mediterranean charm.

1/2 teaspoon dried oregano, crumbled
1/8 teaspoon garlic powder
1/8 teaspoon salt
2 boneless, skinless chicken breast halves (about 4 ounces each), all visible fat discarded
1 teaspoon olive oil and 1 teaspoon olive oil, divided use
1/4 cup dry white wine (regular or nonalcoholic)
1 1/2 tablespoons capers, drained
1 teaspoon grated lemon zest
6 grape tomatoes, quartered

1. In a small bowl, stir together the oregano, garlic powder, and salt. Sprinkle over the smooth side of the chicken. Using your fingertips, firmly press the mixture so it adheres to the chicken.

2. In a medium nonstick skillet, heat 1 teaspoon oil over medium heat, swirling to coat the bottom. Cook the chicken with the seasoned side down, covered, for 4 minutes. Turn over and cook for 4 minutes, or until no longer pink in the center. Transfer the chicken to plates.

3. Return the skillet to the heat. Put the wine, capers, and lemon zest in the skillet. Stir to combine. Cook over medium heat for 1 minute. Stir in the tomatoes and remaining 1 teaspoon oil. Cook for 1 minute, or until the mixture is slightly reduced and the tomatoes are soft. Spoon the mixture over the chicken.

COOK'S TIP: *Be sure to use grape tomatoes for peak flavor and texture.*

Exchanges/Choices
3 Lean Meat
1 Fat

Calories	190	
Calories from Fat	65	
Total Fat	7.0	g
Saturated Fat	1.4	g
Trans Fat	0.0	g
Polyunsaturated Fat	1.1	g
Monounsaturated Fat	4.3	g
Cholesterol	65	mg
Sodium	400	mg
Total Carbohydrate	2	g
Dietary Fiber	1	g
Sugars	1	g
Protein	24	g

Spinach and Orange Salad
with Pumpkin Seeds, page 31
Barbecued Rosemary Chicken, page 88

Sweet and Creamy Corn, page 182
Salmon and Asparagus Gremolata in Parchment, page 60

Quick-Herb Tomato Soup, page 14
Crustless Spinach and Mushroom
Quiche, page 152

FRUIT-FILLED PANCAKE PUFFS, PAGE 193

PUMPKIN CAKES, PAGE 202

LEMONY FRUIT CUPS, PAGE 208

Chicken Lettuce Wraps, page 7

Cherry Tomato Toppers, page 4

Asian Pork Soup, page 27

Salad Greens with Hoisin-Plum Dressing, page 32

GRILLED SHRIMP WITH MINT SALSA VERDE, PAGE 77

YELLOW RICE WITH BROWNED ONIONS, PAGE 186

PEACH-GLAZED CHICKEN

Peach-Glazed Chicken

Serves 2; 3 ounces chicken and 1/2 cup peaches per serving
Preparation time: 10 minutes

Transform everyday chicken into a special treat with a sweet-and-sour fruit glaze and seared peaches.

1/2 (15.25-ounce) can sliced peaches in fruit juice, drained with 1/4 cup juice reserved
1 tablespoon light brown sugar
1 tablespoon cider vinegar
2 teaspoons fresh lemon juice
1 teaspoon dried basil, crumbled
1/4 teaspoon salt
1/8 teaspoon pepper
2 boneless, skinless chicken breast halves (about 4 ounces each), all visible fat discarded, pounded to 1/4-inch thickness
Olive oil spray
1 teaspoon olive oil

1. In a small bowl, stir together the peaches, reserved juice, brown sugar, vinegar, and lemon juice. Set aside.

2. In another small bowl, stir together the basil, salt, and pepper. Sprinkle over both sides of the chicken. Lightly spray both sides with olive oil spray.

3. In a large nonstick skillet, heat the oil over medium-high heat, swirling to coat the bottom. Cook the chicken for 4 to 5 minutes on each side, or until browned on the outside and no longer pink in the center. Push the chicken to one side. With a slotted spoon, transfer the peaches to the pan, reserving the juice. Cook for 1 minute. Turn the peaches over and cook for 1 minute, or until lightly browned.

4. Pour in the reserved juice. Stir to combine the juice, chicken, and peaches. Cook for 3 to 5 minutes, or until most of the liquid has evaporated and the juices are slightly caramelized and glaze the chicken and peaches, stirring occasionally.

Exchanges/Choices		
1 Fruit		
1/2 Carbohydrate		
3 Lean Meat		
Calories	250	
Calories from Fat	45	
Total Fat	5.0	g
Saturated Fat	1.1	g
Trans Fat	0.0	g
Polyunsaturated Fat	0.9	g
Monounsaturated Fat	2.6	g
Cholesterol	65	mg
Sodium	360	mg
Total Carbohydrate	26	g
Dietary Fiber	2	g
Sugars	23	g
Protein	25	g

BARBECUED ROSEMARY CHICKEN

Serves 2; 3 ounces chicken and 2 tablespoons sauce per serving
Preparation time: 10 minutes

The combination of fresh rosemary, balsamic vinegar, and barbecue sauce transforms grilled chicken from ordinary to sensational. Serve with grilled eggplant slices and quartered tomatoes.

2 teaspoons olive oil
1 teaspoon grated lemon zest
1 tablespoon fresh lemon juice
1 medium garlic clove, minced
1 tablespoon chopped fresh rosemary
1/8 teaspoon salt
1/8 teaspoon pepper
2 boneless, skinless chicken breast halves (about 4 ounces each), all visible fat discarded
Cooking spray
3 tablespoons barbecue sauce (lowest sodium available)
1 tablespoon balsamic vinegar
1 teaspoon honey

1. In a nonmetallic bowl, stir together the oil, lemon zest, lemon juice, garlic, rosemary, salt, and pepper. Add the chicken, turning to coat. Cover and refrigerate for 30 minutes to 8 hours. If marinating for more than 30 minutes, turn several times.

2. Lightly spray the grill rack with cooking spray. Preheat the grill on medium.

3. Grill the chicken for 4 to 5 minutes on each side, or until no longer pink in the center. Transfer to plates.

4. Meanwhile, in a small saucepan, whisk together the barbecue sauce, vinegar, and honey. Cook over medium-low heat for 3 to 4 minutes, or until heated through, stirring occasionally. Spoon the mixture over the cooked chicken.

Exchanges/Choices		
1 Carbohydrate		
3 Lean Meat		
1/2 Fat		
Calories	235	
Calories from Fat	65	
Total Fat	7.0	g
Saturated Fat	1.4	g
Trans Fat	0.0	g
Polyunsaturated Fat	1.1	g
Monounsaturated Fat	4.3	g
Cholesterol	65	mg
Sodium	390	mg
Total Carbohydrate	17	g
Dietary Fiber	0	g
Sugars	13	g
Protein	24	g

OATMEAL-CRUSTED BAKED CHICKEN

Serves 2; 3 ounces chicken per serving
Preparation time: 5 minutes

Oatmeal adds an interesting texture and nutty flavor to this savory dish. The longer the chicken marinates, the tenderer and more flavorful it will be.

Cooking spray
2 tablespoons low-fat buttermilk
2 boneless, skinless chicken breast halves (about 4 ounces each), all visible fat discarded
1/2 cup uncooked quick-cooking oatmeal
1/4 teaspoon garlic powder
1/4 teaspoon chili powder
1/4 teaspoon onion powder
1/4 teaspoon paprika
1/4 teaspoon salt
1/4 teaspoon pepper

1. Preheat the oven to 375°F. Lightly spray an 8-inch square baking pan with cooking spray.

2. Put the buttermilk in a shallow bowl. Add the chicken, turning to coat. Cover and refrigerate for 30 minutes to 8 hours to marinate. If marinating for more than 30 minutes, turn several times.

3. In a small bowl, stir together the remaining ingredients.

4. Transfer the chicken to the baking pan. Sprinkle half the oatmeal mixture over the chicken. Lightly spray with cooking spray. Turn the chicken over and repeat on the other side.

5. Bake for 35 to 40 minutes, or until the chicken is no longer pink in the center and the coating is golden brown.

Exchanges/Choices		
1 Starch		
3 Lean Meat		
Calories	215	
Calories from Fat	40	
Total Fat	**4.5**	**g**
Saturated Fat	1.1	g
Trans Fat	0.0	g
Polyunsaturated Fat	1.1	g
Monounsaturated Fat	1.4	g
Cholesterol	**65**	**mg**
Sodium	**370**	**mg**
Total Carbohydrate	**15**	**g**
Dietary Fiber	2	g
Sugars	1	g
Protein	**28**	**g**

Cajun Chicken Pasta

CAJUN CHICKEN PASTA

Serves 2; 1 1/2 cups per serving
Preparation time: 10 minutes

This all-in-one meal comes together quickly and simply. The spicy cream sauce will make this dish a favorite.

1 1/2 ounces uncooked whole-wheat penne
1 teaspoon canola or corn oil
8 ounces boneless, skinless chicken breasts, all visible fat discarded,
    cut into bite-sized pieces
1/2 small onion, diced
1/2 small red bell pepper, chopped
1/2 small green bell pepper, chopped
2 ounces baby portobello mushrooms, sliced
2 medium garlic cloves, minced
2 tablespoons fat-free sour cream
2 tablespoons light tub cream cheese
2 tablespoons fat-free milk
1/2 teaspoon salt-free extra-spicy seasoning blend
2 tablespoons shredded or grated reduced-fat Parmesan cheese

Exchanges/Choices		
1 Starch		
2 Vegetable		
4 Lean Meat		
1/2 Fat		
Calories	340	
Calories from Fat	90	
Total Fat	10.0	g
Saturated Fat	3.3	g
Trans Fat	0.0	g
Polyunsaturated Fat	1.6	g
Monounsaturated Fat	3.6	g
Cholesterol	85	mg
Sodium	260	mg
Total Carbohydrate	29	g
Dietary Fiber	4	g
Sugars	6	g
Protein	32	g

1. Prepare the pasta using the package directions, omitting the salt and oil. Drain well in a colander.

2. Meanwhile, in a medium nonstick skillet, heat the oil over medium heat, swirling to coat the bottom. Cook the chicken for 4 to 5 minutes, or until golden on the outside and no longer pink inside, stirring frequently. Transfer to a plate and set aside.

3. In the same skillet, stir together the onion, bell peppers, mushrooms, and garlic. Cook over medium heat for about 3 minutes, or until tender, stirring frequently. Stir in the chicken and pasta.

4. Whisk together the remaining ingredients except the Parmesan. Pour into the skillet, stirring to heat through. Sprinkle with the Parmesan.

CARIBBEAN CHICKEN AND RICE

Serves 2; 3 ounces chicken and 1 cup fruit and rice per serving
Preparation time: 10 minutes

Fragrant spices from the jerk seasoning mingle with the pineapple-infused brown rice in this incredibly easy baked chicken dish.

1 (8-ounce) can pineapple tidbits in their own juice, drained
1/2 cup fat-free, low-sodium chicken broth
1/2 cup uncooked instant brown rice
2 medium green onions, thinly sliced
2 tablespoons diced red bell pepper
1 teaspoon salt-free jerk seasoning blend
2 boneless, skinless chicken breast halves (about 4 ounces each), all visible fat discarded
2 teaspoons soy sauce (lowest sodium available)

1. Preheat the oven to 375°F.

2. In an 8-inch square baking pan, stir together the pineapple, broth, rice, green onions, and bell pepper.

3. Sprinkle the seasoning blend over both sides of the chicken. Place the chicken on the pineapple mixture. Pour the soy sauce over the chicken.

4. Bake, covered, for 40 to 45 minutes, or until the chicken is no longer pink in the center and the rice is tender.

COOK'S TIP: *If you prefer to make your own jerk seasoning, combine 1/2 teaspoon ground allspice; 1/4 teaspoon dried thyme, crumbled; 1/8 teaspoon ground cinnamon; and 1/8 teaspoon garlic powder. That will give you the exact amount you need for this recipe.*

Exchanges/Choices
2 1/2 Starch
1 Fruit
3 Lean Meat

Calories	365	
Calories from Fat	35	
Total Fat	4.0	g
Saturated Fat	0.9	g
Trans Fat	0.0	g
Polyunsaturated Fat	1.2	g
Monounsaturated Fat	1.5	g
Cholesterol	65	mg
Sodium	295	mg
Total Carbohydrate	51	g
Dietary Fiber	4	g
Sugars	13	g
Protein	30	g

Orange Chicken with Couscous

Serves 2; 3 ounces chicken, 1/4 cup orange slices, and 1/2 cup couscous per serving
Preparation time: 15 minutes

Your kitchen will be filled with aromas of orange and ginger when you prepare this delectable chicken entrée. Serve with steamed sugar snap peas or stir-fried bok choy.

1/4 cup fat-free, low-sodium chicken broth
1 tablespoon all-fruit orange marmalade
1 tablespoon frozen orange juice concentrate
1 tablespoon white wine vinegar
1/2 teaspoon grated peeled gingerroot
2 tablespoons all-purpose flour
8 ounces boneless, skinless chicken breast halves, all visible fat discarded, cut into thin strips
Cooking spray

1 teaspoon canola or corn oil
1/3 cup uncooked couscous
1/2 teaspoon grated orange zest
1 medium orange, peeled and cut crosswise into thin slices

1. In a small bowl, whisk together the broth, marmalade, orange juice concentrate, vinegar, and gingerroot. Set aside.

2. Put the flour on a plate. Add the chicken, turning to coat. Shake off the excess flour. Transfer the chicken to a flat surface, such as a cutting board or piece of aluminum foil. Lightly spray both sides of the chicken with cooking spray.

3. In a large nonstick skillet, heat the oil over medium-high heat, swirling to coat the bottom. Cook the chicken for 4 minutes on each side, or until golden brown on the outside and no longer pink in the center. Pour in the broth mixture. Cook for 1 to 2 minutes, or until the mixture is slightly thickened and warmed through, stirring occasionally.

4. Meanwhile, prepare the couscous using the package directions, omitting the salt and oil. Cover to keep warm.

5. When the chicken is done, spoon the couscous onto plates. Spoon the chicken mixture over the couscous. Garnish with the orange zest and orange slices.

Exchanges/Choices
2 Starch
1 Fruit
3 Lean Meat

Calories	350	
Calories from Fat	45	
Total Fat	5.0	g
Saturated Fat	1.0	g
Trans Fat	0.0	g
Polyunsaturated Fat	1.4	g
Monounsaturated Fat	2.3	g
Cholesterol	65	mg
Sodium	75	mg
Total Carbohydrate	44	g
Dietary Fiber	3	g
Sugars	15	g
Protein	29	g

Chicken and Vegetable Fried Rice

Serves 2; 1 1/2 cups per serving
Preparation time: 10 minutes

Using brown rice instead of white and holding the soy sauce to a splash of the low-sodium variety make this tasty version of the Chinese restaurant favorite a full-speed-ahead choice for a healthier-than-takeout meal.

6 ounces boneless, skinless chicken breasts,
    all visible fat discarded, cut into 1-inch cubes
2 medium garlic cloves, minced
1 teaspoon grated peeled gingerroot
1/2 teaspoon toasted sesame oil
1/4 teaspoon crushed red pepper flakes
1/2 cup uncooked instant brown rice
3/4 cup water
1/2 teaspoon canola or corn oil
2 cups frozen stir-fry vegetables
2 medium green onions, thinly sliced
1 tablespoon soy sauce (lowest sodium available)

1. In a small bowl, stir together the chicken, garlic, gingerroot, sesame oil, and red pepper flakes. Cover and refrigerate for 15 minutes.

2. Meanwhile, in small saucepan, combine the rice with 3/4 cup water. Bring to a boil over high heat. Cover and reduce the heat to low. Simmer for 6 minutes, or until the liquid is absorbed. Remove from heat and let the rice cool, uncovered.

3. While the rice cools, heat the oil in a small nonstick skillet over high heat, swirling to coat the bottom. Cook the chicken mixture for 3 minutes, or until the chicken is lightly browned, stirring constantly. Transfer to a plate.

4. Reduce the heat to medium. Cook the stir-fry vegetables for 4 minutes, or until almost tender-crisp, stirring constantly. Stir in the cooled rice, chicken mixture, green onions, and soy sauce. Reduce the heat to low and cook, covered, for 2 minutes, or until the rice is heated through, stirring frequently.

Exchanges/Choices		
2 1/2 Starch		
2 Vegetable		
2 Lean Meat		
Calories	340	
Calories from Fat	45	
Total Fat	5.0	g
Saturated Fat	0.8	g
Trans Fat	0.0	g
Polyunsaturated Fat	1.8	g
Monounsaturated Fat	2.4	g
Cholesterol	50	mg
Sodium	390	mg
Total Carbohydrate	46	g
Dietary Fiber	5	g
Sugars	5	g
Protein	25	g

GREEK CHICKEN POT PIE

Serves 2; 1 pot pie per serving
Preparation time: 10 minutes

In this savory pie, flaky layers of phyllo make a delicately crisp topping for the dill-laced chicken and spinach nestled beneath.

1 boneless, skinless chicken breast (about 6 ounces), all visible fat discarded,
    cut into 3 pieces
1 cup frozen chopped spinach, thawed and squeezed very dry
5 medium green onions, chopped (about 1/2 cup)
1/4 cup low-fat feta cheese
1 tablespoon dried dillweed, crumbled
2 tablespoons all-purpose flour
2 tablespoons water
1/4 teaspoon salt-free lemon pepper
5 (14 × 9-inch) sheets phyllo dough, thawed
1 tablespoon plus 1 teaspoon olive oil

1. Put the chicken in a small saucepan. Pour in enough water to barely cover (about 1 cup). Bring just to a boil over medium heat. Reduce the heat and simmer for 5 to 6 minutes, or until cooked through, turning once. Transfer the chicken to a plate to cool. Increase the heat to high and boil the poaching liquid for 5 to 6 minutes, or until reduced to 3/4 cup.

2. Meanwhile, put the spinach in a medium bowl. Using a fork, separate the spinach into small clumps. Stir in the green onions, feta, and dillweed.

3. Preheat the oven to 350°F.

4. In a small bowl, whisk together the flour and water until smooth.

5. When the poaching liquid is reduced, reduce the heat to medium low. Whisk in the flour mixture. Cook for 2 to 3 minutes to thicken and remove any floury taste, whisking frequently. Whisk in the lemon pepper. Stir into the spinach mixture.

6. When the chicken is cool enough to handle, cut into 3/4-inch cubes. Stir into the spinach mixture. Divide the mixture between two 1-cup individual pie pans or 10-ounce custard cups.

7. Place one sheet of phyllo on a cutting board. Keep the unused sheets covered with a damp cloth or damp paper towels to prevent drying. Using a pastry brush, lightly brush the first sheet with the oil. Working quickly, repeat with the remaining phyllo and oil, making a stack of the 5 sheets. Cut crosswise into two 9 × 7-inch stacks. Top each pie with one stack. Using scissors, trim around the edge. Discard the scraps.

8. Bake for 30 minutes, or until the phyllo is golden brown and the filling is bubbly.

COOK'S TIP: *Phyllo is usually sold frozen, often with two 8-ounce packages in each box. Remove one of the packages. Let the phyllo thaw in the refrigerator for 6 hours or longer. Remove the amount needed, then wrap the remaining sheets tightly in plastic wrap, return to the box, and refreeze.*

Exchanges/Choices

1 Starch
1 Vegetable
3 Lean Meat
1 Fat

Calories	295	
Calories from Fat	90	
Total Fat	10.0	g
Saturated Fat	2.8	g
Trans Fat	0.0	g
Polyunsaturated Fat	1.4	g
Monounsaturated Fat	4.8	g
Cholesterol	55	mg
Sodium	445	mg
Total Carbohydrate	25	g
Dietary Fiber	5	g
Sugars	2	g
Protein	28	g

Indian-Spiced Chicken Pitas

Serves 2; 3 ounces chicken, 1 pita bread, 2 tablespoons sauce, and 6 tablespoons filling per serving
Preparation time: 15 minutes

"Exotic" and "enticing" describe this chicken sandwich, seasoned with ginger, cumin, paprika, and cayenne. Add a yogurt topping, and the result is irresistible.

Cooking spray
1 tablespoon and 1/4 cup fat-free plain yogurt, divided use
1 teaspoon minced peeled gingerroot
1/4 teaspoon and 1/4 teaspoon ground cumin, divided use
1/4 teaspoon paprika
1/8 teaspoon cayenne
8 ounces boneless, skinless chicken breast, all visible fat discarded, pounded
    to 1/2-inch thickness
1 tablespoon minced fresh cilantro
1 small garlic clove, minced
2 (6-inch) whole-wheat pita breads, each halved
1/2 cup shredded lettuce
1 thin slice red onion, halved, separated into rings
1/4 cup chopped tomato

1. Lightly spray a grill rack with cooking spray. Preheat the grill on medium high. Preheat the oven to 350°F if using to heat pita breads (see the Cook's Tip on page 97).

2. In a small bowl, stir together 1 tablespoon yogurt, gingerroot, 1/4 teaspoon cumin, paprika, and cayenne. Brush lightly over both sides of the chicken.

3. Grill the chicken for 5 to 6 minutes on each side, or until no longer pink in the center. Transfer to a plate. Cover and let stand for 5 minutes. Thinly slice the chicken.

4. Meanwhile, wrap the pita breads in aluminum foil and heat in the oven for about 10 minutes.

5. In a small bowl, whisk together the remaining 1/4 cup yogurt, remaining 1/4 teaspoon cumin, cilantro, and garlic.

6. To serve, spoon about 2 tablespoons lettuce into each pita half. Arrange the onion over the lettuce, then top with the chicken. Dollop with the yogurt mixture. Garnish with the tomato.

COOK'S TIP: *If you prefer to warm the pita breads on the grill, wrap them in aluminum foil and put them on the edge of the grill over indirect heat. Heat for about 10 minutes, turning halfway through. To heat in the microwave, stack the pitas and loosely wrap in paper towels. Heat on 100% power (high) for about 30 seconds, or until warm.*

Exchanges/Choices
2 Starch
1 Vegetable
3 Lean Meat

Calories	330	
Calories from Fat	45	
Total Fat	5.0	**g**
Saturated Fat	1.1	g
Trans Fat	0.0	g
Polyunsaturated Fat	1.4	g
Monounsaturated Fat	1.3	g
Cholesterol	70	**mg**
Sodium	425	**mg**
Total Carbohydrate	41	**g**
Dietary Fiber	5	g
Sugars	4	g
Protein	33	**g**

CHICKEN, RICE, AND ASPARAGUS CASSEROLES

Chicken, Rice, Asparagus

Serves 2; 1/2 cup asparagus and chicken mixture, 1/3 cup rice, and 1/2 cup sauce per serving
Preparation time: 15 minutes

The brown rice adds a healthy twist to this elegant casserole.

1/2 cup uncooked instant brown rice
3 ounces fresh asparagus, trimmed, cut into 2-inch pieces
1/2 cup water
1 teaspoon canola or corn oil
6 ounces boneless, skinless chicken breasts, all visible fat discarded, cut into
    bite-sized pieces
2 tablespoons chopped onion
1 tablespoon all-purpose flour
3/4 cup fat-free milk
1/4 teaspoon dried thyme, crumbled
1/4 teaspoon salt
1/4 teaspoon pepper (coarsely ground preferred)
Cooking spray
1/4 cup shredded Gruyere cheese
1 tablespoon slivered almonds

1. In a small saucepan, prepare the rice using the package directions, omitting the salt and margarine.

2. Preheat the oven to 375°F.

3. In a 10-inch nonstick skillet, bring 1/2 cup water to a boil over high heat. Add the asparagus and return to a boil. Reduce the heat and simmer, covered, for 2 minutes, or until tender-crisp. Drain well in a colander and set aside. Wipe the skillet dry with paper towels.

4. Pour the oil into the skillet, swirling to coat the bottom. Heat over medium-high heat. Cook the chicken for 4 to 5 minutes, or until golden outside and no longer pink inside, stirring frequently. Transfer to a plate and set aside.

5. In the same skillet, cook the onion for about 1 minute, or until tender, stirring frequently to avoid overcooking. Sprinkle the flour over the onion. Stir to blend. Slowly pour in the milk, stirring constantly. Add the thyme, salt, and pepper. Cook for about 1 minute, or until blended and thick, stirring constantly. Remove from the heat.

6. Lightly spray two 8-ounce ramekins (4-inch diameter) with cooking spray. Spoon the rice into the ramekins. Spoon the asparagus and chicken on top. Sprinkle with the Gruyere. Pour the sauce over each ramekin. Sprinkle with the almonds.

7. Bake for 15 to 20 minutes, or until the almonds are slightly golden and the casseroles are heated through.

Exchanges/Choices

2 1/2 Starch
1/2 Fat-Free Milk
1 Vegetable
3 Lean Meat
1/2 Fat

Calories	430	
Calories from Fat	110	
Total Fat	12.0	g
Saturated Fat	3.4	g
Trans Fat	0.0	g
Polyunsaturated Fat	2.5	g
Monounsaturated Fat	5.3	g
Cholesterol	65	mg
Sodium	450	mg
Total Carbohydrate	48	g
Dietary Fiber	3	g
Sugars	6	g
Protein	32	g

Sesame-Herb Chicken Kebabs

Serves 2; 2 kebabs per serving
Preparation time: 10 minutes

Flavored with lemon, herbs, and just a touch of sesame seeds, these chicken and vegetable kebabs will tantalize your taste buds.

3 tablespoons fresh lemon juice
2 tablespoons fat-free, low-sodium chicken broth
2 teaspoons olive oil
1/2 teaspoon dried basil, crumbled
1/2 teaspoon dried thyme, crumbled
1/4 teaspoon garlic powder
8 ounces boneless, skinless chicken breasts, all visible fat discarded, cut into 8 or 10 cubes
1/4 medium red bell pepper, cut into 4 or 6 squares
1/2 small zucchini (about 2 ounces), quartered crosswise
4 small button mushrooms
1 teaspoon sesame seeds

1. Soak four 10-inch wooden skewers for at least 10 minutes in cold water to keep them from charring, or use metal skewers.

2. In a small bowl, stir together the lemon juice, chicken broth, oil, basil, thyme, and garlic powder.

3. Alternately thread the chicken, bell pepper, zucchini, and mushrooms on the skewers. Do not crowd the pieces together. Place the skewers in a single layer in a 13 × 9 × 2-inch nonmetallic pan. Drizzle with 3 table-spoons lemon juice mixture. Turn to coat. Cover and refrigerate for 30 minutes. Cover and refrigerate the remaining lemon juice mixture separately.

4. Preheat the grill on medium high. Grill the skewers for 6 minutes. Turn over and brush generously with the reserved lemon juice mixture. Grill for 5 minutes. Brush with all the remaining lemon juice mixture. Sprinkle with the sesame seeds. Grill for 1 to 2 minutes, or until the chicken is no longer pink and the vegetables are tender-crisp.

Exchanges/Choices		
1 Vegetable		
3 Lean Meat		
1/2 Fat		
Calories	190	
Calories from Fat	65	
Total Fat	7.0	g
Saturated Fat	1.4	g
Trans Fat	0.0	g
Polyunsaturated Fat	1.4	g
Monounsaturated Fat	3.7	g
Cholesterol	65	mg
Sodium	70	mg
Total Carbohydrate	5	g
Dietary Fiber	1	g
Sugars	2	g
Protein	26	g

Slow-Cooker Chicken and Noodles

Serves 2; 1 1/2 cups per serving
Preparation time: 10 minutes

Serve this homey dish in shallow bowls so you can savor every drop of the gravy.

1 medium carrot, cut lengthwise into eighths, then cut crosswise into 2-inch pieces
1/2 medium onion, cut into 1/4-inch wedges
1/3 cup water
1 bone-in skinless chicken breast half (about 9 ounces), all visible fat discarded
1/4 teaspoon dried thyme, crumbled
1/4 teaspoon garlic powder
1/8 teaspoon paprika
2 ounces dried no-yolk egg noodles
1 tablespoon light tub margarine
1/8 teaspoon salt
1/8 teaspoon pepper (coarsely ground preferred)

1. Put the carrot, onion, and water in a 1 1/2- to 2-quart slow cooker. Add the chicken. Sprinkle the thyme, garlic powder, and paprika over the chicken. Cook, covered, on high for 2 hours or on low for 4 hours, or until the carrot pieces are tender-crisp and the chicken is no longer pink in the center. Transfer the chicken to a plate.

2. Stir the noodles into the vegetable mixture. Cook, covered, on high for 30 minutes, or until the noodles are tender.

3. Meanwhile, remove the chicken from the bone and cut into bite-size pieces. When the noodles are tender, stir in the chicken, margarine, salt, and pepper. Let stand, covered, for 5 minutes, or until the chicken is heated through.

Exchanges/Choices
1 1/2 Starch
1 Vegetable
3 Lean Meat

Calories	280	
Calories from Fat	45	
Total Fat	5.0	g
Saturated Fat	1.5	g
Trans Fat	0.0	g
Polyunsaturated Fat	1.4	g
Monounsaturated Fat	2.0	g
Cholesterol	60	mg
Sodium	290	mg
Total Carbohydrate	29	g
Dietary Fiber	3	g
Sugars	5	g
Protein	27	g

Chicken Saté

CHICKEN SATÉ

CHICKEN SATÉ
WITH SPICY PEANUT SAUCE

Serves 2; 1 skewer per serving
Preparation time: 5 minutes

Six ingredients and a short time in the kitchen are all you need for preparing this exotic saté (sah-TAY).

2 1/2 teaspoons creamy peanut butter
1 to 2 teaspoons and 2 tablespoons fresh lime juice, divided use
1/8 teaspoon crushed red pepper flakes, or to taste
1 teaspoon firmly packed light or dark brown sugar
1 teaspoon soy sauce (lowest sodium available)
8 ounces chicken breast tenders, all visible fat discarded

1. In a small bowl, whisk together the peanut butter, 1 to 2 teaspoons lime juice, and red pepper flakes until smooth. Set aside.

2. In a shallow dish, stir together the remaining 2 tablespoons lime juice, brown sugar, and soy sauce. Add the chicken, turning to coat. Cover and refrigerate for 15 minutes, stirring once or twice.

3. Meanwhile, soak two 6- to 8-inch wooden skewers for at least 10 minutes in cold water to keep them from charring, or use metal skewers. Preheat the broiler.

4. Remove the chicken from the dish. Thread half the chicken accordion-style onto each skewer. Place on a baking sheet. Broil 4 to 5 inches from the heat for 3 to 4 minutes on each side, or until no longer pink in the center. Brush the chicken with the peanut sauce.

Exchanges/Choices
1/2 Carbohydrate
3 Lean Meat
1/2 Fat

Calories	180	
Calories from Fat	55	
Total Fat	6.0	g
Saturated Fat	1.4	g
Trans Fat	0.0	g
Polyunsaturated Fat	1.6	g
Monounsaturated Fat	2.6	g
Cholesterol	65	mg
Sodium	190	mg
Total Carbohydrate	5	g
Dietary Fiber	1	g
Sugars	3	g
Protein	26	g

ALMOND-CRUSTED TURKEY TENDERS

Serves 2; 3 ounces turkey per serving
Preparation time: 5 minutes

Turkey is not just for Thanksgiving! When teamed with cranberry sauce flavored with lemon pepper, as in this easily prepared dish, it is a winner at any time of the year.

Cooking spray
2 tablespoons Dijon mustard
1/2 teaspoon and 1/4 teaspoon salt-free lemon pepper, divided use
2 turkey tenders (about 4 ounces each), all visible fat discarded, halved lengthwise
2 tablespoons sliced almonds
1/4 cup whole-berry cranberry sauce

1. Preheat the oven to 350°F. Lightly spray an 8-inch square baking pan with cooking spray.

2. In a small bowl, stir together the mustard and 1/2 teaspoon lemon pepper. Brush on the turkey. Transfer to the baking pan. Sprinkle the almonds over the top and sides of the turkey.

3. Bake for 30 to 35 minutes, or until the turkey is no longer pink in the center and registers 170°F on an instant-read thermometer.

4. Meanwhile, in a small bowl, stir together the cranberry sauce and remaining 1/4 teaspoon lemon pepper. Cover and refrigerate until ready to serve. Spoon the mixture over the turkey.

Exchanges/Choices
1 Carbohydrate
4 Lean Meat

Calories	235	
Calories from Fat	45	
Total Fat	5.0	g
Saturated Fat	0.6	g
Trans Fat	0.0	g
Polyunsaturated Fat	1.3	g
Monounsaturated Fat	3.1	g
Cholesterol	75	mg
Sodium	415	mg
Total Carbohydrate	17	g
Dietary Fiber	2	g
Sugars	14	g
Protein	29	g

BLACK BEAN TURKEY CHILI

Serves 2; 1 1/2 cups per serving
Preparation time: 15 minutes

Coffee is the secret ingredient that gives a deep, rich flavor to this colorful chili.

1 teaspoon olive oil and 2 teaspoons olive oil, divided use
6 ounces ground skinless turkey breast
1 (14-ounce) can fat-free, no-salt-added beef broth
2 medium tomatoes, chopped
1/2 (15-ounce) can no-salt-added black beans, rinsed and drained
1 cup frozen mixed sliced bell peppers (bell pepper stir-fry mix) (about 4 ounces)
1 1/4 to 1 3/4 teaspoons sugar
3/4 teaspoon ground cumin
3/4 teaspoon instant coffee granules
1/8 teaspoon salt

1. In a medium saucepan, heat 1 teaspoon oil over medium heat, swirling to coat the bottom. Cook the turkey for 2 minutes, or until no longer pink, stirring constantly to turn and break up the turkey. Stir in the broth, tomatoes, beans, bell peppers, sugar, cumin, and coffee granules. Increase the heat to high and bring to a boil. Reduce the heat and simmer for 30 minutes, or until thickened, stirring occasionally.

2. Remove from heat. Stir in the remaining 2 teaspoons oil and salt. Let stand for 10 minutes so the flavors blend.

COOK'S TIP: *Some ground turkey includes the skin and/or dark meat. For the leanest product, be sure only skinless breast meat is ground.*

Exchanges/Choices
1 Starch
2 Vegetable
3 Lean Meat
1/2 Fat

Calories	300	
Calories from Fat	70	
Total Fat	8.0	g
Saturated Fat	1.2	g
Trans Fat	0.0	g
Polyunsaturated Fat	1.1	g
Monounsaturated Fat	5.3	g
Cholesterol	55	mg
Sodium	300	mg
Total Carbohydrate	27	g
Dietary Fiber	6	g
Sugars	9	g
Protein	30	g

STUFFED PICADILLO POBLANOS

Serves 2; 2 halves per serving
Preparation time: 10 minutes

This turkey-based picadillo (pee-kah-DEE-yoh) has a tasty twist—instead of the usual raisins, it's made with dried apricots.

2 poblano, or pasilla, peppers, halved lengthwise, seeds and stems discarded
1 teaspoon canola or corn oil
1 small onion, chopped
2 medium garlic cloves, minced
8 ounces ground skinless turkey breast, broken into chunks
1 (8-ounce) can no-salt-added tomato sauce
8 dried apricot halves, chopped
4 medium pimiento-stuffed green olives, chopped
1/4 teaspoon ground cinnamon
1/4 teaspoon pepper
1/4 cup low-fat grated cheddar cheese

1. Put the poblano halves with the cut side up in an 8-inch square baking pan. Put the baking pan in the oven while preheating to 350°F. Remove the peppers after about 15 minutes.

2. Meanwhile, in a medium nonstick skillet, heat the oil over medium heat, swirling to coat the bottom. Cook the onion for about 4 minutes, or until soft. Stir in the garlic. Cook for 30 seconds to 1 minute, or until fragrant. Add the turkey. Cook, stirring to turn and break into small pieces, for about 5 minutes, or until crumbled and no longer pink. Stir in the remaining ingredients except the cheddar cheese.

3. Stuff each pepper half with the turkey mixture. Bake for 25 minutes, or until the peppers are tender-crisp. Top each pepper half with 1 table-spoon cheddar. Bake for 5 minutes.

COOK'S TIP: *Mildly spicy poblano chile peppers, or pasillas, look like elongated, softly triangular bell peppers.*

Exchanges/Choices		
1/2 Fruit		
4 Vegetable		
4 Lean Meat		

Calories	300	
Calories from Fat	55	
Total Fat	6.0	g
Saturated Fat	2.0	g
Trans Fat	0.0	g
Polyunsaturated Fat	1.1	g
Monounsaturated Fat	2.8	g
Cholesterol	80	mg
Sodium	315	mg
Total Carbohydrate	29	g
Dietary Fiber	4	g
Sugars	20	g
Protein	32	g

Cornish Game Hens

LEMON-ROASTED CORNISH GAME HENS

Serves 2; 1/2 Cornish game hen per serving
Preparation time: 5 minutes

The petite Cornish game hen is the perfect size for a fancy dinner for two. Serve with steamed asparagus and Barley and Porcini Pilaf (page 181) on the side.

Cooking spray
1 tablespoon chopped fresh rosemary
2 medium garlic cloves, sliced
1/2 teaspoon dried sage
1/2 teaspoon dried thyme, crumbled
1/4 teaspoon pepper
1 (1-pound) Cornish game hen, thawed if frozen, giblets and all visible fat discarded
2 thin lemon slices, halved

1. Preheat the oven to 325°F. Lightly spray an 8-inch square baking pan or small roasting pan and a rack with cooking spray. Place the rack in the pan.

2. In a small bowl, stir together the rosemary, garlic, sage, thyme, and pepper.

3. Using your fingers, gently loosen the skin from the breast meat of the hen. Evenly distribute the herb mixture under the loosened skin. Place the lemon slices under the skin. Lightly spray the hen with cooking spray.

4. Bake for 1 hour 30 minutes, or until an instant-read thermometer inserted between the thigh and breast meat registers 170°F. You may need to place a small piece of aluminum foil lightly over the top of the hen during the last 15 minutes of cooking to keep it from getting too brown. Remove from the oven and let stand for 10 minutes. Cut the hen in half with a large chef's knife or kitchen scissors, and remove the skin before eating the hen.

COOK'S TIP: *If you prefer, you can roast the hen at 350°F for 1 hour. The longer, slower cooking results in a tenderer hen, though.*

Exchanges/Choices
3 Lean Meat

Calories	135	
Calories from Fat	35	
Total Fat	4.0	g
Saturated Fat	1.0	g
Trans Fat	0.0	g
Polyunsaturated Fat	0.9	g
Monounsaturated Fat	1.2	g
Cholesterol	100	mg
Sodium	60	mg
Total Carbohydrate	2	g
Dietary Fiber	0	g
Sugars	0	g
Protein	23	g

MEATS

FILETS MIGNONS
WITH ROSEMARY-HORSERADISH SAUCE

Serves 2; 1 filet and 1 tablespoon sauce per serving
Preparation time: 5 minutes

Zesty chili powder plus aromatic rosemary equals delicious seasoning for an elegant entrée.

2 tablespoons fat-free sour cream
1/4 teaspoon snipped fresh rosemary
1/4 teaspoon prepared horseradish
1/8 teaspoon salt
1/4 teaspoon chili powder
2 filets mignons without bacon (about 4 ounces each), about 1 inch thick, all visible fat discarded
1 teaspoon canola or corn oil

1. In a small serving bowl, stir together the sour cream, rosemary, horseradish, and salt. Set aside.

2. Sprinkle the chili powder on both sides of the filets.

3. In a large nonstick skillet, heat the oil over medium heat, swirling to coat the bottom. Cook the filets for 5 to 6 minutes on each side, or until the desired doneness. Serve with the sauce.

Exchanges/Choices		
3 Lean Meat		
1 Fat		
Calories	175	
Calories from Fat	70	
Total Fat	8.0	g
Saturated Fat	2.4	g
Trans Fat	0.0	g
Polyunsaturated Fat	0.9	g
Monounsaturated Fat	3.6	g
Cholesterol	60	mg
Sodium	205	mg
Total Carbohydrate	1	g
Dietary Fiber	0	g
Sugars	1	g
Protein	22	g

FILETS MIGNONS WITH SHERRY AU JUS

Serves 2; 1 filet and 2 tablespoons sherry mixture per serving
Preparation time: 5 minutes

Tender filets mignons make any night of the week special.

1/4 teaspoon pepper (coarsely ground preferred)
1/4 teaspoon salt
1/8 teaspoon garlic powder
1/8 teaspoon onion powder
2 filets mignons without bacon (about 4 ounces each), all visible fat discarded
1 teaspoon canola or corn oil
1/4 cup dry sherry
1/2 teaspoon light tub margarine
1 tablespoon snipped fresh parsley

1. In a small bowl, stir together the pepper, salt, garlic powder, and onion powder. Sprinkle over both sides of the filets. Using your fingertips, gently press the mixture so it adheres to the filets.

2. In a medium nonstick skillet, heat the oil over medium-high heat, swirling to coat the bottom. Cook the filets for 3 minutes on each side. Turn the filets back to the first side. Reduce the heat to medium and cook for 2 minutes, or until the desired doneness. Transfer to plates. Let stand for 2 minutes so the meat can release some of its juices.

3. During the standing time, in the same skillet, stir together the sherry and margarine. Bring to a boil over medium heat. Boil for 1 minute, or until the liquid is reduced to 2 tablespoons. Spoon the mixture over the filets. Sprinkle with the parsley.

COOK'S TIP: *The standing time is very important in this recipe. The meaty liquid that is released blends with the sherry mixture to create an even tastier dish.*

Exchanges/Choices		
3 Lean Meat		
1 Fat		
Calories	**185**	
Calories from Fat	70	
Total Fat	**8.0**	**g**
Saturated Fat	2.5	g
Trans Fat	0.0	g
Polyunsaturated Fat	1.0	g
Monounsaturated Fat	3.8	g
Cholesterol	**60**	**mg**
Sodium	**345**	**mg**
Total Carbohydrate	**1**	**g**
Dietary Fiber	0	g
Sugars	0	g
Protein	**21**	**g**

Teriyaki Finger Steaks

Serves 2; 3 ounces steak and 1/2 cup rice per serving
Preparation time: 10 minutes

Instead of discarding the marinade after the steak strips absorb its flavor, you'll use it to make the brown rice in this dish special. Serve it with steamed sugar snap peas and mandarin orange segments.

1 tablespoon soy sauce (lowest sodium available)
1 tablespoon white wine vinegar
1 teaspoon light brown sugar
1 teaspoon grated peeled gingerroot or 1/8 teaspoon dried ginger
1 teaspoon toasted sesame oil
1 medium garlic clove, minced
8 ounces boneless sirloin steak, about 1/2 inch thick, all visible fat discarded,
    cut across the grain into 8 strips
Cooking spray
1/2 cup fat-free, low-sodium chicken broth
1/4 cup uncooked instant brown rice
1 medium green onion, thinly sliced
1 tablespoon sliced almonds, dry-roasted

1. Soak eight (8-inch) wooden skewers in cold water for 10 minutes to keep them from charring, or use metal skewers.

2. Meanwhile, in a medium bowl, stir together the soy sauce, vinegar, brown sugar, ginger, sesame oil, and garlic. Add the steak, stirring to coat. Cover and refrigerate for 20 minutes to 8 hours, stirring occasionally if marinating longer than 20 minutes.

3. Thread one steak strip on each skewer, leaving the marinade in the bowl. Return the skewers to the bowl. (The skewers won't fit into the bowl far enough to continue marinating. You are just avoiding washing an extra bowl or plate.)

4. Lightly spray the grill rack or broiler pan and rack with cooking spray. Preheat the grill on medium or preheat the broiler.

5. Meanwhile, in a small saucepan, bring the broth and reserved marinade to a boil over medium-high heat. Stir in the rice. Reduce the heat and simmer, covered, for 5 minutes. Remove from heat. Let stand for 5 minutes. Fluff with a fork.

6. While the rice cooks, grill the steak strips or broil about 4 inches from the heat for 3 to 5 minutes on each side, or until the desired doneness.

7. Spoon the rice onto plates. Sprinkle with the green onion and almonds. Arrange the steak strips on the rice.

COOK'S TIP: *One way to keep small amounts of fresh gingerroot on hand is to freeze it. Peel it if you wish before cutting it into 1/2-inch slices, or "coins." Arrange the coins in a single layer in a resealable plastic freezer bag. Seal the bag, freeze the ginger for up to four months, and chop the amount you need.*

Exchanges/Choices		
1 1/2 Starch		
3 Lean Meat		
1/2 Fat		
Calories	280	
Calories from Fat	70	
Total Fat	8.0	g
Saturated Fat	2.1	g
Trans Fat	0.1	g
Polyunsaturated Fat	1.7	g
Monounsaturated Fat	3.7	g
Cholesterol	45	mg
Sodium	370	mg
Total Carbohydrate	23	g
Dietary Fiber	2	g
Sugars	4	g
Protein	27	g

Sirloin Steak
with Balsamic Mushrooms

Serves 2; 3 ounces steak and 1/2 cup mushrooms per serving
Preparation time: 10 minutes

The mushroom topping of these pan-seared steaks is infused with balsamic vinegar and beef broth. Serve the steaks with spinach salad and small slices of whole-grain garlic toast.

2 teaspoons and 1 tablespoon balsamic vinegar, divided use
1 medium garlic clove, minced
1/2 teaspoon dried oregano, crumbled
1/8 teaspoon pepper
8 ounces boneless sirloin steak, all visible fat discarded, halved
1 teaspoon and 1 teaspoon olive oil, divided use
6 ounces button mushrooms, sliced
1/4 cup fat-free, no-salt-added beef broth

1. In a medium nonmetallic bowl, stir together 2 teaspoons vinegar, garlic, oregano, and pepper. Add the steak, turning to coat. Cover and refrigerate for 30 minutes to 8 hours, turning several times if marinating for more than 30 minutes.

2. In a large skillet, heat 1 teaspoon oil over medium-high heat, swirling to coat the bottom. Cook the steaks for 4 to 5 minutes on each side, or until browned and the desired doneness. Transfer to plates. Cover with aluminum foil to keep warm.

3. In the same skillet, heat the remaining 1 teaspoon oil, swirling to coat the bottom. Cook the mushrooms over medium heat for 2 to 3 minutes, or until they start releasing their juices. Pour in the remaining 1 tablespoon vinegar and broth, scraping to dislodge any browned bits. Stir in the mushrooms. Cook for 5 minutes, or until most of the liquid has evaporated, stirring occasionally. Serve over the steaks.

Exchanges/Choices
1 Vegetable
3 Lean Meat
1 Fat

Calories	205	
Calories from Fat	80	
Total Fat	9.0	g
Saturated Fat	2.3	g
Trans Fat	0.2	g
Polyunsaturated Fat	0.7	g
Monounsaturated Fat	5.0	g
Cholesterol	40	mg
Sodium	65	mg
Total Carbohydrate	6	g
Dietary Fiber	1	g
Sugars	3	g
Protein	25	g

SIRLOIN WITH ORANGE-SOY SAUCE

Serves 2; 3 ounces steak per serving
Preparation time: 5 minutes

Deglazing, a classic French cooking technique you'll use for this recipe, enriches the pan sauce by incorporating any flavorful caramelized bits that have stuck to the pan.

  1 teaspoon canola or corn oil
  2 boneless sirloin steaks (about 4 ounces each), about 3/4 inch thick, all visible
      fat discarded
  1/2 cup fresh orange juice
  2 teaspoons soy sauce (lowest sodium available)
  1 small garlic clove, minced
  1/4 teaspoon dried thyme, crumbled
  1/8 teaspoon pepper

1. In a large nonstick skillet, heat the oil over medium heat, swirling to coat the bottom. Cook the steaks for 4 to 5 minutes on each side, or until the desired doneness. Transfer to plates. Cover to keep warm.

2. Meanwhile, in a small bowl, stir together the orange juice, soy sauce, garlic, and thyme. When the steaks are done, pour the mixture into the same skillet. Whisk, scraping the bottom to dislodge any browned bits. Increase the heat to medium high. Boil gently for 3 to 5 minutes, or until reduced by half, stirring occasionally. Stir in the pepper. Spoon mixture over the steaks.

Exchanges/Choices		
1/2 Fruit		
3 Lean Meat		
1/2 Fat		
Calories	190	
Calories from Fat	65	
Total Fat	7.0	g
Saturated Fat	1.8	g
Trans Fat	0.2	g
Polyunsaturated Fat	0.9	g
Monounsaturated Fat	3.0	g
Cholesterol	40	mg
Sodium	235	mg
Total Carbohydrate	8	g
Dietary Fiber	0	g
Sugars	7	g
Protein	23	g

Skirt Steaks with Salsa

SKIRT STEAKS WITH SPICY SALSA VERDE

Serves 2; 3 ounces steak and heaping 2 teaspoons salsa per serving
Preparation time: 10 minutes

Give grilled steak some south-of-the-border flair with this easy-to-prepare dish.

Cooking spray
1 teaspoon chili powder
1/2 teaspoon ground cumin
8 ounces skirt steak, about 1/2 inch thick, all visible fat discarded

Salsa Verde

1/4 cup fresh cilantro, finely snipped
2 tablespoons finely snipped fresh Italian (flat-leaf) parsley
2 teaspoons fresh lime juice
1 teaspoon minced pickled jalapeño or 1/2 teaspoon minced fresh jalapeño,
    seeds and ribs discarded
1 teaspoon olive oil (extra-virgin preferred)

1. Lightly spray a grill rack with cooking spray. Preheat the grill on medium high.

2. In a small bowl, stir together the chili powder and cumin. Rub on both sides of the steak.

3. Grill the steak with the grill lid closed for 3 to 4 minutes on each side, or until the desired doneness. Transfer to a cutting board. Cover and let stand for 10 minutes.

4. Meanwhile, in a small bowl, combine the salsa ingredients. Slice the steak against the grain into very thin slices. Arrange on a platter, slightly overlapping the slices. Drizzle the salsa down the center of the steak.

Exchanges/Choices		
3 Lean Meat		
1 Fat		
Calories	205	
Calories from Fat	100	
Total Fat	11.0	g
Saturated Fat	3.6	g
Trans Fat	0.0	g
Polyunsaturated Fat	0.7	g
Monounsaturated Fat	6.2	g
Cholesterol	50	mg
Sodium	80	mg
Total Carbohydrate	2	g
Dietary Fiber	1	g
Sugars	1	g
Protein	23	g

STEAK AND BROCCOLI STIR-FRY

Serves 2; 1 1/2 cups per serving
Preparation time: About 15 minutes

Dry mustard and vinegar join traditional Asian stir-fry seasonings in this version of a classic.

1/4 cup fat-free, no-salt-added beef broth

3 tablespoons and 1/4 cup cold water, divided use

1 tablespoon white vinegar or white wine vinegar

1/2 tablespoon soy sauce (lowest sodium available) or light tamari

1 teaspoon toasted sesame oil

1 teaspoon grated peeled gingerroot

1/8 teaspoon dry mustard

8 ounces flank steak, all visible fat and silver skin discarded, thinly sliced on the diagonal, cut into bite-sized pieces

2 teaspoons canola or corn oil

6 ounces small broccoli florets

1/4 cup chopped leeks, white part only

1/4 medium red or green bell pepper, chopped

1 medium garlic clove, minced

2 teaspoons cornstarch

1. In a small bowl, stir together the broth, 3 tablespoons water, vinegar, soy sauce, sesame oil, gingerroot, and mustard. Set aside.

2. Heat a medium nonstick skillet over medium-high heat. Cook the steak for 3 to 4 minutes, or until browned and the desired doneness, stirring frequently. Transfer to a plate.

3. Heat the same skillet over medium heat. Pour in the oil, swirling to coat the bottom. Cook the broccoli, leeks, bell pepper, and garlic for 3 to 4 minutes, or until the broccoli and leeks are tender-crisp. Return the steak to the skillet. Stir in the broth mixture. Cook for 1 minute, or until hot, stirring occasionally. Put the cornstarch in a small bowl. Add the remaining 1/4 cup cold water and whisk until smooth. Pour into the skillet. Cook for 1 minute, or until thickened, stirring frequently.

Exchanges/Choices		
2 Vegetable		
3 Lean Meat		
1 1/2 Fat		
Calories	260	
Calories from Fat	115	
Total Fat	13.0	g
Saturated Fat	3.2	g
Trans Fat	0.0	g
Polyunsaturated Fat	2.7	g
Monounsaturated Fat	5.9	g
Cholesterol	40	mg
Sodium	230	mg
Total Carbohydrate	11	g
Dietary Fiber	3	g
Sugars	3	g
Protein	26	g

CUBE STEAKS WITH COUNTRY GRAVY

Serves 2; 3 ounces steak and 2 tablespoons sauce per serving
Preparation time: 5 minutes

Balance these hearty steaks with light accompaniments, such as
Zucchini-Tomato Salad (page 37) and steamed carrots.

Cooking spray
1 tablespoon and 1 teaspoon all-purpose flour, divided use
1/4 teaspoon onion powder
1/4 teaspoon garlic powder
1/4 teaspoon paprika
3 tablespoons low-fat buttermilk or fat-free milk
2 beef cube steaks (about 4 ounces each), all visible fat discarded
1/4 cup plain dry bread crumbs
1 teaspoon and 1 teaspoon canola or corn oil, divided use
1/4 cup fat-free milk
1/8 teaspoon pepper
1/8 teaspoon onion powder

1. Preheat the oven to 400°F. Lightly spray a baking sheet with cooking
   spray.

2. In a shallow bowl, stir together 1 tablespoon flour, onion powder, garlic
   powder, and paprika.

3. Pour the buttermilk into another shallow bowl.

4. Set the bowl with the flour mixture, the bowl with the buttermilk, and
   a large piece of aluminum foil in a row, assembly-line fashion. Coat the
   steaks with the flour and then coat with the buttermilk. Place the steaks
   on the foil. Coat the top and sides of each steak with the bread crumbs.
   Lightly spray both sides with cooking spray.

5. In a large nonstick skillet, heat 1 teaspoon oil over medium-high heat, swirling to coat the bottom. Cook the steaks for 3 minutes, or until browned on the bottom. Add the remaining 1 teaspoon oil, swirling to coat the bottom as well as possible. Turn the steaks over. Cook the steaks for 3 minutes or until browned. Transfer to the baking sheet. (You'll use the skillet again.)

6. Bake for 5 to 8 minutes, or until the steaks are no longer pink in the center and the crust is golden brown. Transfer to plates.

7. Meanwhile, in a small bowl, whisk together the milk, pepper, onion powder, and remaining 1 teaspoon flour. Pour into the skillet. Cook over medium heat for 1 to 2 minutes, or until thickened, scraping to dislodge any browned bits and stirring constantly. Spoon over the steaks.

Exchanges/Choices		
1 Starch		
3 Lean Meat		
1 Fat		
Calories	170	
Calories from Fat	100	
Total Fat	11.0	g
Saturated Fat	2.3	g
Trans Fat	0.0	g
Polyunsaturated Fat	1.9	g
Monounsaturated Fat	5.1	g
Cholesterol	65	mg
Sodium	170	mg
Total Carbohydrate	17	g
Dietary Fiber	1	g
Sugars	4	g
Protein	25	g

CAJUN-CREOLE SMOTHERED STEAKS

Serves 2; 3 ounces steak and 1/2 cup vegetables per serving
Preparation time: 10 minutes

Slow braising is the key to successfully tenderizing very lean eye-of-round steaks. Zesty spices and an aromatic vegetable mixture give this dish its Cajun-Creole zip.

2 teaspoons salt-free Cajun-Creole seasoning blend
2 eye-of-round steaks (about 4 ounces each), all visible fat discarded
2 teaspoons olive oil
1/2 (14.5-ounce) can no-salt-added diced tomatoes, undrained (about 1 cup)
1/4 cup water
1/2 medium green bell pepper, chopped
1/2 medium rib of celery, cut into 1/2-inch slices
2 tablespoons chopped onion
1 medium garlic clove, minced
1/4 teaspoon salt

1. Sprinkle the seasoning blend over both sides of the steaks.

2. In a medium skillet, heat the oil over medium-high heat, swirling to coat the bottom. Cook the steaks for 2 minutes on each side, or until browned. Transfer to a plate.

3. In the same skillet, stir together the tomatoes with liquid, water, bell pepper, celery, onion, garlic, and salt. Add the steaks. Spoon the sauce over the steaks. Bring to a simmer. Reduce the heat and simmer for 1 hour 15 minutes, or until tender.

> **TIME-SAVER:** *If you are pressed for time, you can serve the steaks after about 45 minutes of simmering. They should be tender enough by then, though they will be even better with the full simmering time.*

Exchanges/Choices		
2 Vegetable		
3 Lean Meat		
1 Fat		
Calories	225	
Calories from Fat	70	
Total Fat	8.0	g
Saturated Fat	1.9	g
Trans Fat	0.0	g
Polyunsaturated Fat	0.7	g
Monounsaturated Fat	4.9	g
Cholesterol	50	mg
Sodium	390	mg
Total Carbohydrate	10	g
Dietary Fiber	3	g
Sugars	6	g
Protein	28	g

HUNGARIAN GOULASH

Hungarian Goulash

Serves 2; 1 cup goulash and 3/4 cup pasta per serving
Preparation time: 10 minutes

This goulash has all the flavor of traditional recipes for the comforting dish but uses whole-wheat pasta, no-salt-added tomatoes, and fat-free sour cream to make it healthier.

1 teaspoon canola or corn oil

8 ounces boneless round steak, all visible fat discarded, cut into 1/4- to 1/2-inch cubes

1/4 cup finely chopped onion

1 small garlic clove, minced

1 tablespoon all-purpose flour

1 teaspoon paprika

1/4 teaspoon dried thyme, crumbled

1 (14.5-ounce) can no-salt-added tomatoes, undrained, cut in small pieces

3 ounces dried whole-wheat penne or rotini

1/4 cup fat-free sour cream

1/8 teaspoon salt

1/8 teaspoon pepper

1 tablespoon snipped fresh parsley (optional)

1. In a medium saucepan, heat the oil over medium heat, swirling to coat the bottom. Cook the steak, onion, and garlic for 4 to 5 minutes, or until the steak is no longer pink and the onion is tender, stirring occasionally.

2. Stir in the flour, paprika, and thyme. Stir in the tomatoes. Increase the heat to medium and bring to a boil. Reduce the heat and simmer, covered, for 10 minutes. Stir. Simmer, uncovered, for 10 to 15 minutes, or until the meat is tender and the sauce is thickened, stirring occasionally. Meanwhile, cook the pasta using the package directions, omitting the salt and oil. Drain well in a colander.

3. Stir the sour cream, salt, and pepper into the goulash, then spoon over the pasta. If you prefer, spoon the goulash over the pasta, then top with the sour cream mixture. Garnish with the parsley.

Exchanges/Choices		
2 1/2 Starch		
2 Vegetable		
3 Lean Meat		
1 Fat		
Calories	430	
Calories from Fat	80	
Total Fat	9.0	g
Saturated Fat	2.2	g
Trans Fat	0.1	g
Polyunsaturated Fat	1.4	g
Monounsaturated Fat	3.8	g
Cholesterol	80	mg
Sodium	290	mg
Total Carbohydrate	51	g
Dietary Fiber	9	g
Sugars	10	g
Protein	35	g

Beef and Bell Pepper Stew

SLOW-COOKER BEEF AND BELL PEPPER STEW

Serves 2; 1 1/2 cups per serving
Preparation time: 15 minutes

Full of vegetables and meat and enticing with its spicy overtones, this stew is comfort food at its best.

1 teaspoon and 1 teaspoon olive oil, divided use
8 ounces boneless top round steak, all visible fat discarded, cut into 1-inch cubes
1 medium green bell pepper, cut into 1-inch pieces
4 small red potatoes (about 2 ounces each), quartered
1/2 medium onion, cut into 1/2-inch wedges
1/2 medium rib of celery, cut into 1/2-inch pieces
2 tablespoons no-salt-added ketchup
2 tablespoons and 2 tablespoons medium picante sauce (lowest sodium available), divided use
1 medium bay leaf
1/2 teaspoon instant coffee granules
1/4 teaspoon salt

1. In a medium nonstick skillet, heat 1 teaspoon oil over medium-high heat, swirling to coat the bottom. Cook the steak for 1 to 2 minutes, or until lightly browned. Transfer to a 1 1/2- to 2-quart slow cooker.

2. Stir in the bell pepper, potatoes, onion, celery, ketchup, 2 tablespoons picante sauce, bay leaf, and coffee granules. Cook, covered, on high for 4 hours or on low for 8 hours, or until the steak is tender.

3. Stir in the remaining 2 tablespoons picante sauce, remaining 1 teaspoon oil, and salt. Cook, covered, on high for 30 minutes. Discard the bay leaf before serving the stew.

COOK'S TIP: *Many small slow cookers have only an on/off switch. The "on" switch is the high setting.*

Exchanges/Choices
1 1/2 Starch
1/2 Carbohydrate
1 Vegetable
3 Lean Meat
1/2 Fat

Calories	330	
Calories from Fat	70	
Total Fat	**8.0**	**g**
Saturated Fat	1.8	g
Trans Fat	0.0	g
Polyunsaturated Fat	0.8	g
Monounsaturated Fat	4.6	g
Cholesterol	**60**	**mg**
Sodium	**595**	**mg**
Total Carbohydrate	**37**	**g**
Dietary Fiber	5	g
Sugars	10	g
Protein	**27**	**g**

Vietnamese Lettuce Wraps

Serves 2; 2 lettuce wraps per serving
Preparation time: 5 minutes

Warm, spicy beef served in crisp lettuce leaves makes a distinctive main dish.

8 ounces extra-lean ground beef
1/4 medium red onion, chopped
2 medium garlic cloves, minced
1/2 large red bell pepper, chopped
1/2 large rib of celery, chopped
1 teaspoon minced peeled gingerroot
1/8 teaspoon crushed red pepper flakes
2 tablespoons white wine vinegar
1 tablespoon soy sauce (lowest sodium available)
1 tablespoon minced fresh mint
2 tablespoons dry-roasted unsalted peanuts
4 large lettuce leaves, such as romaine, Boston, or iceberg, carefully removed
    and kept whole

1. In a medium skillet, cook the beef, onion, and garlic over medium heat for 5 minutes, or until the beef is browned and the onion is soft, stirring frequently to turn and break up the beef. Drain well in a colander. Wipe the skillet with paper towels. Return the mixture to the skillet.

2. Stir in the bell pepper, celery, gingerroot, and red pepper flakes. Cook over medium heat for 3 minutes, stirring frequently. Stir in the vinegar, soy sauce, and mint. Cook for 1 minute. Stir in the peanuts.

3. Place the lettuce leaves on plates. Spoon the meat mixture into the center of each leaf. Roll up loosely.

Exchanges/Choices		
2 Vegetable		
3 Lean Meat		
1 Fat		
Calories	250	
Calories from Fat	100	
Total Fat	11.0	g
Saturated Fat	3.3	g
Trans Fat	0.1	g
Polyunsaturated Fat	1.9	g
Monounsaturated Fat	4.7	g
Cholesterol	70	mg
Sodium	380	mg
Total Carbohydrate	11	g
Dietary Fiber	3	g
Sugars	5	g
Protein	27	g

Tex-Mex Meat Loaves

INDIVIDUAL TEX-MEX MEAT LOAVES

Serves 2; 1 meat loaf per serving
Preparation time: 5 minutes

Punch up the flavor of mini meat loaves with poblano pepper and picante sauce.

8 ounces extra-lean ground beef
1/2 cup frozen whole-kernel corn
1/2 medium poblano pepper, seeds and stem discarded, finely chopped
3 tablespoons uncooked quick-cooking oats
3 tablespoons and 2 tablespoons mild picante sauce (lowest sodium available), divided use
1 large egg white
1/4 teaspoon ground cumin

1. Preheat the oven to 350°F. Line a baking sheet with aluminum foil.

2. In a medium bowl, using a spoon or your hands, work together all the ingredients except the 2 tablespoons picante sauce just until blended. Divide in half and place on the baking sheet. Shape into 2 oval loaves, each about 3 1/2 × 3 × 1 inches, smoothing the tops. Spread 1 tablespoon remaining picante sauce over the tops and sides of each loaf.

3. Bake for 50 minutes, or until the internal temperature registers 160°F on an instant-read thermometer. Remove from the oven. Let stand for 5 minutes so the flavors blend.

COOK'S TIP: *You can make a single meat loaf, about 7 × 3 × 1 inches, if you prefer. The baking time remains the same.*

Exchanges/Choices
1 Starch
3 Lean Meat
1/2 Fat

Calories	240	
Calories from Fat	65	
Total Fat	7.0	g
Saturated Fat	2.8	g
Trans Fat	0.1	g
Polyunsaturated Fat	0.6	g
Monounsaturated Fat	2.7	g
Cholesterol	70	mg
Sodium	410	mg
Total Carbohydrate	17	g
Dietary Fiber	3	g
Sugars	2	g
Protein	27	g

SLOPPY JOE PASTA

Sloppy Joe Pasta

Serves 2; 3/4 cup pasta and 1 cup sauce per serving
Preparation time: 10 minutes

This hearty beef dish has all the flavor of a Sloppy Joe sandwich but is neatly served over whole-wheat pasta.

8 ounces extra-lean ground beef
1/4 cup finely chopped onion
1 small garlic clove, minced
2 to 3 ounces shiitake mushrooms, tough stems discarded, chopped
1 (8-ounce) can no-salt-added tomato sauce
1 teaspoon chili powder
1/4 teaspoon red hot-pepper sauce
3 ounces dried whole-wheat rotini or penne
2 teaspoons snipped fresh cilantro (optional)

1. In a medium saucepan, cook the beef, onion, and garlic over medium heat for 6 to 8 minutes, or until no longer pink, stirring occasionally to turn and break up the beef. Drain well in a colander. Wipe the pan with paper towels. Return the mixture to the pan. Stir in the mushrooms. Cook for 4 to 6 minutes, or until the mushrooms are soft, stirring occasionally.

2. Stir in the tomato sauce, chili powder, and hot-pepper sauce. Increase the heat to medium high and bring to a boil. Reduce the heat and simmer for 10 minutes, or until the desired consistency.

3. Meanwhile, prepare the pasta using the package directions, omitting the salt and oil. Drain well in a colander. Transfer to plates. Spoon the sauce over the pasta. Sprinkle with the cilantro.

Exchanges/Choices		
2 Starch		
2 Vegetable		
3 Lean Meat		
Calories	360	
Calories from Fat	65	
Total Fat	7.0	g
Saturated Fat	2.8	g
Trans Fat	0.1	g
Polyunsaturated Fat	0.7	g
Monounsaturated Fat	2.6	g
Cholesterol	70	mg
Sodium	120	mg
Total Carbohydrate	42	g
Dietary Fiber	7	g
Sugars	9	g
Protein	31	g

Luleh Kebabs
with Yogurt-Cucumber Sauce

Serves 2; 1 kebab per serving
Preparation time: 10 minutes

A Middle Eastern specialty typically made with seasoned ground lamb, luleh can be formed around skewers for kebabs or shaped into oblong patties.

Yogurt-Cucumber Sauce
1/4 cup fat-free plain yogurt
2 tablespoons finely chopped, peeled, and seeded cucumber
1/8 teaspoon dried dillweed, crumbled
Dash of pepper

Kebabs
8 ounces extra-lean ground beef
2 tablespoons finely chopped onion
2 tablespoons snipped fresh parsley
1/4 teaspoon ground coriander
1/4 teaspoon ground cumin
1/8 teaspoon garlic powder
1/8 teaspoon salt

1. If making kebabs, not patties, soak two 8-inch wooden skewers for at least 10 minutes in cold water to keep them from charring, or use metal skewers.

2. Meanwhile, in a small bowl, stir together the sauce ingredients. Cover and refrigerate until ready to serve.

3. Preheat the broiler.

4. In a medium bowl, using your hands or a large spoon, combine the kebab ingredients. Using your hands, shape the mixture into two 6 × 1 1/2-inch logs. Insert the skewers into the center of the logs. (Or shape the mixture into two oblong patties about 3/4 inch thick.) Place on a baking sheet.

5. Broil 4 to 5 inches from the heat for 4 to 5 minutes on each side, or until no longer pink in the center (the internal temperature should be 160°F). Serve with the sauce.

Exchanges/Choices		
3 Lean Meat		
Calories	165	
Calories from Fat	55	
Total Fat	6.0	g
Saturated Fat	2.5	g
Trans Fat	0.1	g
Polyunsaturated Fat	0.3	g
Monounsaturated Fat	2.3	g
Cholesterol	65	mg
Sodium	220	mg
Total Carbohydrate	4	g
Dietary Fiber	0	g
Sugars	3	g
Protein	23	g

BEEF AND BEAN CHILI

Serves 2; 1 1/4 cups per serving
Preparation time: 5 minutes

Choose your favorite canned beans and adjust the heat with the amount and kind of chili powder you use so the finished dish is just the way you like it.

1 teaspoon olive oil
1/2 large onion, chopped
1/4 medium green bell pepper, chopped
4 ounces extra-lean ground beef
2 (8-ounce) cans no-salt-added tomato sauce
1/2 (15-ounce) can no-salt-added black, pinto, or kidney beans, rinsed and drained
1/3 cup light beer (regular or nonalcoholic), fat-free, low-sodium chicken broth, or water
1 tablespoon chili powder (mild, regular, or hot), or to taste
1/2 teaspoon ground cumin
1/4 teaspoon ground coriander

1. In a medium saucepan, heat the oil over medium-low heat, swirling to coat the bottom. Cook the onion and bell pepper for about 5 minutes, or until soft. Stir in the beef. Cook for about 3 minutes, or until no longer pink, stirring occasionally to turn and break up the beef. Drain well in a colander. Wipe the pan with paper towels. Return the mixture to the pan.

2. Stir in the remaining ingredients. Cook for 20 minutes so the flavors blend and the sauce thickens to the desired consistency.

Exchanges/Choices

1 1/2 Starch
2 Vegetable
2 Lean Meat
1/2 Fat

Calories	290	
Calories from Fat	55	
Total Fat	6.0	g
Saturated Fat	1.7	g
Trans Fat	0.1	g
Polyunsaturated Fat	0.9	g
Monounsaturated Fat	3.1	g
Cholesterol	35	mg
Sodium	220	mg
Total Carbohydrate	39	g
Dietary Fiber	10	g
Sugars	18	g
Protein	19	g

Beefy Manicotti Alfredo

Beefy Manicotti Alfredo

Serves 2; 2 stuffed shells and 1/2 cup sauce per serving
Preparation time: 15 minutes (see Time-Saver, page 127)

This luscious dish, with its herb-enhanced Alfredo sauce, does take time, but the results are well worth the wait. Serve with a crisp green salad that you prepare while the manicotti bakes.

Cooking spray
4 dried manicotti shells

Filling

1 teaspoon olive oil
1 medium leek (white and light green parts) halved lengthwise, cut crosswise into
    1/4-inch slices (about 3/4 cup)
2 medium garlic cloves, minced
5 ounces extra-lean ground beef
1/2 teaspoon Italian seasoning blend, crumbled
1/3 cup chopped roasted red bell pepper, rinsed and drained if bottled
1/4 cup fat-free ricotta cheese
2 tablespoons fat-free sour cream
2 tablespoons egg substitute

Sauce

1 1/2 tablespoons all-purpose flour
2/3 cup fat-free milk
1/2 cup fat-free half-and-half
1 medium garlic clove, minced
1 tablespoon shredded or grated Parmesan cheese
1/2 teaspoon Italian seasoning blend, crumbled
1/8 teaspoon white pepper

TIME-SAVER: *This recipe goes together faster if you wait to measure the filling ingredients until you start to heat the water for boiling the pasta. You save even more time by cooking the filling while the noodles boil on the next burner.*

1. Lightly spray a 9-inch glass pie pan with cooking spray. Set aside.

2. Prepare the pasta using the package directions, omitting the salt and oil. Drain, rinse under cold water, and pat dry, being careful not to tear the pasta. Set aside.

3. Meanwhile, in a small nonstick skillet, heat the oil over medium heat, swirling to coat the bottom. Cook the leek and 2 minced garlic cloves for 2 to 3 minutes, or until the leek begins to soften, stirring frequently. Set aside 2 teaspoons mixture for garnish.

4. Stir the beef and 1/2 teaspoon seasoning blend into the remaining leek mixture in the skillet. Increase the heat to medium high and cook for 2 minutes, or until the beef is browned, stirring frequently to turn and break up the beef. Drain well in a colander. Pat the meat mixture and wipe the skillet with paper towels. Return the mixture to the skillet (the heat should be off). Stir in the remaining filling ingredients. Set aside.

5. Preheat the oven to 350°F.

6. In a small saucepan, whisk together the flour, milk, half-and-half, and remaining minced garlic. Bring to a simmer over medium-high heat, whisking constantly. Reduce the heat and simmer for 2 to 3 minutes, or until thickened, whisking constantly. Remove from the heat.

7. Stir in the Parmesan, seasoning blend, and pepper, whisking constantly until the Parmesan is melted.

8. To assemble, spread about 1/3 cup sauce in the pie pan. The sauce will "bounce" back when you spread it. Stuff the shells with the filling, being careful not to tear them. Place on the sauce. Spread the remaining sauce on the shells. Sprinkle with the reserved 2 teaspoons leek mixture.

9. Bake for 35 minutes, or until the sauce is hot and the shells are tender and heated through.

Exchanges/Choices		
2 Starch		
1 Fat-Free Milk		
1 Vegetable		
3 Lean Meat		
Calories	**405**	
Calories from Fat	80	
Total Fat	**9.0**	**g**
Saturated Fat	3.1	g
Trans Fat	0.1	g
Polyunsaturated Fat	0.9	g
Monounsaturated Fat	3.8	g
Cholesterol	**60**	**mg**
Sodium	**290**	**mg**
Total Carbohydrate	**49**	**g**
Dietary Fiber	3	g
Sugars	13	g
Protein	**31**	**g**

Pork Medallions

Pork Medallions
with Apricot-Sage Sauce

Serves 2; 3 ounces pork and 3 tablespoons sauce per serving
Preparation time: 5 minutes

Fresh sage, with its distinctive flavor, is perfectly balanced against tangy apricot preserves in a delicious sauce.

8 ounces pork tenderloin, all visible fat discarded, cut into 1/2-inch slices
1/8 teaspoon pepper
1 teaspoon olive oil
1 tablespoon finely chopped shallot or onion
1/2 cup fat-free, low-sodium chicken broth
1 large or 2 medium fresh sage leaves
2 tablespoons all-fruit apricot spread

1. Season the pork on both sides with the pepper. In a large nonstick skillet, heat the oil over medium-high heat. Cook the pork for 6 to 8 minutes, or until just slightly pink in the center, turning once. Transfer to a plate. Cover with aluminum foil to keep warm.

2. Put the shallot in the skillet. Cook for 1 minute, stirring constantly. Pour the broth into the skillet, stirring to dislodge any browned bits. Let boil for about 5 minutes, or until the liquid is reduced to about half (about 1/4 cup).

3. Meanwhile, chop the sage. Whisk the sage and apricot spread into the sauce. Spoon over the pork.

COOK'S TIP: *Chop the sage leaves right before adding them to the sauce. If they stand too long, the cut edges will turn brown.*

Exchanges/Choices
1 Fruit
3 Lean Meat

Calories	185	
Calories from Fat	45	
Total Fat	5.0	g
Saturated Fat	1.4	g
Trans Fat	0.0	g
Polyunsaturated Fat	0.5	g
Monounsaturated Fat	2.8	g
Cholesterol	60	mg
Sodium	70	mg
Total Carbohydrate	11	g
Dietary Fiber	0	g
Sugars	8	g
Protein	23	g

GERMAN PORK TENDERLOIN
WITH BRAISED CABBAGE

Serves 2; 3 ounces pork, 1 1/2 tablespoons sauce, and 1/2 cup cabbage per serving
Preparation time: 5 minutes

A quick mustard and sour cream sauce tops tangy cabbage and peppery pork medallions. During warm weather, grill the pork tenderloin, then slice it and serve with the cabbage and sauce.

1 tablespoon cider vinegar
8 ounces green cabbage, core discarded, coarsely chopped
8 ounces pork tenderloin, all visible fat discarded
1/2 teaspoon pepper (coarsely ground preferred)
1 teaspoon canola or corn oil
1 tablespoon whole-grain mustard
2 teaspoons Dijon mustard
2 tablespoons light sour cream

1. Fill a medium saucepan 2/3 full of water. Add the vinegar. Bring to a boil over medium-high heat. Add the cabbage. Reduce the heat and simmer for 10 to 15 minutes, or until just tender. Drain well in a colander and set aside.

2. Meanwhile, cut the pork crosswise into 4 slices. Pound each slice to flatten into a medallion about 3/8-inch thick. Sprinkle on both sides with the pepper.

3. In a medium nonstick skillet, heat the oil over medium-high heat, swirling to coat the bottom. Cook the pork for 3 minutes. Reduce the heat to medium. Turn the pork over and cook for 3 minutes. Transfer to a plate and cover to keep warm.

4. In the same skillet, whisk together the mustards and sour cream. Cook the mixture over medium heat for 1 to 2 minutes, or until heated through.

5. Spoon the cabbage onto plates. Place the pork on top. Drizzle with the mustard sauce.

Exchanges/Choices		
1 Vegetable		
3 Lean Meat		
1/2 Fat		
Calories	200	
Calories from Fat	65	
Total Fat	7.0	g
Saturated Fat	2.2	g
Trans Fat	0.0	g
Polyunsaturated Fat	1.1	g
Monounsaturated Fat	2.8	g
Cholesterol	65	mg
Sodium	195	mg
Total Carbohydrate	8	g
Dietary Fiber	3	g
Sugars	5	g
Protein	25	g

Pork Medallions with Cherry-Balsamic Sauce

Serves 2; 3 ounces pork and 2 tablespoons sauce per serving
Preparation time: 5 minutes

A super-quick balsamic reduction brings out the well-blended flavors of pork and dark cherries.

1/2 cup fresh or frozen unsweetened pitted dark cherries (about 12)
8 ounces pork tenderloin (about 3 inches long), all visible fat discarded
1/4 teaspoon salt
1/8 teaspoon pepper
1/8 teaspoon dried sage
2 teaspoons and 1/2 teaspoon olive oil, divided use
1 tablespoon minced shallot
1/3 cup balsamic vinegar

1. If using frozen cherries, remove from the freezer and cut in half. Set aside to thaw slightly while preparing the pork.

2. Slice the tenderloin into 6 medallions, each about 1/2 inch thick. Place between sheets of wax paper. Using the smooth side of a meat mallet or a heavy pan, pound meat to 1/4-inch thickness.

3. In a small bowl, stir together the salt, pepper, and sage. Sprinkle on both sides of the pork. Using your fingertips, gently press the mixture so it adheres to the pork.

4. In a large skillet, heat 2 teaspoons oil over medium-high heat, swirling to coat the bottom. Cook the pork without stirring for about 3 minutes, or until a golden crust forms and the pork releases easily from the skillet. Turn over and cook for about 3 minutes. Transfer to a plate and keep warm.

5. Reduce the heat to low. Add the remaining 1/2 teaspoon oil and shallot to the skillet. Cook for 1 minute, stirring to dislodge any browned bits. Add the vinegar and cherries. (The mixture will boil vigorously.) Slightly increase the heat and cook for about 2 minutes, or until all the browned bits release into the sauce and the cherries are heated through, stirring constantly.

6. Return the pork and any accumulated juices to the skillet. Stir to coat the pork with the sauce.

Exchanges/Choices
1 Fruit
1/2 Carbohydrate
3 Lean Meat
1/2 Fat

Calories	245	
Calories from Fat	80	
Total Fat	9.0	g
Saturated Fat	1.8	g
Trans Fat	0.0	g
Polyunsaturated Fat	0.8	g
Monounsaturated Fat	5.4	g
Cholesterol	60	mg
Sodium	330	mg
Total Carbohydrate	21	g
Dietary Fiber	2	g
Sugars	14	g
Protein	22	g

CHIMICHURRI-STYLE PORK

Serves 2; 3 ounces pork and 2 tablespoons sauce per serving
Preparation time: 5 minutes

Transform a pork chop into something very special with this flavorful sauce, reminiscent of an Argentinean favorite.

1 boneless center-cut loin pork chop (about 8 ounces), about 3/4 inch thick, all visible fat discarded
1 teaspoon olive oil

Chimichurri Sauce

1/4 cup fresh lime juice
1 tablespoon red wine vinegar
1 tablespoon very finely snipped fresh parsley
1 teaspoon minced fresh jalapeño, seeds and ribs discarded
1 medium garlic clove, minced
1 teaspoon dried oregano, crumbled
1/8 teaspoon salt

1. Put the pork chop in a small dish. Drizzle the oil over the pork.

2. In a small bowl, stir together the sauce ingredients. Drizzle 2 tablespoons sauce over the pork. Cover the pork and refrigerate for 30 minutes. Cover the remaining sauce and set aside.

3. Preheat the grill on medium high.

4. Drain the pork, discarding the marinade.

5. Grill the pork for 5 minutes. Turn over and grill for 3 to 5 minutes, or until the pork is no longer pink in the center or registers 160°F on an instant-read thermometer for medium doneness. Transfer to a plate. Cover with aluminum foil and let stand for 5 to 10 minutes. Slice into thin strips. Spoon the reserved sauce over the pork.

Exchanges/Choices

3 Lean Meat
1 Fat

Calories	185	
Calories from Fat	80	
Total Fat	9.0	g
Saturated Fat	2.9	g
Trans Fat	0.0	g
Polyunsaturated Fat	0.7	g
Monounsaturated Fat	4.9	g
Cholesterol	60	mg
Sodium	180	mg
Total Carbohydrate	3	g
Dietary Fiber	0	g
Sugars	1	g
Protein	21	g

Pork Chops with Garlic-Fennel Rub

Serves 2; 1 pork chop per serving
Preparation time: 5 minutes

These tender-moist pork chops will draw rave reviews for their robust seasoning.

Rub

3/4 teaspoon garlic powder
1/2 teaspoon dried fennel seeds, finely chopped
1/4 teaspoon Italian seasoning blend, crumbled

****

2 boneless pork loin chops (about 4 ounces each), about 1 inch thick, all visible fat discarded, patted dry
1 teaspoon olive oil
1/4 cup dry white wine (regular or nonalcoholic) or water

1. In a small bowl, stir together the rub ingredients. Using your fingertips, gently press the rub so it adheres to both sides of the pork chops.

2. In a small nonstick skillet, heat the oil over medium-low heat, swirling to coat the bottom. Cook the pork for 3 minutes on each side. Turn over and cook for 2 minutes on each side, or until the pork is no longer pink in the center or the internal temperature registers 150°F on an instant-read thermometer. Transfer to plates.

3. Pour the wine into the skillet. Cook for 1 to 2 minutes, or until reduced to about 1 tablespoon, scraping to dislodge any browned bits. Drizzle over the pork.

Exchanges/Choices		
3 Lean Meat		
1 Fat		
Calories	195	
Calories from Fat	90	
Total Fat	10.0	g
Saturated Fat	2.9	g
Trans Fat	0.0	g
Polyunsaturated Fat	0.7	g
Monounsaturated Fat	5.0	g
Cholesterol	60	mg
Sodium	50	mg
Total Carbohydrate	1	g
Dietary Fiber	0	g
Sugars	0	g
Protein	21	g

VEGETARIAN ENTRÉES

Herbed Asparagus and Pasta

HERBED ASPARAGUS AND PASTA TOSS

Serves 2; about 1 1/2 cups per serving
Preparation time: 10 minutes

The light gournay cheese in this dish melts into a creamy sauce for the hot pasta and asparagus combo. Gournay is a type of cream cheese created by François Boursin, who named it after the small town in France where he grew up.

4 ounces dried multigrain rotini or penne
4 ounces fresh asparagus, trimmed and cut diagonally into 2-inch pieces
4 ounces light gournay cheese with garlic and herbs
1/2 cup fat-free milk
1 medium garlic clove, minced
1/4 teaspoon pepper (coarsely ground preferred)
1/8 teaspoon salt
1 medium Italian plum tomato, diced
1 to 2 tablespoons finely chopped fresh basil

1. In a large saucepan, prepare the pasta using the package directions, omitting the salt and oil, adding the asparagus during the last 2 minutes of cooking time. Remove from heat. Drain well in a colander. Return to the pan. Stir in the gournay cheese, milk, garlic, pepper, and salt until well blended. Sprinkle with the tomato and basil.

COOK'S TIP: *For a change, sprinkle the pasta with a combination of fresh herbs, such as thyme, parsley, and a small amount of rosemary, instead of basil.*

Exchanges/Choices
3 Starch
1 Vegetable
2 Lean Meat

Calories	340	
Calories from Fat	65	
Total Fat	7.0	g
Saturated Fat	3.4	g
Trans Fat	0.0	g
Polyunsaturated Fat	1.5	g
Monounsaturated Fat	1.2	g
Cholesterol	10	mg
Sodium	470	mg
Total Carbohydrate	51	g
Dietary Fiber	8	g
Sugars	8	g
Protein	20	g

WHOLE-WHEAT PENNE
WITH TOASTED ALMOND PESTO

Serves 2; heaping 1 1/2 cups per serving
Preparation time: 10 minutes

Cherry tomatoes add a burst of color and juiciness to this interesting dish.

4 ounces dried whole-wheat penne
1/3 cup firmly packed fresh basil
2 tablespoons slivered almonds, dry-roasted
1 medium garlic clove
1/8 teaspoon salt
1/8 teaspoon pepper
1 tablespoon olive oil
1 tablespoon firmly packed Parmesan cheese
6 cherry tomatoes, halved

1. In a medium saucepan, prepare the pasta using the package directions, omitting the salt and oil. Immediately before draining the pasta, reserve 1/4 cup cooking water. Set the cooking water aside. Drain the pasta well in a colander.

2. In a mini food processor, process the basil, almonds, garlic, salt, and pepper for 30 seconds, or until finely minced. Add the oil and 1 tablespoon reserved pasta cooking water. Process for 15 seconds. Transfer the pesto to the same saucepan.

3. Stir in the Parmesan and pasta. Stir in the remaining 3 tablespoons pasta cooking water. Stir in the tomatoes. Heat over low heat for 3 to 5 minutes, or until hot.

Exchanges/Choices		
3 Starch		
2 1/2 Fat		
Calories	350	
Calories from Fat	115	
Total Fat	13.0	g
Saturated Fat	2.1	g
Trans Fat	0.0	g
Polyunsaturated Fat	2.1	g
Monounsaturated Fat	8.1	g
Cholesterol	5	mg
Sodium	230	mg
Total Carbohydrate	49	g
Dietary Fiber	8	g
Sugars	4	g
Protein	11	g

MUSHROOM STROGANOFF
WITH BROWN RICE

Serves 2; 1 1/2 cups per serving
Preparation time: 15 minutes

A medley of exotic and domestic mushrooms helps make an elegant vegetarian version of Beef Stroganoff. The mushrooms cook just long enough to be tender without releasing all their liquids, giving substance to the dish.

1/2 cup uncooked instant brown rice
1 teaspoon olive oil
1 large portobello mushroom (about 5 ounces), halved lengthwise, cut crosswise into 1/4-inch slices
2 ounces shiitake mushrooms, sliced
1 medium onion, thinly sliced
5 ounces button mushrooms, sliced
2 medium garlic cloves, minced
1 teaspoon all-purpose flour
1 tablespoon low-sodium vegetable broth
2 teaspoons dry sherry (optional)
1/2 cup fat-free sour cream, room temperature
2 tablespoons fat-free milk
1/8 teaspoon white pepper
1/8 teaspoon ground nutmeg
1 teaspoon finely snipped fresh Italian (flat-leaf) parsley

1. Prepare the rice using the package directions, omitting the salt and margarine.

2. Meanwhile, in a small nonstick skillet, heat the oil over medium-high heat, swirling to coat the bottom. Cook the portobello and shiitake mushrooms and onion for 5 minutes, or until the mushrooms begin to soften, stirring constantly. Add the button mushrooms and garlic. Cook for 2 minutes, stirring constantly. Reduce the heat to medium. Sprinkle the flour over all. Cook for 1 minute, stirring constantly. Add the broth. Cook for 1 minute, stirring constantly. Stir in the remaining ingredients except the parsley. Cook for 2 to 3 minutes, or until heated through, stirring constantly.

3. Spoon the rice onto plates. Spoon the mushroom mixture and sauce over the rice. Sprinkle with the parsley.

COOK'S TIP: *Portobello mushrooms are meatier and hold their shape much better than the shiitake and button varieties. You may substitute other mushrooms for the shiitakes or the button, but use the portobelos or too much of the mushrooms' bulk will cook away.*

Exchanges/Choices
2 1/2 Starch
3 Vegetable
1 Fat

Calories	325	
Calories from Fat	35	
Total Fat	4.0	g
Saturated Fat	0.4	g
Trans Fat	0.0	g
Polyunsaturated Fat	1.0	g
Monounsaturated Fat	2.2	g
Cholesterol	5	mg
Sodium	75	mg
Total Carbohydrate	57	g
Dietary Fiber	6	g
Sugars	7	g
Protein	13	g

Vegetable Stir-Fry with Walnuts

Serves 2; heaping 1 1/2 cups per serving
Preparation time: 20 minutes

The varied textures and colors of this stir-fry make it a sure winner. Whole-grain instant rice really speeds up the cooking process, while retaining the nutritional benefits of its longer-cooking counterpart.

1/2 cup uncooked instant brown rice
1/2 teaspoon grated peeled gingerroot
1/4 teaspoon dried tarragon, crumbled
2 teaspoons canola or corn oil
4 ounces fresh shiitake mushrooms, entire stems discarded, caps cut into strips
1/2 medium red or green bell pepper, chopped
1 medium carrot, coarsely chopped
1/2 small onion (yellow preferred), finely chopped
1 medium garlic clove, minced
3/4 cup snow peas or sugar snap peas, trimmed if fresh, thawed and patted dry if frozen
1/4 cup canned sliced water chestnuts, drained
1/8 teaspoon pepper
1/4 cup low-sodium vegetable broth
1/4 cup water
3 tablespoons walnuts, coarsely chopped, dry-roasted

1. In a small saucepan, prepare the rice using the package directions, adding the gingerroot and tarragon with the water and omitting the salt and margarine. Remove from heat. Let stand for 10 minutes.

2. During the standing time, in a medium nonstick skillet, heat the oil over medium heat, swirling to coat the bottom. Cook the mushrooms, bell pepper, carrot, onion, and garlic for 5 to 6 minutes, or until the pepper and carrot are tender-crisp, stirring frequently. Stir in the snow peas, water chestnuts, and pepper. Cook for 2 minutes, or until the snow peas are tender. Stir in the broth and water. Cook for 1 minute, or until the liquids are hot.

3. Spoon the rice onto plates. Top with the vegetable mixture. Sprinkle with walnuts.

Exchanges/Choices
2 1/2 Starch
3 Vegetable
2 Fat

Calories	360	
Calories from Fat	115	
Total Fat	13.0	g
Saturated Fat	1.1	g
Trans Fat	0.0	g
Polyunsaturated Fat	7.3	g
Monounsaturated Fat	4.2	g
Cholesterol	0	mg
Sodium	75	mg
Total Carbohydrate	56	g
Dietary Fiber	7	g
Sugars	7	g
Protein	8	g

GRILLED VEGETABLES WITH ORZO

Serves 2; 1 cup vegetables and 1/2 cup orzo per serving
Preparation time: 15 minutes

Tart lemon juice and crunchy almonds enhance the variety of vegetables in this tasty main dish.

1/3 cup plus 2 tablespoons dried orzo
Cooking spray
1/2 small red bell pepper, halved lengthwise,
1/2 medium green bell pepper, cut lengthwise in thirds
1/2 small yellow summer squash (about 2 ounces), cut lengthwise into thirds
2 small button mushrooms
1 medium green onion, sliced
8 grape tomatoes, halved
1/4 cup fresh basil, chopped
2 tablespoons fresh lemon juice
2 teaspoons olive oil
1 large garlic clove, minced
2 tablespoons fat-free feta cheese
2 tablespoons slivered almonds, dry-roasted

1. Prepare the orzo using the package directions, omitting the salt and oil. Drain well in a colander. Transfer to a large bowl.

2. Meanwhile, lightly spray a grill rack with cooking spray. Preheat the grill on medium high.

3. Grill the bell peppers, squash, and mushrooms, covered, for 5 to 6 minutes, or until just tender, turning once. Transfer to a cutting board. Coarsely chop.

4. Stir the grilled vegetables into the orzo. Gently stir in the green onion, tomatoes, and basil.

5. In a small bowl, whisk together the lemon juice, olive oil, and garlic. Pour over the orzo mixture, tossing gently to coat. Sprinkle with the feta and almonds.

Exchanges/Choices		
2 Starch		
2 Vegetable		
2 Fat		
Calories	290	
Calories from Fat	90	
Total Fat	10.0	g
Saturated Fat	1.1	g
Trans Fat	0.0	g
Polyunsaturated Fat	1.9	g
Monounsaturated Fat	6.1	g
Cholesterol	0	mg
Sodium	155	mg
Total Carbohydrate	41	g
Dietary Fiber	5	g
Sugars	8	g
Protein	11	g

Barley Risotto
with Roasted Vegetables

Serves 2; 1 1/2 cups per serving
Preparation time: 10 minutes

Risotto is usually made with arborio rice and can take up to 30 minutes of actual cooking time, with quite a bit of stirring. By using quick-cooking barley, you can cut that time in half. Add a variety of roasted vegetables to create a filling entrée.

Cooking spray
1 small sweet potato (about 4 ounces), peeled and cut into 1/2-inch cubes
1 small red bell pepper, cut into 1-inch pieces
1 small parsnip, peeled and cut crosswise into 1/2-inch slices
1/2 small red onion, cut into 1-inch strips
1/4 teaspoon pepper
2 teaspoons olive oil
1 medium garlic clove, minced
1/4 teaspoon dried oregano, crumbled
1/4 teaspoon dried basil, crumbled
1/4 cup uncooked quick-cooking barley
1/2 cup and 1/2 cup low-sodium vegetable broth, divided use
2 tablespoons shredded or grated Parmesan cheese

1. Preheat the oven to 400°F. Lightly spray an 8-inch square baking pan with cooking spray.

2. In the baking pan, stir together the sweet potato, bell pepper, parsnip, and onion. Sprinkle the pepper over the vegetables. Lightly spray with cooking spray.

3. Bake for 15 minutes. Remove from the oven. Stir the vegetables and lightly spray with cooking spray. Bake for 15 minutes, or until tender.

4. Meanwhile, in a medium saucepan, heat the oil over medium-low heat, swirling to coat the bottom. Cook the garlic, oregano, and basil for 15 to 20 seconds, or until the garlic is tender-crisp, stirring occasionally.

5. Stir in the barley. Increase the heat to medium and cook for 30 seconds to lightly toast. Slowly pour in 1/2 cup broth, about 2 tablespoons at a time, stirring constantly and waiting until the liquid is absorbed before adding the next 2 tablespoons.

6. Stir in the remaining 1/2 cup broth all at once. Bring to a simmer over medium heat. Reduce the heat and simmer, covered, for 8 to 9 minutes, or until the barley is tender. Remove from the heat. Let stand for 5 minutes. Stir in the Parmesan. Spoon onto plates. Top with the vegetables.

Exchanges/Choices
  2 Starch
  1 Vegetable
  1 Fat

Calories	235	
Calories from Fat	70	
Total Fat	8.0	g
Saturated Fat	2.2	g
Trans Fat	0.0	g
Polyunsaturated Fat	0.9	g
Monounsaturated Fat	4.0	g
Cholesterol	10	mg
Sodium	210	mg
Total Carbohydrate	37	g
Dietary Fiber	5	g
Sugars	7	g
Protein	7	g

BULGUR AND BUTTERNUT SQUASH

Serves 2; 1 1/2 cups per serving
Preparation time: 15 minutes

Now that butternut squash is available fresh or frozen all year, you don't need to save this dish just for the colder months. It offers a variety of colors, tastes, and textures that is delightful at any time.

1/2 cup low-sodium vegetable broth
1/4 cup uncooked bulgur
1 tablespoon chopped pecans, dry-roasted
1 teaspoon olive oil
1/2 small red onion, thinly sliced
1/2 medium red bell pepper, thinly sliced
1 medium garlic clove, minced
6 ounces frozen diced butternut squash, thawed
1 cup no-salt-added canned diced tomatoes, undrained
1/2 cup soy crumbles (about 3 ounces)
1/4 teaspoon dried oregano, crumbled
1/4 teaspoon dried basil, crumbled
1/4 teaspoon salt
1/8 teaspoon pepper

1. In a medium saucepan, bring the broth to a simmer over medium-high heat. Stir in the bulgur. Reduce the heat and simmer, covered, for 15 minutes, or until the broth is absorbed. Remove from the heat. Let stand for 5 minutes. Stir in the pecans. Fluff with a fork.

2. Meanwhile, in a large nonstick skillet, heat the oil over medium-high heat, swirling to coat the bottom. Cook the onion, bell pepper, and garlic for 3 to 4 minutes, or until tender, stirring occasionally.

3. Stir in the remaining ingredients. Bring to a simmer. Reduce the heat and simmer for 6 to 8 minutes, or until the mixture is heated through and the flavors have blended, stirring occasionally. Spoon the bulgur onto plates. Top with the squash mixture.

Exchanges/Choices		
1 1/2 Starch		
2 Vegetable		
1 Fat		
Calories	230	
Calories from Fat	55	
Total Fat	6.0	g
Saturated Fat	0.6	g
Trans Fat	0.0	g
Polyunsaturated Fat	1.4	g
Monounsaturated Fat	3.3	g
Cholesterol	0	mg
Sodium	350	mg
Total Carbohydrate	39	g
Dietary Fiber	10	g
Sugars	8	g
Protein	12	g

BLACK-EYED PEAS WITH BROWN RICE

Serves 2; 1 cup black-eyed pea mixture and 1/2 cup rice per serving
Preparation Time: 10 minutes

A quick sauté and simmer and you'll be enjoying this simple but satisfying meal. Try a slice of chilled melon on the side as a balance for the heat from the jalapeño.

1 teaspoon olive oil
1/2 medium onion, diced
1/2 medium bell pepper (yellow preferred), diced
1 medium rib of celery, diced
1 medium fresh jalapeño, seeds and ribs discarded, diced
1 medium garlic clove, minced
1/2 (15-ounce) can no-salt-added black-eyed peas, rinsed and drained
1 cup low-sodium vegetable broth
1/4 teaspoon paprika
1/4 teaspoon ground cumin
1/4 teaspoon salt
1/2 cup uncooked instant brown rice

1. In a medium saucepan, heat the oil over medium heat, swirling to coat the bottom. Cook the onion, bell pepper, celery, jalapeño, and garlic for 3 to 4 minutes, or until tender, stirring occasionally.

2. Stir in the remaining ingredients except the rice. Increase the heat to medium high and bring to a simmer. Reduce the heat and simmer, covered, for 10 to 15 minutes, or until the flavors have blended.

3. Meanwhile, prepare the rice using the package directions, omitting the salt and margarine. Spoon the rice into bowls. Top with the black-eyed pea mixture.

Exchanges/Choices		
3 Starch		
2 Vegetable		
1/2 Fat		
Calories	315	
Calories from Fat	35	
Total Fat	4.0	g
Saturated Fat	0.4	g
Trans Fat	0.0	g
Polyunsaturated Fat	1.0	g
Monounsaturated Fat	2.3	g
Cholesterol	0	mg
Sodium	405	mg
Total Carbohydrate	61	g
Dietary Fiber	7	g
Sugars	7	g
Protein	11	g

MAC AND CHEESE WITH VEGGIES

Serves 2; 1 1/2 cups per serving
Preparation time: 10 minutes

Classic macaroni and cheese gets a nutritious twist with whole-wheat pasta and the addition of a colorful vegetable trio.

> 1/2 cup dried whole-wheat elbow macaroni
> Cooking spray
> 1 teaspoon olive oil
> 1/2 medium red bell pepper, chopped
> 4 ounces broccoli florets, chopped
> 1 small yellow summer squash or zucchini (about 4 ounces), thinly sliced crosswise
> 2 tablespoons water
> 1/2 cup fat-free half-and-half
> 1/4 cup low-sodium vegetable broth
> 1 tablespoon plus 1 teaspoon all-purpose flour
> 1/8 teaspoon salt
> 1/8 teaspoon pepper
> 1/3 cup low-fat shredded cheddar cheese
> 1 tablespoon shredded or grated part-skim asiago cheese or Parmesan cheese
> 1 tablespoon plain dry bread crumbs

1. Prepare the pasta using the package directions, omitting the salt and oil. Drain well in a colander. Lightly spray an 8-inch square baking pan with cooking spray. Pour the pasta into the baking pan.

2. Meanwhile, preheat the oven to 350°F.

3. In a large skillet, heat the oil over medium heat, swirling to coat the bottom. Cook the bell pepper for 2 to 3 minutes, or until tender-crisp, stirring occasionally. Stir in the broccoli and squash. Cook for 1 minute. Stir in the water and cook for 2 to 3 minutes, or until tender, stirring occasionally.

4. Meanwhile, in a small bowl, whisk together the half-and-half, broth, flour, salt, and pepper. Pour into the cooked bell pepper mixture. Increase heat to medium high and bring to a simmer, stirring occasionally. Remove from heat. Stir in the cheddar and asiago until melted. Stir into the pasta. Sprinkle with the bread crumbs.

5. Bake for 20 to 25 minutes, or until the casserole is heated through and the top is golden brown.

COOK'S TIP: *Asiago cheese is similar to Parmesan in texture, although asiago is a little more intensely flavored and nuttier, and it is somewhat more aromatic. You can substitute asiago for Parmesan in most recipes, such as for lasagna, quiche, and pizza, and as a soup and salad garnish. Just remember that a little asiago goes a long way.*

Exchanges/Choices
2 Starch
1/2 Fat-Free Milk
1 Vegetable
1 Fat

Calories	265	
Calories from Fat	70	
Total Fat	8.0	g
Saturated Fat	3.2	g
Trans Fat	0.0	g
Polyunsaturated Fat	0.8	g
Monounsaturated Fat	3.0	g
Cholesterol	15	mg
Sodium	410	mg
Total Carbohydrate	40	g
Dietary Fiber	6	g
Sugars	8	g
Protein	13	g

STUFFED BELL PEPPERS
WITH FRESH TOMATO-BASIL SAUCE

Serves 2; 2 stuffed bell pepper halves per serving
Preparation time: 15 minutes

Turn stuffed peppers into a vegetarian entrée by substituting kasha for the usual ground meat, then topping them with a sauce of fresh cherry tomatoes and basil.

1 cup water
1/2 cup medium kasha
1 large egg white or 2 tablespoons egg white substitute
Cooking spray
2 teaspoons olive oil
10 ounces frozen chopped spinach, thawed and squeezed dry
5 ounces button or baby portobello mushrooms, stems discarded, finely chopped
1 small onion, finely chopped
2 medium garlic cloves, minced
1/4 teaspoon dried marjoram, crumbled
1/8 teaspoon pepper
2 large red or green bell peppers, or a combination, halved lengthwise
2 tablespoons finely chopped walnuts
1 (8-ounce) can no-salt-added tomato sauce
1/4 cup low-sodium vegetable broth or water
4 large grape tomatoes or cherry tomatoes, finely chopped
1 tablespoon chopped fresh basil or 1/2 teaspoon dried basil, crumbled

1. In a small saucepan, bring the water to a boil over medium-high heat. In a medium nonstick saucepan, stir together the kasha and egg white. Cook over medium-low heat for 3 to 4 minutes, or until the kasha is lightly toasted and the egg white is absorbed, stirring frequently to break up any lumps. Stir the boiling water slowly into the kasha mixture. Reduce the heat to low and cook, covered, for 9 to 11 minutes, or until the kasha is tender and the liquid is absorbed. Remove the pan from the heat. Let stand for 10 minutes. Fluff with a fork. Transfer to a medium bowl.

2. Preheat the oven to 375°F. Lightly spray an 11 × 7 × 2-inch glass baking pan with cooking spray.

3. In a medium nonstick skillet, heat the oil over medium heat, swirling to coat the bottom. Cook the spinach, mushrooms, onion, garlic, marjoram, and pepper for 7 to 8 minutes, or until the onion is soft and any liquid has evaporated. Stir into the kasha.

4. Put the bell peppers with the cut side up in the baking dish. Stuff the peppers with the kasha mixture. Sprinkle the nuts over the stuffed peppers.

5. In a small bowl, stir together the remaining ingredients. Pour over and around the stuffed peppers.

6. Cover the dish loosely with aluminum foil. Bake for 30 minutes. Bake, uncovered, for 15 to 20 minutes, or until the stuffed peppers are tender and easily pierced with the tip of a sharp knife.

COOK'S TIP: *Look for kasha, or buckwheat groats, in the ethnic aisle of supermarkets or in specialty and health food stores. It is available in fine, medium, and coarse textures.*

Exchanges/Choices
2 Starch
5 Vegetable
2 Fat

Calories	375	
Calories from Fat	110	
Total Fat	12.0	g
Saturated Fat	1.5	g
Trans Fat	0.0	g
Polyunsaturated Fat	4.9	g
Monounsaturated Fat	4.3	g
Cholesterol	0	mg
Sodium	200	mg
Total Carbohydrate	60	g
Dietary Fiber	15	g
Sugars	20	g
Protein	17	g

Couscous with Chick-Peas

COUSCOUS WITH CHICK-PEAS AND VEGETABLES

Serves 2; 1 1/4 cups vegetable and chick-pea mixture and 1/3 cup couscous per serving
Preparation time: 10 minutes

Couscous is a mild-tasting grain that usually absorbs the flavors of the foods with which it is combined. Here, however, you add the seasonings to the dry couscous instead.

2 teaspoons olive oil
1/2 small zucchini (about 2 ounces), chopped
1/2 small yellow summer squash (about 2 ounces), chopped
1/2 medium red or green bell pepper, chopped
1 medium shallot, chopped
1 medium garlic clove, minced
1/2 cup canned no-salt-added chick-peas, rinsed and drained well
1/4 cup low-sodium vegetable broth
1/2 cup water
1/4 cup uncooked couscous (whole-wheat preferred)
1/8 teaspoon ground turmeric
1/8 teaspoon ground cumin
1/8 teaspoon pepper
1 tablespoon snipped fresh cilantro or parsley

1. In a medium nonstick skillet, heat the oil over medium heat, swirling to coat the bottom. Cook the zucchini, squash, bell pepper, shallot, and garlic for 4 to 5 minutes, or until the vegetables are tender-crisp, stirring frequently.

2. Stir in the chick-peas and broth. Cook for 1 to 2 minutes, or until the vegetables are tender, stirring occasionally.

3. Meanwhile, in a small saucepan, bring the water to a boil over high heat. Stir in the couscous, turmeric, cumin, and pepper. Remove the pan from the heat. Cover and let stand for 5 minutes. Fluff with a fork. Spoon the mixture onto plates. Top with the vegetable mixture. Sprinkle with the cilantro.

Exchanges/Choices		
1 1/2 Starch		
1 Vegetable		
1 Fat		
Calories	210	
Calories from Fat	55	
Total Fat	6.0	g
Saturated Fat	0.9	g
Trans Fat	0.0	g
Polyunsaturated Fat	1.2	g
Monounsaturated Fat	3.7	g
Cholesterol	0	mg
Sodium	30	mg
Total Carbohydrate	33	g
Dietary Fiber	6	g
Sugars	5	g
Protein	8	g

POBLANO FRITTATA

Serves 2; 2 wedges, 2 tablespoons picante sauce, and 1 tablespoon sour cream per serving
Preparation time: 10 minutes

An Italian frittata goes south of the border with the addition of poblano pepper, cilantro, and picante sauce.

1/2 cup egg substitute
2 tablespoons fat-free milk
1 tablespoon snipped fresh cilantro
1/2 teaspoon olive oil
1 medium poblano pepper, seeds and stem discarded, chopped
1 1/2 cups frozen whole-kernel corn, thawed
1 medium green onion, chopped
2 tablespoons shredded low-fat sharp cheddar cheese
1/4 cup mild picante sauce (lowest sodium available)
2 tablespoons fat-free sour cream

1. In a small bowl, whisk together the egg substitute, milk, and cilantro.

2. In a small nonstick skillet, heat the oil over medium heat, swirling to coat the bottom. Cook the poblano for 3 minutes, or until beginning to brown on the edges, stirring frequently. Stir in the corn and green onion. Reduce the heat to medium low and carefully pour the egg substitute mixture over all. Cook, covered, for 10 minutes, or until the mixture is just set on the edge and is still a bit soft in the center (don't overcook or it will become tough and rubbery). Remove from heat.

3. Sprinkle with the cheddar. Let stand for 5 minutes to continue cooking and to melt the cheddar. Cut into 4 wedges. Place 2 wedges on each plate. Top with the picante sauce and sour cream.

Exchanges/Choices		
1 1/2 Starch		
1 Vegetable		
1 Lean Meat		
Calories	200	
Calories from Fat	30	
Total Fat	3.5	g
Saturated Fat	1.1	g
Trans Fat	0.0	g
Polyunsaturated Fat	0.5	g
Monounsaturated Fat	1.4	g
Cholesterol	5	mg
Sodium	450	mg
Total Carbohydrate	32	g
Dietary Fiber	4	g
Sugars	6	g
Protein	14	g

CRUSTLESS SPINACH AND MUSHROOM QUICHE

Serves 2; 1 quiche per serving

Preparation time: 10 minutes

This quiche is heartier than most, with added texture from meaty portobello mushrooms.

Cooking spray

1 teaspoon canola or corn oil

6 ounces portobello mushrooms, stemmed and sliced

3 medium green onions, chopped

2 tablespoons port

2 medium garlic cloves, minced

1 cup (about 2 1/2 ounces) frozen chopped spinach, thawed and squeezed dry

1 teaspoon cornstarch

3/4 cup fat-free milk

1/2 cup egg substitute

1/4 cup plus 2 tablespoons shredded part-skim mozzarella cheese

1 tablespoon shredded or grated Parmesan cheese

1/8 teaspoon pepper

Pinch of nutmeg

1. Preheat the oven to 350°F. Lightly spray two 10-ounce ovenproof custard cups or individual pie pans with cooking spray. Place on a shallow baking sheet.

2. In a large nonstick skillet, heat the oil over medium heat, swirling to coat the bottom. Cook the mushrooms and green onions for 2 minutes, stirring occasionally. Stir in the port. Reduce the heat to medium low and cook for 3 to 4 minutes, or until all the liquid is absorbed. Stir in the garlic and cook for 30 seconds to 1 minute, or until fragrant. Remove from heat. Add the spinach. Using a spoon, separate it into small pieces.

3. Put the cornstarch in a medium bowl. Pour in the milk, whisking to dissolve. Whisk in the remaining ingredients. Stir in the mushroom mixture. Pour into the custard cups.

4. Bake for 30 minutes, or until the centers are puffed and set (don't jiggle when gently shaken). Let stand for 5 minutes before serving.

COOK'S TIP: *Never soak fresh mushrooms to clean them. They will absorb some of the water. Give them a quick wipe with a damp cloth or mushroom brush instead, or rinse them quickly under cold running water and pat dry with a paper towel.*

Exchanges/Choices
1/2 Fat-Free Milk
2 Vegetable
2 Lean Meat
1/2 Fat

Calories	205	
Calories from Fat	65	
Total Fat	7.0	**g**
Saturated Fat	3.2	g
Trans Fat	0.0	g
Polyunsaturated Fat	1.0	g
Monounsaturated Fat	2.6	g
Cholesterol	20	**mg**
Sodium	395	**mg**
Total Carbohydrate	16	**g**
Dietary Fiber	3	g
Sugars	8	g
Protein	20	**g**

Portobello Benedict

Serves 2; 1/2 English muffin, 1/2 cup vegetables, and 2 tablespoons sauce per serving
Preparation time: 10 minutes

A portobello mushroom and red bell pepper replace poached egg and pork to provide a delightful vegetarian twist to traditional eggs Benedict.

1 teaspoon and 2 teaspoons olive oil, divided use
1/2 medium onion (yellow preferred), thinly sliced and slices cut in half
1/2 teaspoon sugar
Cooking spray
1 medium portobello mushroom (about 4 inches in diameter), stem discarded and gills scraped off
1/2 large red bell pepper, halved
2 tablespoons water
1/4 teaspoon dried thyme, crumbled
1/3 cup fat-free milk
1 teaspoon cornstarch
1/8 teaspoon dry mustard
1/2 tablespoon egg substitute
1/2 tablespoon fresh lemon juice
1/8 teaspoon salt
1/8 teaspoon pepper (coarsely ground preferred)
1 whole-wheat English muffin, split

1. In a small skillet, heat 1 teaspoon olive oil over medium heat, swirling to coat the bottom. Add the onion and stir to coat. Sprinkle the sugar over the onion. Cook for 2 minutes, or until hot. Reduce the heat to low and cook for 20 to 30 minutes, or until golden brown, stirring frequently.

2. Meanwhile, preheat the oven to 425°F. Lightly spray a baking sheet with cooking spray.

3. Brush the mushroom and bell pepper with the remaining 2 teaspoons oil. Transfer the bell pepper with the skin side up to the baking sheet.

4. Bake for 13 minutes. Add the mushroom with the stem side down. Bake for 7 minutes, or until the bell pepper is blistered and slightly charred and the mushroom is hot. Remove the baking sheet from the oven, leaving the mushroom on it. Transfer the bell pepper to a small bowl. Cover loosely with a cloth. Let the mushroom and bell pepper stand for 5 to 10 minutes, or until cool enough to handle. With the tip of a sharp knife, remove the skin from the bell pepper. Cut the bell pepper and mushroom into 1/2-inch squares.

5. Stir the bell pepper, mushroom, water, and thyme into the cooked onions. Cook over low heat for 2 to 3 minutes, or until hot. Cover with aluminum foil to keep warm. Set aside.

6. In a small saucepan, stir together the milk, cornstarch, and mustard until the cornstarch is completely dissolved. Cook over medium heat for 3 to 4 minutes, or until the mixture begins to boil and has thickened, stirring constantly. Remove from heat.

7. Pour the egg substitute into a small bowl. Stir in about 1 tablespoon hot milk mixture. Stir into the milk mixture in the saucepan. Cook over low heat for 1 to 2 minutes, or until the mixture bubbles, stirring constantly. Remove from heat. Stir in the lemon juice, salt, and pepper.

8. Toast the English muffin halves. Transfer with the cut sides up to plates. Top with the vegetable mixture. Drizzle with the sauce.

Exchanges/Choices
1 Starch
2 Vegetable
1 1/2 Fat

Calories	195	
Calories from Fat	70	
Total Fat	8.0	g
Saturated Fat	1.1	g
Trans Fat	0.0	g
Polyunsaturated Fat	1.1	g
Monounsaturated Fat	5.2	g
Cholesterol	0	mg
Sodium	340	mg
Total Carbohydrate	27	g
Dietary Fiber	4	g
Sugars	10	g
Protein	7	g

Vegetable Lasagna

Serves 2; two 1 1/2-inch slices per serving
Preparation time: 15 minutes

A wide variety of vegetables and herbs will make this satisfying no-pasta lasagna appeal to vegetarians and meat lovers alike. You don't need to simmer the easy sauce on the stove. Just stir in the herbs and spices, and the flavors will blend as the lasagna bakes.

Olive oil spray
1 small eggplant (about 12 ounces)
1 (8-ounce) can no-salt-added tomato sauce
1 teaspoon Italian seasoning blend, crumbled
1/2 teaspoon garlic powder
1/2 teaspoon onion powder
1/8 teaspoon pepper
1/8 teaspoon salt
1/2 teaspoon and 1/2 teaspoon olive oil, divided use
1/2 medium onion, sliced into 1/8-inch-wide half-circles
3 ounces button mushrooms, sliced
1 medium garlic clove, minced
1/3 cup fat-free ricotta cheese
1/4 cup frozen chopped spinach, thawed and squeezed dry
2 teaspoons egg substitute
1/8 teaspoon ground nutmeg
2 tablespoons shredded part-skim mozzarella cheese

1. Preheat the oven to 425°F. Lightly spray a 6 × 3-inch aluminum foil mini loaf pan with olive oil spray. Line a baking sheet with aluminum foil. Place a cooling rack on the baking sheet.

2. Cut four 1/4-inch slices, crosswise, from the bottom end of the eggplant. Halve the slices. Put the eggplant on the rack. Lightly spray with olive oil spray. Bake the eggplant for 15 minutes, turning once. Transfer to a plate. Remove the rack. Wipe the aluminum foil with a paper towel. Set the baking sheet aside.

3. Meanwhile, in a small measuring cup or bowl, stir together the tomato sauce, seasoning blend, garlic powder, onion powder, pepper, and salt.

4. In a small nonstick skillet, heat 1/2 teaspoon oil over medium-high heat, swirling to coat the bottom. Add the onion. Reduce the heat to medium. Stir. Cook for 6 minutes, or until light brown, stirring frequently. Transfer to a small bowl. Set aside.

5. In the same skillet, heat the remaining 1/2 teaspoon oil over medium-high heat, swirling to coat the bottom. Cook the mushrooms and garlic for 2 to 3 minutes, or until the mushrooms are soft, stirring frequently. Remove from heat. Stir in half the reserved tomato sauce mixture.

6. In a small bowl, stir together the ricotta, spinach, egg substitute, and nutmeg.

7. In the loaf pan, layer, in order, all the mushroom mixture, half the eggplant slices in a single layer, all the onion, all the ricotta mixture, the remaining eggplant slices, and the remaining sauce. Cover with aluminum foil. Transfer to the baking sheet.

8. Bake for 20 minutes. Sprinkle with the mozzarella. Bake, uncovered, for 10 minutes, or until the lasagna is hot and bubbly and the mozzarella has melted. Let stand for 5 minutes to make slicing and serving easier. Cut into 4 slices.

COOK'S TIP: *For a crunchy topping for salads, cut leftover eggplant into cubes, lightly spray with olive oil spray, and bake at 400°F to the desired doneness.*

Exchanges/Choices		
5 Vegetable		
1 Fat		
Calories	**175**	
Calories from Fat	35	
Total Fat	**4.0**	**g**
Saturated Fat	1.2	g
Trans Fat	0.0	g
Polyunsaturated Fat	0.5	g
Monounsaturated Fat	2.0	g
Cholesterol	**20**	**mg**
Sodium	**300**	**mg**
Total Carbohydrate	**25**	**g**
Dietary Fiber	6	g
Sugars	13	g
Protein	**11**	**g**

Artichoke-Cannellini Pitas

ARTICHOKE-CANNELLINI PITAS

Serves 2; 1 pita half and 1/2 cup salad mixture per serving
Preparation time: 10 minutes

Stuff this garlicky bean mixture in a pita pocket half and serve with juicy tomato wedges on the side for a simple lunch. For a change, substitute a large leaf of red-tipped lettuce for each pita half.

1 (15-ounce) can no-salt-added cannellini beans, rinsed and drained
2 tablespoons water
1/4 cup finely chopped red bell pepper
2 tablespoons marinated artichoke hearts, drained and chopped
1 small garlic clove, minced
1/4 teaspoon Italian seasoning blend, crumbled
1/8 teaspoon pepper
1 (6-inch) pita pocket, halved
1 cup fresh baby spinach leaves

1. In a food processor or blender, process the beans and water until creamy, scraping the side as needed. (For a coarser mixture, put the beans and water in a medium bowl and mash with a fork.) Transfer to a medium bowl. Stir in the bell pepper, artichokes, garlic, seasoning blend, and pepper.

2. Line the pita pocket halves with the spinach. Spoon the bean mixture into the pitas.

Exchanges/Choices		
3 Starch		
1 Lean Meat		
Calories	280	
Calories from Fat	15	
Total Fat	1.5	g
Saturated Fat	0.2	g
Trans Fat	0.0	g
Polyunsaturated Fat	0.9	g
Monounsaturated Fat	0.2	g
Cholesterol	0	mg
Sodium	205	mg
Total Carbohydrate	52	g
Dietary Fiber	11	g
Sugars	5	g
Protein	16	g

Posole-Style Corn Casserole

Serves 2; 1 1/2 cups per serving
Preparation time: 10 minutes

We've kept the classic influence of posole's zesty seasonings but substituted corn for the traditional hominy, which is higher in sodium.

Cooking spray
1 cup frozen whole-kernel corn, thawed
2 teaspoons olive oil
1 medium red bell pepper, thinly sliced
1/2 medium red onion, thinly sliced
1 medium garlic clove, minced
3/4 cup soy crumbles (about 4 ounces)
1 medium Italian plum tomato, diced
2 tablespoons canned diced green chiles

1/4 teaspoon chili powder
1/4 teaspoon ground cumin
1/4 cup fat-free sour cream
1/4 cup low-fat shredded cheddar cheese

1. Preheat the oven to 350°F.

2. Lightly spray a shallow 1-quart casserole dish with cooking spray. Spread the corn in the dish. Set aside.

3. In a large skillet, heat the oil over medium-high heat, swirling to coat the bottom. Cook the bell pepper, onion, and garlic for 3 to 4 minutes, or until soft, stirring occasionally.

4. Stir in the soy crumbles, tomato, green chiles, chili powder, and cumin. Cook for 1 to 2 minutes, or until slightly warmed. Remove from the heat. Stir in the sour cream. Pour over the corn. Sprinkle with the cheddar.

5. Bake, covered, for 20 to 25 minutes, or until the ingredients are warmed through and the cheddar has melted.

Exchanges/Choices
1 Starch
1/2 Carbohydrate
2 Vegetable
2 Lean Meat
1/2 Fat

Calories	275	
Calories from Fat	80	
Total Fat	9.0	g
Saturated Fat	2.6	g
Trans Fat	0.0	g
Polyunsaturated Fat	1.1	g
Monounsaturated Fat	4.5	g
Cholesterol	15	mg
Sodium	440	mg
Total Carbohydrate	34	g
Dietary Fiber	8	g
Sugars	9	g
Protein	22	g

Pita Pizza Margherita

PITA PIZZA MARGHERITA

Serves 2; 1 pizza per serving
Preparation time: 10 minutes

Thick slices of tomato, fresh basil leaves, and shredded mozzarella and Parmesan are baked atop whole-wheat pitas to create individual pizzas. The crowning touch is a fresh gremolata, made with the usual parsley, lemon zest, and garlic.

Olive oil spray
2 (6-inch) whole-wheat pita breads
1/4 cup no-salt-added tomato sauce
1/4 teaspoon dried oregano, crumbled
1/4 teaspoon garlic powder
2 Italian plum tomatoes, cut into 1/2-inch slices
8 medium fresh basil leaves
1/4 cup shredded part-skim mozzarella cheese
1 tablespoon shredded or grated Parmesan cheese
2 tablespoons snipped fresh parsley (Italian [flat-leaf] preferred)

1/2 teaspoon grated lemon zest
1 small garlic clove, minced

Exchanges/Choices

2 Starch
1 Vegetable
1 Fat

Basic Nutritional Values:

Calories	245	
Calories from Fat	45	
Total Fat	**5.0**	**g**
Saturated Fat	2.2	g
Trans Fat	0.0	g
Polyunsaturated Fat	0.9	g
Monounsaturated Fat	1.2	g
Cholesterol	**10**	**mg**
Sodium	**465**	**mg**
Total Carbohydrate	**41**	**g**
Dietary Fiber	6	g
Sugars	4	g
Protein	**12**	**g**

1. Preheat the oven to 375°F. Lightly spray a baking sheet with olive oil spray.

2. Place the pitas on the baking sheet. Lightly spray the tops with olive oil spray. Bake for 8 to 10 minutes, or until golden brown.

3. Meanwhile, in a small bowl, stir together the tomato sauce, oregano, and garlic powder. Spread over the baked pita breads.

4. Arrange the tomato slices on the pitas. Top with the basil. Sprinkle the mozzarella and Parmesan over each pita.

5. Bake for 5 minutes, or until the topping is warmed through and the mozzarella and Parmesan are melted.

6. Meanwhile, in a small bowl, stir together the parsley, lemon zest, and garlic. Sprinkle over each pizza just before serving.

SZECHUAN TOFU STIR-FRY

Serves 2; 2/3 cup tofu mixture and 1 cup noodles per serving
Preparation time: 10 minutes

Just a small amount of chili-garlic sauce adds heat and flavor to stir-fries, marinades, and homemade barbecue sauces.

1/2 (12.3-ounce) package light extra-firm tofu (see Cook's Tip)
1/2 medium red bell pepper
1 1/2 ounces fresh shiitake mushrooms
1 tablespoon low-sodium vegetable broth
1 tablespoon plain rice vinegar
2 teaspoons firmly packed light or dark brown sugar

1 teaspoon chili-garlic sauce
1/2 teaspoon toasted sesame oil
1 teaspoon canola or corn oil
4 ounces dried soba noodles
2 tablespoons thinly sliced green onions

1. Place the tofu on several layers of paper towels. Top with additional paper towels, then weight the tofu down with a plate. (These steps remove excess moisture.) Set aside.

2. Meanwhile, cut the bell pepper into slivers. Discard the stems of the mushrooms. Cut the mushrooms.

3. In a small bowl, stir together the broth, vinegar, brown sugar, chili-garlic sauce, and sesame oil. Set aside. Cut the prepared tofu into 1/2-inch cubes.

4. In a large nonstick skillet, heat the oil over medium-high heat, swirling to coat the bottom. Cook the bell pepper and mushrooms for 3 to 4 minutes, or until tender-crisp, stirring constantly. Gently stir in the tofu. Cook for 1 to 2 minutes, or until heated through. Add the reserved sauce mixture, stirring to coat well. Cover to keep warm. Set aside.

5. Prepare the noodles using the package directions, omitting the salt and oil. Serve the tofu mixture over the noodles. Top with the green onions.

> **COOK'S TIP:** *To make it easier to extract the moisture and have the proper thickness for cutting into cubes, cut the package of tofu lengthwise into two long, thin pieces. Use one for this recipe and save the other for a different meal.*

Exchanges/Choices
2 1/2 Starch
1 Vegetable
1 Lean Meat

Calories	255	
Calories from Fat	35	
Total Fat	**4.0**	**g**
Saturated Fat	0.5	g
Trans Fat	0.0	g
Polyunsaturated Fat	1.6	g
Monounsaturated Fat	1.9	g
Cholesterol	**0**	**mg**
Sodium	**220**	**mg**
Total Carbohydrate	**43**	**g**
Dietary Fiber	3	g
Sugars	10	g
Protein	**15**	**g**

Soft Vegetable Tacos
with Smoky Poblano Sauce

Serves 2; 2 tacos per serving
Preparation time: 20 minutes

This hearty vegetarian entrée packs an intense flavor punch.

1 small red onion
1 small red bell pepper, cut into 2-inch pieces
3 ounces broccoli florets
1 poblano pepper, seeds and stem discarded, cut into 2-inch pieces
1 teaspoon and 2 teaspoons olive oil, divided use
1/8 teaspoon pepper
4 (6-inch) corn tortillas
1 medium garlic clove, chopped
1/8 teaspoon ground cumin
1/8 teaspoon chili powder
1/8 teaspoon paprika
1/8 teaspoon salt
1/2 cup low-sodium vegetable broth
1 medium Italian plum tomato, chopped
1/4 cup chopped fresh cilantro
1/2 ounce shredded fat-free Monterey Jack cheese

1. Preheat the oven to 400°F.

2. Cut the onion in half. Set half aside. Cut the remaining half into 1-inch pieces. Put the onion pieces, bell pepper, broccoli, and poblano in a single layer on a rimmed baking sheet, keeping the poblano separate. Drizzle the vegetables with 1 teaspoon olive oil. Sprinkle with the pepper.

3. Roast for about 20 minutes, or until the vegetables are tender and browned in spots, stirring halfway through. Remove from the oven.

4. Meanwhile, wrap the tortillas in aluminum foil. Dice the reserved red onion half.

5. When the vegetables are roasted, lower the oven temperature to warm. Put the tortillas in the oven until needed.

6. Finely chop half the roasted poblano pieces.

7. In a medium saucepan, heat the remaining 2 teaspoons oil over medium heat, swirling to coat the bottom. Cook the remaining diced onion, garlic, cumin, chili powder, paprika, and salt for about 5 minutes, or until the onion has softened, stirring occasionally. Stir in the finely chopped poblano, broth, tomato, and cilantro. Increase the heat to medium high and bring to a simmer. Reduce the heat and cook at a steady simmer for about 15 minutes, or until the liquid has reduced slightly and the vegetables are very soft, stirring occasionally. Pour into a small food processor and process until smooth to make the sauce.

8. Remove the tortillas from the oven. Spoon the roasted vegetables, including the remaining poblano pieces, down the center of each tortilla. Sprinkle with the Monterey Jack. Fold the tortillas over the filling. Drizzle with the sauce.

Exchanges/Choices		
1 1/2 Starch		
2 Vegetable		
1 1/2 Fat		

Calories	255	
Calories from Fat	90	
Total Fat	10.0	g
Saturated Fat	2.1	g
Trans Fat	0.0	g
Polyunsaturated Fat	1.7	g
Monounsaturated Fat	5.8	g
Cholesterol	5	mg
Sodium	285	mg
Total Carbohydrate	38	g
Dietary Fiber	7	g
Sugars	8	g
Protein	8	g

VEGETABLES AND SIDE DISHES

MEDITERRANEAN ASPARAGUS AND CHERRY TOMATOES

Serves 2; 1/2 cup per serving
Preparation time: 10 minutes

Need a fast, bright, delicious side dish? Try this Greek- and Italian-inspired veggie combo.

1/2 teaspoon olive oil
1 medium garlic clove, minced
1/2 teaspoon dried basil, crumbled
1/8 teaspoon pepper
4 ounces fresh asparagus, trimmed and cut diagonally into 1/2-inch pieces
4 medium cherry tomatoes, halved
2 tablespoons snipped fresh parsley (Italian [flat-leaf] preferred)
1/2 teaspoon grated lemon zest
1 tablespoon crumbled fat-free feta cheese
1 teaspoon shredded or grated Parmesan cheese

1. In a large nonstick skillet, heat the oil over medium heat, swirling to coat the bottom. Cook the garlic, basil, and pepper for 10 to 15 seconds. Stir in the asparagus. Cook for 2 to 3 minutes, or until tender-crisp, stirring occasionally. Stir in the tomatoes, parsley, and lemon zest. Cook for 1 to 2 minutes, or until the tomatoes are tender and heated through. Stir in the feta and Parmesan.

Exchanges/Choices
1 Vegetable
1/2 Fat

Calories	40	
Calories from Fat	20	
Total Fat	2.0	g
Saturated Fat	0.4	g
Trans Fat	0.0	g
Polyunsaturated Fat	0.2	g
Monounsaturated Fat	1.0	g
Cholesterol	0	mg
Sodium	100	mg
Total Carbohydrate	5	g
Dietary Fiber	1	g
Sugars	2	g
Protein	3	g

GREEN BEAN RELISH

Serves 2; 1/2 cup per serving
Preparation time: 5 minutes

For year-round enjoyment, you can serve this side dish warm or chilled.

1/3 cup water
3 ounces fresh green beans, trimmed, cut into 1-inch pieces
2 tablespoons chopped red onion
3 tablespoons chopped red bell pepper
2 teaspoons red wine vinegar
1/8 teaspoon salt
1/8 teaspoon pepper

1. In a small saucepan, heat the water, green beans, and onion, covered, over high heat until the water boils. Reduce the heat to medium and cook for 5 minutes. Stir in the bell pepper. Cook for 2 to 3 minutes, or until the vegetables are tender-crisp. Remove from heat.

2. Stir in the vinegar, salt, and pepper. Serve warm or transfer to a small bowl and refrigerate, covered, to serve chilled.

Exchanges/Choices		
1 Vegetable		
Calories	20	
Calories from Fat	0	
Total Fat	0.0	g
Saturated Fat	0.0	g
Trans Fat	0.0	g
Polyunsaturated Fat	0.1	g
Monounsaturated Fat	0.0	g
Cholesterol	0	mg
Sodium	155	mg
Total Carbohydrate	5	g
Dietary Fiber	2	g
Sugars	2	g
Protein	1	g

Five-Spice Green Beans

FIVE-SPICE GREEN BEANS

Serves 2; 1/2 cup per serving
Preparation time: 5 minutes

Dress up green beans with a dusting of Chinese five-spice powder—a wonderful blend of star anise, cinnamon, cloves, fennel seeds, and Szechuan peppercorns—for an exotic side dish.

2 cups water
4 ounces fresh green beans, trimmed, cut into 3-inch pieces
1 teaspoon soy sauce (lowest sodium available)
1 teaspoon toasted sesame oil
1/2 teaspoon five-spice powder

1. In a small saucepan, bring the water to a boil over medium-high heat. Cook the green beans for 3 to 5 minutes, or until tender-crisp. Drain well in a colander. Transfer to a small bowl.

2. Add the soy sauce and oil. Toss to coat. Sprinkle with the five-spice powder. Toss to coat.

COOK'S TIP: *Five-spice powder is a great way to boost flavor without turning to the salt shaker. Sprinkle it on roasted vegetables or steamed carrots, use it to season pork tenderloin or salmon, and add to Asian dishes for an extra dimension.*

Exchanges/Choices
  1 Vegetable
  1/2 Fat

Calories	40	
Calories from Fat	20	
Total Fat	2.5	g
Saturated Fat	0.4	g
Trans Fat	0.0	g
Polyunsaturated Fat	1.0	g
Monounsaturated Fat	0.9	g
Cholesterol	0	mg
Sodium	95	mg
Total Carbohydrate	4	g
Dietary Fiber	2	g
Sugars	1	g
Protein	1	g

BROCCOLI WITH LEMON-DIJON SAUCE

Serves 2; 3/4 cup per serving
Preparation time: 5 minutes

Just a tip of Dijon is all you need to give a bit of zing to this broccoli dish.

3 ounces broccoli florets, broken into bite-sized pieces
1/3 cup water
1 1/2 tablespoons light tub margarine
1/4 teaspoon grated lemon zest
1/2 teaspoon fresh lemon juice
1/2 teaspoon Dijon mustard

1. In a medium nonstick skillet, bring the broccoli and water to a boil over medium-high heat. Reduce the heat and simmer, covered, for 2 minutes, or until just tender-crisp. Using a slotted spoon or tongs, transfer the broccoli to paper towels. Drain well.

2. Dry the skillet. Place over low heat. Put the remaining ingredients in the skillet. Stir. Heat for about 30 seconds or just until the margarine melts. Stir. Add the broccoli. Stir gently.

Exchanges/Choices		
1 Vegetable		
1/2 Fat		
Calories	45	
Calories from Fat	35	
Total Fat	4.0	g
Saturated Fat	1.2	g
Trans Fat	0.0	g
Polyunsaturated Fat	1.2	g
Monounsaturated Fat	1.5	g
Cholesterol	0	mg
Sodium	105	mg
Total Carbohydrate	3	g
Dietary Fiber	1	g
Sugars	1	g
Protein	1	g

Roasted Brussels Sprouts

ROASTED BRUSSELS SPROUTS
WITH BALSAMIC-DIJON VINAIGRETTE

Serves 2; 1/2 cup per serving
Preparation time: 5 minutes

The caramelized flavor of roasted Brussels sprouts harmonizes with robust balsamic vinaigrette. Serve warm or chilled with hearty sirloin steaks or delicate broiled fish fillets.

Olive oil spray
4 ounces fresh Brussels sprouts (about 12 small), loose or yellow leaves discarded, trimmed and cut in half lengthwise
1 tablespoon balsamic vinegar
1 teaspoon coarse-grained or Dijon mustard
1 teaspoon olive oil (extra-virgin preferred)
1 teaspoon honey
1 teaspoon fresh lemon juice
1/2 teaspoon grated lemon zest
1/8 teaspoon pepper

1. Preheat the oven to 400°F. Lightly spray an 8-inch baking pan with olive oil spray.

2. Place the Brussels sprouts in a single layer in the baking pan. Lightly spray with olive oil spray.

3. Bake for 20 to 25 minutes, or until tender when pierced with the tip of a sharp knife, stirring once.

4. Meanwhile, in a medium bowl, whisk together the remaining ingredients. Add the Brussels sprouts, stirring to coat. Serve hot, or cover and refrigerate for up to two days to serve chilled.

Exchanges/Choices
1/2 Carbohydrate
1 Vegetable
1/2 Fat

Calories	60	
Calories from Fat	20	
Total Fat	2.5	g
Saturated Fat	0.3	g
Trans Fat	0.0	g
Polyunsaturated Fat	0.4	g
Monounsaturated Fat	1.7	g
Cholesterol	0	mg
Sodium	70	mg
Total Carbohydrate	10	g
Dietary Fiber	2	g
Sugars	6	g
Protein	2	g

Roasted Carrots
with Shallots and Sage

Serves 2; 1/2 cup per serving
Preparation time: 5 minutes

Try pairing these carrots with baked chicken or roast pork for great complementary flavors.

3/4 cup baby carrots
2 large shallots, halved lengthwise
1 tablespoon balsamic vinegar
1 teaspoon olive oil
1 tablespoon finely chopped fresh sage
1/8 teaspoon garlic powder
1/8 teaspoon salt
1/8 teaspoon pepper

1. Preheat the oven to 400°F.

2. In an 8- or 9-inch shallow nonstick baking dish, toss the carrots and shallots with the vinegar and oil to coat.

3. Roast for 25 to 30 minutes, or until the vegetables are tender and deeply browned, turning twice. Transfer to a serving bowl.

4. Meanwhile, in a small bowl, stir together the sage, garlic powder, salt, and pepper. Sprinkle over the roasted vegetables. Stir well.

Exchanges/Choices		
2 Vegetable		
1/2 Fat		
Calories	65	
Calories from Fat	20	
Total Fat	2.5	g
Saturated Fat	0.3	g
Trans Fat	0.0	g
Polyunsaturated Fat	0.3	g
Monounsaturated Fat	1.7	g
Cholesterol	0	mg
Sodium	190	mg
Total Carbohydrate	11	g
Dietary Fiber	2	g
Sugars	4	g
Protein	1	g

Roasted Cauliflower

ROASTED CAULIFLOWER WITH INDIAN SPICES

Serves 2; 1/2 cup per serving
Preparation time: 10 minutes

A fragrant blend of spices roasts into cauliflower florets, bringing a touch of an Indian restaurant right to your home table.

Cooking spray
5 ounces cauliflower florets (about 1/4 medium head), broken into bite-sized pieces
1/2 cup medium-thick onion slices (yellow preferred) (about 1/3 small), separated into rings
1 teaspoon canola or corn oil
1 teaspoon ground ginger
1/2 teaspoon ground coriander
1/4 teaspoon ground cumin
1/8 teaspoon cayenne
1/8 teaspoon powdered turmeric
Scant 1/8 teaspoon salt
1 teaspoon fresh lemon juice

Exchanges/Choices		
1 Vegetable		
1/2 Fat		
Calories	50	
Calories from Fat	20	
Total Fat	2.5	g
Saturated Fat	0.2	g
Trans Fat	0.0	g
Polyunsaturated Fat	0.8	g
Monounsaturated Fat	1.4	g
Cholesterol	0	mg
Sodium	175	mg
Total Carbohydrate	7	g
Dietary Fiber	2	g
Sugars	3	g
Protein	2	g

1. Preheat the oven to 425°F.

2. Lightly spray an 8-inch square glass baking dish with cooking spray. Put the cauliflower and onion in the dish. Drizzle the oil over the vegetables. Toss to coat.

3. In a small bowl, stir together the remaining ingredients except the lemon juice. Sprinkle over the vegetables, tossing to coat. Lightly spray with cooking spray.

4. Roast for 20 minutes, or until the cauliflower is tender when pierced with a fork, stirring frequently. Remove from the oven. Stir in the lemon juice.

COOK'S TIP: *Give this dish a try even if you are not true cauliflower lovers. The dry heat of roasting cooks the cauliflower without releasing any of the juices that keep some people from enjoying this versatile vegetable.*

EGGPLANT WITH AVOCADO SALSA

Serves 2; 2 slices eggplant and 1/2 cup salsa per serving
Preparation time: 10 minutes

Use a small eggplant in this recipe—the skin will be thin and easy to cut, and the eggplant will have a remarkably sweet flavor.

Avocado Salsa

1 small ripe avocado, chopped
1 1/2 ounces grape tomatoes, chopped (about 1/4 cup)
1 tablespoon finely chopped red onion
1 tablespoon snipped fresh cilantro
1 tablespoon fresh lime juice
✳✳✳✳✳✳✳
4 (1/2-inch) slices from small eggplant (about 8 ounces)
1/2 teaspoon salt-free southwestern seasoning blend
1/8 teaspoon salt
Cooking spray

1. In a small bowl, gently stir together the avocado salsa ingredients. Set aside.

2. Preheat the broiler. Place the eggplant slices on a baking sheet. Sprinkle with half the seasoning blend and half the salt. Lightly spray the tops with cooking spray. Turn the slices over. Repeat.

3. Broil 4 to 5 inches from the heat for 3 to 4 minutes on each side, or until tender and lightly browned. Serve the slices topped with the salsa.

> **COOK'S TIP:** *Spraying the eggplant slices with cooking spray after sprinkling with the seasoning blend helps keep the seasoning on the slices and also helps keep the slices from burning before they are tender.*

Exchanges/Choices		
3 Vegetable		
1 1/2 Fat		
Calories	125	
Calories from Fat	70	
Total Fat	**8.0**	**g**
Saturated Fat	1.1	g
Trans Fat	0.0	g
Polyunsaturated Fat	1.1	g
Monounsaturated Fat	5.0	g
Cholesterol	**0**	**mg**
Sodium	**160**	**mg**
Total Carbohydrate	**16**	**g**
Dietary Fiber	7	g
Sugars	5	g
Protein	**2**	**g**

Braised Kale and Cabbage

Serves 2; 1/2 cup per serving
Preparation time: 10 minutes

Mustard seeds and bacon bits add a zesty smokiness to tender braised kale and cabbage. Serve this dish with broiled pork chops or grilled chicken breasts or tilapia.

1 teaspoon olive oil
2 tablespoons chopped onion
1 tablespoon imitation bacon bits (lowest sodium available)
1/4 teaspoon mustard seeds, crushed in a mortar and pestle,
    or 1 tablespoon coarse-grained mustard
3 ounces fresh kale, coarsely chopped (about 3 cups)
2 ounces green cabbage, coarsely chopped (about 1 cup)
2 tablespoons fat-free, low-sodium chicken broth
2 teaspoons Dijon mustard
1/8 teaspoon pepper

1. In a medium saucepan, heat the oil over medium heat, swirling to coat the bottom. Cook the onion, bacon bits, and mustard seeds for 2 minutes, or until the onion is tender-crisp, stirring occasionally.

2. Stir in the kale and cabbage. Cook for 3 to 4 minutes, or until wilted, stirring occasionally.

3. Stir in the broth, mustard, and pepper. Bring to a simmer. Reduce the heat and simmer, covered, for 10 to 15 minutes, or until the vegetables are tender, stirring occasionally.

COOK'S TIP: *Don't let any leftover kale go to waste. Coarsely chop it and braise with chick-peas or frozen black-eyed peas or add it to vegetable soup, minestrone, or stew. You can even layer cooked kale in your favorite healthful version of lasagna made with whole-wheat pasta.*

Exchanges/Choices		
2 Vegetable		
1/2 Fat		
Calories	85	
Calories from Fat	30	
Total Fat	3.5	g
Saturated Fat	0.5	g
Trans Fat	0.0	g
Polyunsaturated Fat	0.7	g
Monounsaturated Fat	2.0	g
Cholesterol	0	mg
Sodium	200	mg
Total Carbohydrate	11	g
Dietary Fiber	4	g
Sugars	3	g
Protein	4	g

BAKED OKRA

Baked Okra

Serves 2; 1/2 cup per serving
Preparation time: 10 minutes

This crunchy coating is so good that you'll want to eat the extra crumbles that bake with the okra.

Cooking spray
4 ounces fresh okra, stems discarded, cut into 1/2-inch slices, or 2 cups frozen sliced okra, thawed and patted dry
1 tablespoons all-purpose flour
1 large egg white
1/4 teaspoon salt-free lemon pepper
3/4 cup cornflakes, finely crushed
2 tablespoons shredded or grated Parmesan cheese

1. Preheat the oven to 400°F. Lightly spray an 8-inch square baking pan with cooking spray.

2. In a shallow bowl, stir together the okra and flour to coat.

3. In a second shallow bowl, whisk the egg white for 30 seconds, or until frothy. Whisk in the lemon pepper.

4. In a third shallow bowl, stir together the cornflakes and Parmesan.

5. Set the bowl with the okra, the bowl with the egg white, the bowl with the cornflake mixture, and the baking sheet in a row, assembly-line fashion. Using a slotted spoon, transfer the okra in batches to the egg-white mixture, stirring to coat. Transfer to the cornflake mixture, stirring to coat. Arrange the okra in a single layer on the baking sheet, leaving space between the pieces so they brown evenly. Repeat with the remaining ingredients. Sprinkle any remaining cornflake mixture over the okra. Lightly spray the okra with cooking spray.

6. Bake for 10 to 12 minutes, or until golden brown.

Exchanges/Choices		
1 Starch		
1/2 Fat		
Calories	105	
Calories from Fat	20	
Total Fat	2.0	g
Saturated Fat	1.0	g
Trans Fat	0.0	g
Polyunsaturated Fat	0.2	g
Monounsaturated Fat	0.6	g
Cholesterol	5	mg
Sodium	150	mg
Total Carbohydrate	16	g
Dietary Fiber	2	g
Sugars	2	g
Protein	6	g

GERMAN RED CABBAGE AND APPLES

Serves 2; 1/2 cup per serving
Preparation time: 5 minutes

Typically sweet and sour, this classic German dish is perfect to serve with lean pork chops and a spinach salad.

1 teaspoon olive oil
1/2 small onion, thinly sliced
1/2 small apple (Granny Smith, Gala, or Golden Delicious), peeled, cored, and thinly sliced
1 cup shredded red cabbage (about 2 ounces)
1 tablespoon frozen unsweetened apple juice concentrate
1 tablespoon cider vinegar
1/8 teaspoon salt
1/8 teaspoon pepper

1. In a small saucepan, heat the oil over medium heat, swirling to coat the bottom. Cook the onion for 2 to 3 minutes, or until tender-crisp, stirring occasionally.

2. Stir in the apple and cabbage. Cook for 1 to 2 minutes, or until tender-crisp, stirring occasionally. Stir in the remaining ingredients. Increase the heat to medium high and bring to a simmer. Reduce the heat and simmer, covered, for 10 to 15 minutes, or until the cabbage and apple are tender, stirring occasionally.

Exchanges/Choices
1/2 Fruit
1 Vegetable
1/2 Fat

Calories	70	
Calories from Fat	20	
Total Fat	2.5	g
Saturated Fat	0.3	g
Trans Fat	0.0	g
Polyunsaturated Fat	0.3	g
Monounsaturated Fat	1.7	g
Cholesterol	0	mg
Sodium	160	mg
Total Carbohydrate	12	g
Dietary Fiber	2	g
Sugars	9	g
Protein	1	g

SPEEDY SNOW PEAS

Serves 2; 1/2 cup per serving
Preparation time: 5 minutes

Brighten up your meal with this extra-quick side. It's a nice accompaniment with pork, chicken, or fish.

    1 tablespoon fresh lime juice
    2 teaspoons sugar
    1/2 tablespoon soy sauce (lowest sodium available)
    1 teaspoon canola or corn oil
    6 ounces fresh or frozen snow peas, trimmed if fresh, thawed and well dried if frozen
        (fresh preferred)

1. In a small bowl, stir together the lime juice, sugar, and soy sauce.

2. In a large skillet, heat the oil over medium-high heat, swirling to coat the bottom. Cook the snow peas for 2 minutes, or until just tender-crisp, stirring constantly. Remove from the heat. Stir in the lime juice mixture.

Exchanges/Choices
1/2 Carbohydrate
1 Vegetable
1/2 Fat

Calories	75	
Calories from Fat	20	
Total Fat	2.5	**g**
Saturated Fat	0.2	g
Trans Fat	0.0	g
Polyunsaturated Fat	0.7	g
Monounsaturated Fat	1.3	g
Cholesterol	0	**mg**
Sodium	145	**mg**
Total Carbohydrate	11	**g**
Dietary Fiber	2	g
Sugars	8	g
Protein	3	**g**

Creamy Spinach and Onions

CREAMY SPINACH AND ONIONS

Serves 2; 1/2 cup per serving
Preparation time: 5 minutes

Using frozen chopped spinach and frozen pearl onions makes this delightful homemade version of a favorite side dish very easy to put together. Serve it with grilled salmon, chicken, or pork tenderloin or for a touch of elegance, spoon it into Whole-Wheat Popovers (page 190).

1 teaspoon olive oil
15 frozen pearl onions, halved lengthwise
1 1/3 cups frozen chopped spinach (about 3 1/2 ounces)
2 tablespoons water
1 ounce (2 tablespoons) fat-free cream cheese
2 tablespoons fat-free half-and-half
1/4 teaspoon white pepper
1/8 teaspoon ground nutmeg

1. In a small saucepan, heat the oil over medium heat for 1 minute, swirling to coat the bottom. Cook the onions for 3 minutes, or until just beginning to soften, stirring frequently.

2. Stir in the spinach and water. Cook for 4 minutes, or until the spinach is tender and most of the water has cooked away, stirring frequently.

3. Stir in remaining ingredients. Cook for 2 minutes, or until the cream cheese melts and the sauce begins to bubble, stirring constantly.

Exchanges/Choices
2 Vegetable
1/2 Fat

Calories	90	
Calories from Fat	25	
Total Fat	3.0	g
Saturated Fat	0.5	g
Trans Fat	0.0	g
Polyunsaturated Fat	0.3	g
Monounsaturated Fat	1.7	g
Cholesterol	5	mg
Sodium	180	mg
Total Carbohydrate	12	g
Dietary Fiber	3	g
Sugars	8	g
Protein	5	g

Lemon-Ginger Acorn Squash

LEMON-GINGER ACORN SQUASH

Serves 2; 1 squash half per serving
Preparation time: 5 minutes

A very small amount of fresh ginger adds a lot of flavor to acorn squash in this microwaved side dish.

1/4 cup water
1 medium acorn squash (about 3/4 pound), halved, seeds and strings discarded, skin
    pierced in several places
2 teaspoons sugar
2 teaspoons light tub margarine
1/2 teaspoon grated lemon zest
1/4 teaspoon grated peeled gingerroot

1. Pour the water into a microwaveable 11 × 7 × 2-inch baking dish. Put the squash halves with the cut side down in the dish. Cover. Microwave on 100% power (high) for 7 minutes, or until a knife tip inserted in the skin comes out easily. Transfer with the cut side up to plates.

2. Meanwhile, in a small bowl, stir together the remaining ingredients. Put the mixture in the hollow of each cooked squash half.

COOK'S TIP: *Piercing the skin of the raw squash allows steam to be released and helps the squash cook evenly and quickly.*

Exchanges/Choices		
1 Starch		
Calories	85	
Calories from Fat	20	
Total Fat	2.0	g
Saturated Fat	0.5	g
Trans Fat	0.0	g
Polyunsaturated Fat	0.6	g
Monounsaturated Fat	0.7	g
Cholesterol	0	mg
Sodium	35	mg
Total Carbohydrate	18	g
Dietary Fiber	4	g
Sugars	8	g
Protein	1	g

Zucchini and Red Bell Pepper

ZUCCHINI AND RED BELL PEPPER TOSS

Serves 2; 3/4 cup per serving
Preparation time: 5 minutes

The rich and tangy taste of blue cheese adds interest to even the mildest vegetable dish.

1/2 teaspoon canola or corn oil
1 medium zucchini (about 6 ounces), cut lengthwise into eighths, then cut crosswise into 2-inch pieces
1/2 medium red bell pepper, thinly sliced
3 tablespoons crumbled low-fat blue cheese
1 tablespoon snipped fresh parsley

1. In a medium skillet, heat the oil over medium-high heat, swirling to coat the bottom. Cook the zucchini and bell pepper for 5 minutes, or until tender-crisp, stirring frequently. Sprinkle with the blue cheese and parsley. Remove from the heat. Cover and let stand for 2 minutes so the flavors blend and the blue cheese melts slightly.

COOK'S TIP: *Using two utensils makes it easy to stir the vegetables and helps them brown evenly.*

Exchanges/Choices
1 Vegetable
1/2 Fat

Calories	65	
Calories from Fat	25	
Total Fat	3.0	g
Saturated Fat	1.4	g
Trans Fat	0.0	g
Polyunsaturated Fat	0.5	g
Monounsaturated Fat	1.2	g
Cholesterol	5	mg
Sodium	150	mg
Total Carbohydrate	6	g
Dietary Fiber	2	g
Sugars	3	g
Protein	4	g

BARLEY AND PORCINI PILAF

Serves 2; 1/2 cup per serving
Preparation time: 5 minutes

Barley's naturally nutty flavor blends beautifully with the earthiness of dried porcini mushrooms.

1/3 cup dried porcini mushrooms
1 cup warm water
Olive oil cooking spray
1/3 cup baby carrots, cut into 1/2-inch slices
3 medium green onions, white part chopped and 2 tablespoons green part thinly sliced
1/3 cup quick-cooking pearl barley
1/8 teaspoon salt

1. Put the mushrooms in a small bowl. Pour in the water. Soak for 20 to 30 minutes, or until rehydrated. Strain through a coffee filter or paper towel into a small bowl to remove any dirt or grit. Chop the mushrooms. Reserve the liquid.

2. Lightly spray a small saucepan with cooking spray. Cook the carrots and white part of the green onions over medium-low heat for 2 minutes.

3. Add the strained soaking liquid and the mushrooms. Bring to a simmer, still on medium low.

4. Stir in the barley and salt. Reduce the heat and simmer, covered, for 10 to 12 minutes, or until the barley is tender. Remove from the heat. Let stand, covered, for 5 minutes. Stir in the green part of the green onions.

Exchanges/Choices		
1 Starch		
1 Vegetable		
Calories	110	
Calories from Fat	5	
Total Fat	0.5	g
Saturated Fat	0.0	g
Trans Fat	0.0	g
Polyunsaturated Fat	0.3	g
Monounsaturated Fat	0.1	g
Cholesterol	0	mg
Sodium	175	mg
Total Carbohydrate	25	g
Dietary Fiber	4	g
Sugars	2	g
Protein	3	g

Sweet and Creamy Corn

SWEET AND CREAMY CORN

Serves 2; 1/2 cup per serving
Preparation time: 5 minutes

Even when you think you have only enough time to open a can of vegetables, you can make this tasty side dish instead.

1 cup frozen whole-kernel corn, thawed
2 tablespoon fat-free sour cream
1 tablespoon plus 1 teaspoon light tub margarine
1/2 teaspoon Dijon mustard (country-style preferred)
1/8 to 1/4 teaspoon sugar
1/8 teaspoon pepper (coarsely ground preferred)

1. In a small skillet, cook the corn over medium-high heat for 2 to 3 minutes, or until heated through. Stir in the remaining ingredients. Cook for 30 seconds, or until just bubbly—do not boil—stirring constantly. Remove from heat. Let stand, covered, for 3 minutes so the flavors blend.

COOK'S TIP: *Make sure the sour cream mixture does not come to a boil. It will break down and curdle if the mixture becomes too hot.*

Exchanges/Choices
1 Starch
1/2 Fat

Calories	110	
Calories from Fat	35	
Total Fat	4.0	g
Saturated Fat	1.1	g
Trans Fat	0.0	g
Polyunsaturated Fat	1.2	g
Monounsaturated Fat	1.5	g
Cholesterol	0	mg
Sodium	100	mg
Total Carbohydrate	17	g
Dietary Fiber	2	g
Sugars	2	g
Protein	3	g

EDAMAME SUCCOTASH

Edamame Succotash

Serves 2; 1/2 cup per serving
Preparation time: 5 minutes

Quick and colorful, this side dish is perfect for a picnic or a backyard barbecue, especially since it doesn't need to be served hot.

3 cups water
1/2 cup frozen edamame (shelled green soybeans)
1/3 cup fresh or frozen whole-kernel corn
1 teaspoon minced shallot
1 teaspoon Dijon mustard
1 teaspoon white wine vinegar
Pinch of pepper
2 teaspoons olive oil (extra-virgin preferred)
1/3 medium red bell pepper, diced
1 medium fresh basil leaf, thinly sliced

1. In a small saucepan, bring the water to a boil over high heat. Stir in the edamame and corn. Reduce the heat to medium high and cook for 4 minutes, or until tender. Drain in a colander and rinse for 30 seconds under cold running water. Shake the colander to remove the excess water. Drain well.

2. In a small serving bowl, whisk together the shallot, mustard, vinegar, and pepper. Gradually whisk in the oil.

3. Stir in the edamame, corn, and bell pepper. Toss to coat. Sprinkle with the basil. Serve at room temperature, or cover and refrigerate until needed.

Exchanges/Choices		
1 Starch		
1 Fat		
Calories	115	
Calories from Fat	65	
Total Fat	7.0	g
Saturated Fat	0.8	g
Trans Fat	0.0	g
Polyunsaturated Fat	1.6	g
Monounsaturated Fat	3.8	g
Cholesterol	0	mg
Sodium	65	mg
Total Carbohydrate	11	g
Dietary Fiber	3	g
Sugars	3	g
Protein	5	g

Couscous

Couscous
with Apricots and Pistachios

Serves 2; heaping 1/2 cup per serving
Preparation time: 5 minutes

Robust spices and sweet apricots pair with mildly nutty tasting whole-wheat couscous to create an exotic yet easy side dish. Perfect with grilled salmon, garlic-studded lean lamb, or grilled chicken breasts.

1/2 cup water
1/4 cup plus 1 tablespoon uncooked whole-wheat couscous
2 tablespoons chopped dried apricots
1 teaspoon olive oil
1/2 teaspoon finely grated orange zest
1/4 teaspoon ground cinnamon
1/4 teaspoon ground nutmeg
1/8 teaspoon salt
14 dry-roasted unsalted pistachios, chopped

1. In a small saucepan, bring the water to a boil over medium-high heat. Remove from the heat. Stir in the couscous. Let stand, covered, for 5 minutes or until the water is absorbed.

2. Meanwhile, put the apricots in a small microwaveable measuring cup or bowl. Stir in the oil. Microwave, covered, on 100% power (high) for 30 seconds, or until softened.

3. In a small bowl, stir together the orange zest, cinnamon, nutmeg, and salt. Stir into the apricots. Spoon over the hot couscous. Fluff with a fork, distributing the spices. Spoon onto plates. Sprinkle with the pistachios.

COOK'S TIP: *To prevent dried apricots and other dried fruits from sticking to your knife, run it under hot water and dry it just before you start to chop the fruit. Another way is to lightly spray the knife blade with cooking spray.*

Exchanges/Choices
1 Starch
1/2 Fruit
1 Fat

Calories	155	
Calories from Fat	45	
Total Fat	5.0	g
Saturated Fat	0.8	g
Trans Fat	0.0	g
Polyunsaturated Fat	1.2	g
Monounsaturated Fat	3.0	g
Cholesterol	0	mg
Sodium	155	mg
Total Carbohydrate	25	g
Dietary Fiber	3	g
Sugars	6	g
Protein	5	g

GARLIC-ROASTED POTATO WEDGES

Serves 2; 1/2 cup per serving
Preparation time: 5 minutes

Garlic takes on a rich, mellow flavor as it roasts, making it a tasty spread for topping these potato wedges.

Olive oil spray
6 medium garlic cloves, unpeeled
6 ounces red potatoes (about 2 medium), cut into 1/2-inch wedges
1/4 teaspoon pepper

1. Preheat the oven to 450°F. Lightly spray an 8-inch square glass baking dish with olive oil spray.

2. Put the garlic on a cutting board. Gently press the garlic with the palm of your hand to flatten slightly. Lightly spray the garlic with olive oil spray, tossing to coat.

3. Put the potatoes in a medium bowl. Lightly spray the potatoes with olive oil spray, tossing to coat. Place with the flesh side up in a single layer in the center of the baking dish. Put the garlic cloves on the potatoes.

4. Roast for 30 to 35 minutes, or until the potatoes are tender when pierced with a fork and some of the bottoms are crisp and brown. Sprinkle with the pepper. Squeeze the garlic cloves out of their skins and onto the potatoes, discarding the skins, or discard the garlic cloves without squeezing.

Exchanges/Choices		
1 Starch		
Calories	80	
Calories from Fat	0	
Total Fat	0.0	g
Saturated Fat	0.0	g
Trans Fat	0.0	g
Polyunsaturated Fat	0.1	g
Monounsaturated Fat	0.0	g
Cholesterol	0	mg
Sodium	10	mg
Total Carbohydrate	18	g
Dietary Fiber	2	g
Sugars	1	g
Protein	2	g

Yellow Rice with Onions

Yellow Rice with Browned Onions

Serves 2; 1/2 cup per serving
Preparation time: 5 minutes

A little bit of turmeric gives brown rice a sunny yellow color, nicely complementing the foods of any cuisine.

1/2 cup water
1/3 cup uncooked instant brown rice
1/8 teaspoon ground turmeric
1/8 teaspoon ground cumin
1/8 teaspoon garlic powder
1 teaspoon olive oil
1/2 medium onion, chopped (yellow preferred)
1/8 teaspoon salt

1. In a small saucepan, bring the water, rice, turmeric, cumin, and garlic powder to a boil over medium-high heat. Reduce the heat and simmer, covered, for 10 minutes, or until the liquid is absorbed.

2. Meanwhile, in a medium skillet, heat the oil over medium-high heat, swirling to coat the bottom. Cook the onion for 6 minutes, or until richly browned, stirring frequently. Stir in the cooked rice and salt.

TIME-SAVER: *For an even quicker dish, omit the onion and stir 1/4 cup finely chopped green onions into the cooked rice.*

Exchanges/Choices
1 1/2 Starch
1 Vegetable
1/2 Fat

Calories	150	
Calories from Fat	25	
Total Fat	3.0	g
Saturated Fat	0.3	g
Trans Fat	0.0	g
Polyunsaturated Fat	0.6	g
Monounsaturated Fat	2.0	g
Cholesterol	0	mg
Sodium	170	mg
Total Carbohydrate	28	g
Dietary Fiber	2	g
Sugars	2	g
Protein	3	g

APRICOT-SPICE SWEET POTATO

Serves 2; 1 sweet potato half and 1 tablespoon margarine mixture per serving
Preparation time: 4 minutes

Leave the sugar in the sugar bowl and instead enjoy this fruit-and-spice topping to bring out the best in your sweet potato.

1 medium sweet potato (about 8 ounces), skin pierced in several places
2 tablespoons all-fruit apricot spread
1 tablespoon light tub margarine
1/4 teaspoon curry powder
1/8 teaspoon ground cinnamon

1. Pierce the sweet potato in several places with a fork. On a plate or paper towel, microwave on 100% power (high) for 5 minutes, or until tender. Cut the sweet potato in half lengthwise. Using a fork, fluff the pulp in each half.

2. Meanwhile, in a small bowl, whisk together the remaining ingredients. Spoon over the cooked sweet potato halves.

COOK'S TIP: *The fruit spread mixture will be a bit lumpy when combined, but it will melt into a creamy topping when spooned over the hot sweet potato halves.*

Exchanges/Choices		
1 Starch		
1/2 Carbohydrate		
1/2 Fat		
Calories	130	
Calories from Fat	25	
Total Fat	3.0	g
Saturated Fat	0.9	g
Trans Fat	0.0	g
Polyunsaturated Fat	0.9	g
Monounsaturated Fat	1.2	g
Cholesterol	0	mg
Sodium	60	mg
Total Carbohydrate	25	g
Dietary Fiber	3	g
Sugars	14	g
Protein	2	g

Cherry Apples

CHERRY APPLES

Serves 2; 1/2 cup per serving
Preparation time: 5 minutes

You can serve this versatile dish as a side for breakfast or dinner or as a quick snack or dessert.

1/2 teaspoon canola or corn oil
1 large unpeeled sweet-tart apple, such as Gala, Fuji, or Granny Smith, cut into 1/4-inch slices
2 tablespoons chopped pecans, dry-roasted
2 tablespoons dried tart cherries
1 tablespoon firmly packed dark brown sugar
2 1/2 teaspoons light tub margarine
1/4 teaspoon vanilla extract
1/8 teaspoon ground cinnamon

1. In a large skillet, heat the oil over medium heat, swirling to coat the bottom. Cook the apple for 4 minutes, or until tender-crisp, stirring frequently. Remove from the heat.

2. Stir in the remaining ingredients until thoroughly combined.

Variation: Substitute a firm pear for the apple, and raisins for the dried cherries.

Exchanges/Choices
2 Fruit
1 1/2 Fat

Calories	200	
Calories from Fat	80	
Total Fat	9.0	g
Saturated Fat	1.2	g
Trans Fat	0.0	g
Polyunsaturated Fat	2.4	g
Monounsaturated Fat	4.5	g
Cholesterol	0	mg
Sodium	40	mg
Total Carbohydrate	33	g
Dietary Fiber	4	g
Sugars	26	g
Protein	1	g

BREADS AND BREAKFAST DISHES

Whole-Wheat Popovers

WHOLE-WHEAT POPOVERS

Serves 2; 1 popover per serving
Preparation time: 5 minutes

Requiring very little hands-on time, these airy popovers make a dramatic appearance. They are a great bread choice for Sunday brunch and elevate an everyday soup, stew, or tuna salad to special-occasion status.

2 tablespoons whole-wheat flour
2 tablespoons all-purpose flour
1/4 cup fat-free milk
1/4 cup egg substitute
1 teaspoon canola or corn oil
Cooking spray

1. In a small bowl, stir together the flours.

2. In a 1- or 2-cup liquid measuring cup, stir together the milk, egg substitute, and oil. Gently stir the flour mixture into the liquids, continuing until all the flour is moistened. Let the batter stand at room temperature for 30 minutes.

3. Meanwhile, preheat the oven to 450°F. Lightly spray two 8-ounce custard cups with cooking spray. Place on a baking sheet. After the batter has stood, put the baking sheet with the custard cups in the oven for 2 minutes. Transfer to a cooling rack.

4. Quickly stir the batter and immediately pour into the custard cups, filling each about halfway. Return to the oven.

5. Bake for 15 minutes without opening the oven door. Peeking can cause the popovers to fall. Reduce the heat to 325°F. Bake for 25 to 30 minutes, or until the popovers are puffy and deep golden brown. Gently remove the popovers from the cups. Serve immediately.

Variation: Stir 1 tablespoon grated Parmesan cheese into the flours.

Exchanges/Choices		
1 Starch		
1/2 Fat		
Calories	100	
Calories from Fat	20	
Total Fat	2.5	g
Saturated Fat	0.2	g
Trans Fat	0.0	g
Polyunsaturated Fat	0.8	g
Monounsaturated Fat	1.4	g
Cholesterol	0	mg
Sodium	75	mg
Total Carbohydrate	14	g
Dietary Fiber	1	g
Sugars	2	g
Protein	6	g

Peach Melba Breakfast Parfaits

Serves 2; 3/4 cup per serving
Preparation time: 5 minutes

You'll always have time for breakfast with these attractive breakfast parfaits in your repertoire.

1 large peach, peeled and sliced, or 3/4 cup frozen unsweetened sliced peaches, thawed
1 (6-ounce) container fat-free vanilla yogurt
1/2 cup low-fat granola
1/2 cup fresh or frozen unsweetened raspberries, partially thawed if frozen

1. In two wine glasses or 6-ounce glass custard cups, layer the ingredients in each as follows: half the peach slices, about 2 tablespoons yogurt, half the granola, and the remaining yogurt. Top with the raspberries. Serve immediately.

COOK'S TIP: *When buying granola, look for a brand that's high in whole grains and low in saturated fats and calories. Frozen raspberries won't look as pretty as fresh but will still taste delicious.*

Exchanges/Choices		
2 Carbohydrate		
Calories	160	
Calories from Fat	15	
Total Fat	1.5	g
Saturated Fat	0.3	g
Trans Fat	0.1	g
Polyunsaturated Fat	0.4	g
Monounsaturated Fat	0.6	g
Cholesterol	0	mg
Sodium	95	mg
Total Carbohydrate	34	g
Dietary Fiber	4	g
Sugars	18	g
Protein	5	g

Oatmeal Oatmeal Pancakes with Bananas

Serves 2; 2 pancakes plus 1/4 cup bananas, 1/2 tablespoon pecans,
and 2 tablespoons syrup per serving
Preparation time: 10 minutes

Banana slices, dry-roasted nuts, and a drizzle of pancake syrup top these hearty pancakes.

1/2 cup all-purpose flour
1/4 cup uncooked quick-cooking oatmeal
2 teaspoons light brown sugar
1 teaspoon baking powder
1/4 teaspoon ground cinnamon
1/2 cup fat-free milk
1 large egg white, lightly beaten
2 tablespoons unsweetened applesauce
1 teaspoon canola or corn oil
1/2 teaspoon vanilla extract
Cooking spray
1 small banana, thinly sliced
1 tablespoon finely chopped pecans, dry-roasted
1/4 cup sugar-free pancake syrup

Exchanges/Choices		
2 Starch		
1 Fruit		
1/2 Carbohydrate		
1 Fat		
Calories	310	
Calories from Fat	55	
Total Fat	6.0	g
Saturated Fat	0.6	g
Trans Fat	0.0	g
Polyunsaturated Fat	1.7	g
Monounsaturated Fat	3.0	g
Cholesterol	0	mg
Sodium	270	mg
Total Carbohydrate	55	g
Dietary Fiber	4	g
Sugars	18	g
Protein	10	g

1. In a medium bowl, whisk together the flour, oatmeal, brown sugar, baking powder, and cinnamon. Make a well in the center and pour in the milk, egg white, applesauce, oil, and vanilla. Whisk just until the dry ingredients are moistened and no flour is visible. Do not overmix or the pancakes will be tough.

2. Lightly spray a griddle or large skillet with cooking spray. Heat over medium heat. Using a 1/4-cup measure, pour the batter onto the griddle to make 4 pancakes. Cook for 2 to 3 minutes, or until the tops are bubbly all over and the cooked side is golden brown. Turn the pancakes over. Cook for 2 to 3 minutes, or until golden brown.

3. Serve the pancakes topped with the banana slices, pecans, and pancake syrup.

FRUIT-FILLED PANCAKE PUFFS

Serves 2; 1 pancake and 1/2 cup fruit per serving
Preparation time: 5 minutes

Tired of the same old breakfast selections? This elegant puffed pancake will become a favorite! Try different fruit and yogurt combinations to add variety.

Cooking spray
1/4 cup egg substitute
2 tablespoons all-purpose flour
2 tablespoons fat-free milk
2 teaspoons canola or corn oil
1/4 teaspoon vanilla extract
1/8 teaspoon salt
2 1/2 ounces fresh raspberries
6 small strawberries, sliced
2 tablespoons fat-free mixed-berry yogurt

1. Preheat the oven to 400°F. Lightly coat two 8-ounce ramekins (4-inch diameter) with cooking spray. Set aside.

2. In a medium bowl, whisk together the egg substitute, flour, milk, oil, vanilla, and salt until smooth. Pour half the batter into each ramekin. Set the filled ramekins on a baking sheet.

3. Bake for 20 to 25 minutes, or until golden brown and puffy. Remove from the oven. Using the tip of a knife, gently pierce each pancake in one place. Allow to stand for 5 minutes so you don't burn your fingers when handling the ramekins.

4. Meanwhile, in a small bowl, gently stir together the raspberries and strawberries. Spoon over each cooled pancake. Dollop each with yogurt.

Exchanges/Choices		
1/2 Carbohydrate		
1 Fat		
Calories	100	
Calories from Fat	45	
Total Fat	5.0	g
Saturated Fat	0.3	g
Trans Fat	0.0	g
Polyunsaturated Fat	1.5	g
Monounsaturated Fat	2.7	g
Cholesterol	0	mg
Sodium	225	mg
Total Carbohydrate	10	g
Dietary Fiber	3	g
Sugars	4	g
Protein	5	g

Spiced Sweet Potato Waffles

SPICED SWEET POTATO WAFFLES

Serves 2; 2 4-inch waffles per serving
Preparation time: 5 minutes

A jar of baby food provides a hint of sweet potato flavor to these tender waffles.

1/2 cup whole-wheat pastry flour
1/4 cup all-purpose flour
1 teaspoon pumpkin pie spice
1/2 teaspoon baking powder
1/2 teaspoon ground ginger
1/8 teaspoon ground allspice
1/2 cup low-fat buttermilk
1/4 cup fat-free sour cream
1 (4-ounce) jar baby food pureed sweet potatoes
2 tablespoons egg substitute
2 teaspoons light brown sugar, firmly packed
1 teaspoon vanilla extract
1 teaspoon canola or corn oil
Cooking spray
2 large egg whites, at room temperature

1. In a large bowl, whisk together the flours, pumpkin pie spice, baking powder, ginger, and allspice. Make a well in the center. Set aside.

2. In a medium bowl, whisk together the buttermilk, sour cream, sweet potatoes, egg substitute, brown sugar, vanilla, and oil. Set aside.

3. Lightly spray the waffle iron with cooking spray. Preheat the iron.

4. In a small glass, stainless steel, or copper mixing bowl, use an electric mixer on medium low to beat the egg whites until foamy. Gradually increasing the speed, continue beating until soft, glossy peaks form. The whites should form a peak when you lift the beaters out of the egg whites.

5. Pour the buttermilk mixture into the well in the flour mixture. Stir just to blend. Spoon 1/3 of the egg whites over the mixture. Gently stir into the batter. Spoon the remaining egg whites over the batter. Using a rubber scraper, gently fold in the whites just until all the flour mixture is moistened (bits of egg whites may still be visible).

6. Following the manufacturer's recommendation for amounts, gently spoon the batter into the waffle iron. Using a wooden spoon, push the batter to the edges of the iron. Bake as directed by the manufacturer until the waffles are golden brown and firm to the touch. Serve immediately.

COOK'S TIP: *Beaten egg whites help the waffles rise with less baking powder, reducing the sodium in the recipe to a heart-healthy level.*

Exchanges/Choices
3 Starch
1/2 Fat-Free Milk
1/2 Fat

Calories	320	
Calories from Fat	30	
Total Fat	3.5	g
Saturated Fat	0.7	g
Trans Fat	0.0	g
Polyunsaturated Fat	1.0	g
Monounsaturated Fat	1.6	g
Cholesterol	5	mg
Sodium	270	mg
Total Carbohydrate	53	g
Dietary Fiber	5	g
Sugars	12	g
Protein	14	g

Zucchini-Walnut Scones

Serves 2; 1 scone per serving
Preparation time: 25 minutes

You'll hear an enthusiastic "yum" when you serve this healthful alternative to coffee shop pastries.

Cooking spray
1/4 cup whole-wheat pastry flour
1/4 cup all-purpose flour
1 tablespoon firmly packed light brown sugar
1/4 teaspoon baking powder
1/4 teaspoon ground cinnamon
1/8 teaspoon ground nutmeg
1/3 cup finely grated unpeeled zucchini (about 3 ounces)
1 tablespoon low-fat buttermilk or fat-free milk

1 tablespoon egg substitute
2 teaspoons canola or corn oil
1 teaspoon finely chopped walnuts

Exchanges/Choices		
2 Starch		
1 Fat		
Calories	200	
Calories from Fat	55	
Total Fat	6.0	g
Saturated Fat	0.6	g
Trans Fat	0.0	g
Polyunsaturated Fat	2.1	g
Monounsaturated Fat	2.8	g
Cholesterol	0	mg
Sodium	75	mg
Total Carbohydrate	33	g
Dietary Fiber	3	g
Sugars	8	g
Protein	5	g

1. Preheat the oven to 375°F. Lightly spray a baking sheet with cooking spray.

2. In a medium bowl, stir together the flours, brown sugar, baking powder, cinnamon, and nutmeg.

3. In a small bowl, stir together the remaining ingredients except the walnuts. Add to the dry ingredients. Stir gently just until the dry ingredients are moistened. Do not overmix or the scones may be tough.

4. Transfer the dough to the baking sheet. Shape into a ball. Using the palm of your hand, flatten the dough into a circle 3 1/2 inches in diameter. Fold the dough in half, making a half-circle. Fold in half again, making a quarter-circle. Pat down lightly. Sprinkle with the walnuts. Score the dough into 2 wedges by making a cut about 1/4-inch deep; do not cut all the way through.

5. Bake for 20 minutes, or until the scones are golden brown and a wooden toothpick or cake tester inserted in the center comes out clean. Remove from the oven. Immediately cut into 2 wedges along the scored cut. Serve warm or at room temperature.

FRENCH TOAST
WITH ORANGE-STRAWBERRY SAUCE

Serves 2; 2 slices toast, 1/2 cup plus 2 tablespoons sauce, and 1/4 cup yogurt per serving
Preparation time: 5 minutes

Always a favorite, French toast is topped with sweet strawberries, citrusy sauce, and creamy yogurt.

1 cup egg substitute
1/2 teaspoon vanilla extract
4 slices light whole-wheat bread
1 teaspoon canola or corn oil
1/4 teaspoon grated orange zest
1/3 cup fresh orange juice
1 tablespoon sugar
1/2 teaspoon cornstarch
1 cup whole medium strawberries, quartered
1 (6-ounce) container fat-free vanilla yogurt

1. In a shallow dish, whisk together the egg substitute and vanilla. Dip each bread slice in the mixture, coating both sides. Let any excess drip off. Set aside on a plate.

2. In a large nonstick skillet, heat the oil over medium heat, swirling to coat the bottom. Cook the bread for 4 minutes on each side, or until golden brown.

3. Meanwhile, in a small saucepan, combine the orange zest, orange juice, sugar, and cornstarch, stirring until the cornstarch is dissolved. Bring to a boil over medium-high heat. Boil for 1 minute, stirring frequently. Remove from the heat. Set aside to cool slightly.

4. Just before serving, stir the strawberries into the orange sauce until coated. Spoon over the bread. Top with the yogurt.

Exchanges/Choices		
2 1/2 Carbohydrate		
1 Lean Meat		
1/2 Fat		
Calories	250	
Calories from Fat	30	
Total Fat	3.5	g
Saturated Fat	0.3	g
Trans Fat	0.0	g
Polyunsaturated Fat	1.3	g
Monounsaturated Fat	1.5	g
Cholesterol	0	mg
Sodium	430	mg
Total Carbohydrate	43	g
Dietary Fiber	7	g
Sugars	19	g
Protein	15	g

Blueberry Oatmeal Brûlée

BLUEBERRY OATMEAL BRÛLÉE

Serves 2; 1 cup per serving
Preparation time: 5 minutes

As they are being quickly broiled, blueberries make a sweet, syrupy sauce in this homemade version of a spa favorite.

Cooking spray
1 cup uncooked rolled oats
1/2 teaspoon ground cinnamon
1/8 teaspoon ground allspice
1 3/4 cups fat-free milk
1 (4.4-ounce) container fresh blueberries (about 1 cup)
2 teaspoons light brown sugar
1/8 teaspoon ground nutmeg

1. Preheat the broiler. Lightly spray two 8-ounce ramekins (4-inch diameter) or glass custard cups with cooking spray. Put on a baking sheet.

2. In a medium saucepan, stir together the oats, cinnamon, and allspice. Stir in the milk. Cook over medium heat for 8 minutes, or until the oatmeal is thick and creamy, stirring constantly. Spoon into the ramekins. Sprinkle the blueberries over the oatmeal.

3. In a small bowl, stir together the brown sugar and nutmeg. Sprinkle over the blueberries.

4. Broil in the upper third of the oven for 6 to 8 minutes, or until the blueberries are bubbly and the sugar is crisp.

> **COOK'S TIP:** *Frozen blueberries do not work well in this dish. They lose too much of their juice, even when thawed and drained before sprinkling them on the oatmeal.*

Exchanges/Choices		
2 Starch		
1/2 Fruit		
1 Fat-Free Milk		
Calories	295	
Calories from Fat	25	
Total Fat	3.0	g
Saturated Fat	0.6	g
Trans Fat	0.0	g
Polyunsaturated Fat	1.1	g
Monounsaturated Fat	0.9	g
Cholesterol	5	mg
Sodium	120	mg
Total Carbohydrate	54	g
Dietary Fiber	6	g
Sugars	23	g
Protein	15	g

Mexican-Italian Omelets

MEXICAN-ITALIAN OMELETS

Serves 2; 1 omelet per serving
Preparation time: 5 minutes

Enjoy these part Tex-Mex, part Italian omelets at any time of the day. Add chopped green onions or snipped fresh cilantro to liven up the salsa if you wish.

1/2 teaspoon and 1/2 teaspoon canola or corn oil, divided use
1/2 cup and 1/2 cup egg substitute, divided use
1 tablespoon and 1 tablespoon chunky salsa (lowest sodium available), divided use
1 tablespoon and 1 tablespoon shredded part-skim mozzarella cheese, divided use

1. In an 8-inch nonstick skillet, heat 1/2 teaspoon oil over medium heat, swirling to coat the bottom. Pour in 1/2 cup egg substitute. As it sets, push the egg substitute toward the center of the skillet and tilt the skillet so the uncooked portion flows to the edge. (A rubber scraper works wells for this.) When the egg substitute is just set, 3 to 4 minutes, spoon 1 tablespoon salsa down the center. Top the salsa with 1 tablespoon mozzarella. Lift one half of the omelet with the rubber scraper and fold over the other half. Slide the omelet onto a warm plate. Let stand for 1 to 2 minutes, or until the mozzarella melts.

2. Meanwhile, repeat with the remaining ingredients to make a second omelet.

COOK'S TIP: *When cooking for two, try to buy egg substitute in small containers unless you use it frequently. Once opened, the liquid needs to be used within one week, so the twin pack may be better suited to your needs.*

Exchanges/Choices		
2 Lean Meat		
Calories	**100**	
Calories from Fat	30	
Total Fat	**3.5**	**g**
Saturated Fat	0.9	g
Trans Fat	0.0	g
Polyunsaturated Fat	0.7	g
Monounsaturated Fat	1.6	g
Cholesterol	**5**	**mg**
Sodium	**375**	**mg**
Total Carbohydrate	**3**	**g**
Dietary Fiber	0	g
Sugars	2	g
Protein	**14**	**g**

WHOLE-WHEAT BREAKFAST PIZZAS

Serves 2; 1/2 English muffin and 1/2 cup egg mixture
Preparation time: 5 minutes

Breakfast pizzas are worth waking up for!

1 teaspoon light tub margarine
2 small green onions, finely chopped
2 small button mushrooms, sliced
1/2 small red bell pepper, diced
1/2 cup egg substitute
2 tablespoons fat-free milk
1 whole-wheat or multigrain English muffin, split in half
1/4 cup low-fat shredded Colby and Monterey Jack cheese mixture
1 small tomato, seeded and chopped

1. Preheat the oven to 375°F.

2. In a small nonstick skillet, heat the margarine over medium heat until melted, swirling to coat the bottom. Cook the green onions, mushrooms, and bell pepper over medium-high heat for 3 minutes, or until tender, stirring frequently.

3. In a small bowl, whisk together the egg substitute and milk. Pour over the vegetables. Reduce the heat to medium. Cook without stirring until the mixture begins to set on the bottom and around the edge. As it sets, push the mixture toward the center of the skillet and tilt the skillet so the uncooked portion flows to the edge and all the egg substitute is fully cooked, 3 to 4 minutes. (A rubber scraper works well for this.)

4. Put the English muffin halves with the cut side up on a baking sheet. Sprinkle each with 1 tablespoon Colby and Monterey Jack mixture. Spoon the egg mixture over the cheese. Top with the remaining cheese. Sprinkle with the tomato.

5. Bake for 5 to 8 minutes, or until the cheese is melted.

Exchanges/Choices
1 Starch
1 Vegetable
1 Lean Meat
1/2 Fat

Calories	170	
Calories from Fat	40	
Total Fat	4.5	g
Saturated Fat	2.2	g
Trans Fat	0.0	g
Polyunsaturated Fat	0.8	g
Monounsaturated Fat	1.3	g
Cholesterol	10	mg
Sodium	415	mg
Total Carbohydrate	20	g
Dietary Fiber	3	g
Sugars	6	g
Protein	14	g

DESSERTS

Pumpkin Cakes

Serves 2; 1 cake per serving
Preparation time: 10 minutes

Moist and tender though compact, these individual cakes are fragrant with pumpkin and spices. Add cream cheese icing and a sprinkling of nuts for the final touches to a perfect cool-weather dessert. For a tasty breakfast treat, forgo the icing and pair the cake with a steaming cup of tea.

Cooking spray

Cakes

1/4 cup all-purpose flour
3 tablespoons whole-wheat pastry flour
1/4 teaspoon baking powder
1/2 teaspoon ground cinnamon
1/4 teaspoon ground allspice
1/8 teaspoon ground ginger
1/8 teaspoon ground nutmeg
1/16 teaspoon ground cloves
1/4 cup plus 1 tablespoon canned solid-pack pumpkin (not pie filling)
3 tablespoons egg substitute
2 tablespoons sugar
2 teaspoons canola or corn oil
1/2 teaspoon vanilla extract

Icing (optional)

1 tablespoon light tub cream cheese
2 teaspoons confectioners' sugar
1/4 teaspoon vanilla extract
✳✳✳✳✳✳
1 teaspoon finely chopped walnuts

(With Icing)

Exchanges/Choices

3 Carbohydrate
1 Fat

Calories	255	
Calories from Fat	65	
Total Fat	7.0	g
Saturated Fat	1.3	g
Trans Fat	0.0	g
Polyunsaturated Fat	2.1	g
Monounsaturated Fat	3.2	g
Cholesterol	5	mg
Sodium	120	mg
Total Carbohydrate	41	g
Dietary Fiber	4	g
Sugars	17	g
Protein	6	g

1. Preheat the oven to 350°F. Lightly spray two cups of a muffin pan with cooking spray.

2. In a small bowl, whisk together the flours, baking powder, cinnamon, allspice, ginger, nutmeg, and cloves.

3. In a medium bowl, combine the remaining cake ingredients, whisking until smooth. Pour the flour mixture over the pumpkin mixture and gently fold in. Spoon into the prepared muffin cups. Put 1 tablespoon water in each of the empty cups.

4. Bake for 15 minutes, or until a wooden toothpick or cake tester inserted in the center comes out clean. Transfer the pan to a cooling rack. Let cool for 5 minutes. Remove the cakes from the pan. Let cool completely on the rack.

5. Meanwhile, put the cream cheese, confectioners' sugar, and vanilla in a small mixing bowl. Using an electric mixer on low speed, beat until smooth. Using a rubber spatula, spread the icing on the cooled cakes. Sprinkle with the nuts.

COOK'S TIP: *Use leftover pumpkin in soups, sauces, and chilis for extra flavor and fiber. Freeze it in ice-cube trays and store the cubes in a resealable plastic container or plastic bag. Frozen pumpkin will keep for up to three months.*

COOK'S TIP: *Putting water in unfilled muffin pan cups prevents the empty cups from warping or being burned in the oven.*

(Without Icing)		
Exchanges/Choices		
2 1/2 Carbohydrate		
1 Fat		
Calories	220	
Calories from Fat	45	
Total Fat	5.0	g
Saturated Fat	0.5	g
Trans Fat	0.0	g
Polyunsaturated Fat	1.5	g
Monounsaturated Fat	2.7	g
Cholesterol	0	mg
Sodium	90	mg
Total Carbohydrate	38	g
Dietary Fiber	3	g
Sugars	14	g
Protein	5	g

Raspberry-Citrus Cheesecakes

RASPBERRY-CITRUS CHEESECAKES

Serves 2; 1 cheesecake per serving
Preparation time: 5 minutes

This stir-together, no-bake dessert features raspberry, lemon, and lime plus a creamy filling.

1/3 cup frozen unsweetened raspberries
1 tablespoon fresh lemon juice
1/2 teaspoon unflavored gelatin
Cooking spray
2 low-fat vanilla wafers, very finely crushed
1/2 cup fat-free ricotta cheese
1 tablespoon low-fat cream cheese
1 tablespoon sugar
2 teaspoons fresh lime juice

1. Line a plate with paper towels. Place the frozen raspberries in a single layer on the plate to thaw.

2. Meanwhile, pour the lemon juice into a small microwaveable cup. Sprinkle the gelatin on top and stir. Let stand for 5 minutes.

3. Meanwhile, place paper bake cups in two cups of a muffin pan. Very lightly spray the bottoms of the cups with cooking spray. Put the crumbs in the cups. Set aside.

4. Stir the gelatin mixture. Cover and microwave on 100% power (high) for 30 seconds. Set aside to cool, about 3 minutes.

5. Meanwhile, in a small bowl, whisk together the ricotta, cream cheese, sugar, and lime juice. The mixture will not be completely smooth. Whisk in the cooled gelatin mixture.

6. Sprinkle the raspberries over the mixture and fold them in. (It is fine if the raspberries have not thawed completely.) Spoon over the cookie crumbs. Using a spatula, smooth the filling. Cover with plastic wrap and refrigerate for 3 hours, or until firm.

7. To serve, run a flat knife around the outside of each bake cup. Carefully slip the tip of the knife under the bottom of the bake cup and lift the wrapper and cheesecake out of the muffin pan. Invert the cheesecakes onto saucers. Carefully peel off the bake cups.

Exchanges/Choices
 1 Carbohydrate
 1 Lean Meat

Calories	125	
Calories from Fat	20	
Total Fat	2.0	**g**
Saturated Fat	1.2	g
Trans Fat	0.0	g
Polyunsaturated Fat	0.2	g
Monounsaturated Fat	0.7	g
Cholesterol	25	**mg**
Sodium	90	**mg**
Total Carbohydrate	18	**g**
Dietary Fiber	0	g
Sugars	14	g
Protein	10	**g**

Apple Pie Tartlets

APPLE PIE TARTLETS

Serves 2; 1 tartlet per serving
Preparation time: 5 minutes

Making tartlet crust is a breeze when you start with lightly sweetened wonton wrappers. They won't completely cover the muffin cups, but don't worry: The fit is just right to hold the creamy apple filling.

Cooking spray
1 teaspoon light tub margarine
1 teaspoon sugar
2 wonton wrappers (about 3 1/2 × 3 1/2 inches)
1/2 cup finely chopped unpeeled Granny Smith apple
1/4 teaspoon ground cinnamon
2 tablespoons fat-free tub cream cheese
1 tablespoon egg substitute
1 teaspoon sugar
1/4 teaspoon vanilla extract
1/2 teaspoon confectioners' sugar

1. Preheat the oven to 350°F. Lightly spray two cups of a muffin pan with cooking spray.

2. In a small microwaveable bowl, stir together the margarine and sugar. Microwave, covered, on 100% power (high) for 20 seconds, or until the margarine melts. Stir.

3. Place the wonton wrappers on a flat surface. Using a pastry brush, brush with the margarine mixture. Carefully place the wrappers with the margarine side up in the prepared muffin cups, pressing down gently so each wrapper forms a cup. Pour 1 tablespoon water into each of the empty cups.

4. Bake for 5 minutes, or until the wrappers just begin to brown. Transfer to a cooling rack.

5. Meanwhile, in a small bowl, gently stir together the apple and cinnamon. Stir in the remaining ingredients except the confectioners' sugar. Stir into the baked crusts.

6. Bake for 15 minutes, or until the filling jiggles very slightly when gently shaken and the wrappers are golden brown. Let cool in the pan for 10 minutes. Carefully transfer to plates. Serve warm or at room temperature, sifting the confectioners' sugar over the tartlets just before serving.

COOK'S TIP: *Substitute another variety of baking apple for the Granny Smith if you prefer. Choose one that is firm enough to hold up in the oven, but not so hard that it requires a long baking time. Among the many varieties that would work well are Rome Beauty, Jonathan, and McIntosh. And don't forget to experiment with regional apples as well. If you are unsure what to select, ask someone in the produce department for help.*

Exchanges/Choices
1 Carbohydrate

Calories	90	
Calories from Fat	10	
Total Fat	1.0	g
Saturated Fat	0.3	g
Trans Fat	0.0	g
Polyunsaturated Fat	0.3	g
Monounsaturated Fat	0.4	g
Cholesterol	5	mg
Sodium	190	mg
Total Carbohydrate	15	g
Dietary Fiber	1	g
Sugars	9	g
Protein	4	g

LEMONY FRUIT CUPS

Serves 2; 1 bowl per serving
Preparation time: 10 minutes

Add a touch of elegance to dinner with these individual creamy fruit cups.

1/2 cup fat-free frozen whipped topping, thawed in refrigerator
1/4 teaspoon grated lemon zest
2 teaspoons fresh lemon juice
1 tablespoon sliced almonds, dry-roasted, crushed
1 medium kiwifruit, peeled and cut into 4 slices
4 medium strawberries, quartered
1/2 teaspoon confectioners' sugar

1. In a small bowl, gently stir together the whipped topping, lemon zest, and lemon juice. Spoon into two small custard cups or ramekins.

2. Sprinkle the almonds over the whipped topping. Arrange the kiwifruit and strawberries on top. Using a fine sieve, sift the confectioners' sugar over all. Serve immediately, or refrigerate until serving time. If refrigerated, the sugar will dissolve and give the fruit a glazed appearance.

Exchanges/Choices
1 Carbohydrate
1/2 Fat

Calories	90	
Calories from Fat	20	
Total Fat	2.5	g
Saturated Fat	0.2	g
Trans Fat	0.0	g
Polyunsaturated Fat	0.7	g
Monounsaturated Fat	1.4	g
Cholesterol	0	mg
Sodium	15	mg
Total Carbohydrate	15	g
Dietary Fiber	2	g
Sugars	7	g
Protein	1	g

MIXED BERRY CRISP WITH ALMOND STREUSEL

2 servings; 1 cup per serving
Preparation time: 5 minutes

Appealing is the word for this crisp with its crunchy almonds and oats crowning a layer of baked mixed berries. As a bonus, the recipe calls for frozen fruit, making the crisp a great dessert for any season.

1 (12-ounce) bag frozen unsweetened mixed berries
1 teaspoon cornstarch
1/8 teaspoon and 1/8 teaspoon ground cinnamon, divided use
1/4 teaspoon vanilla extract
1/4 cup old-fashioned rolled oats
2 tablespoons sliced almonds
1 tablespoon whole-wheat pastry flour or all-purpose flour
2 teaspoons firmly packed light brown sugar
1/8 teaspoon salt
1 tablespoon light tub margarine, melted

1. Preheat the oven to 350°F. In a microwaveable bowl, thaw the fruit by microwaving on 10% power (low) in 1-minute increments, until it just begins to release its juices.

2. In a small dish, stir together the cornstarch and 1/8 teaspoon cinnamon. Add 1 tablespoon juice from the thawed fruit, stirring until the cornstarch is dissolved. Stir in the vanilla. Pour the juice mixture over the fruit. Toss to coat. Spoon into two 6-ounce ovenproof dishes, such as crème brûlée dishes or custard cups.

3. In a small bowl, stir together the oats, almonds, flour, brown sugar, salt, and remaining 1/8 teaspoon cinnamon. Drizzle with the melted margarine. Pinch with your fingertips to blend until the mixture is like coarse sand with some pea-size pieces. Sprinkle over the fruit.

4. Bake for 25 minutes, or until browned and bubbly. Let stand to cool for at least 10 minutes. Serve warm or at room temperature.

Exchanges/Choices		
1 Starch		
1 Fruit		
1 Fat		
Calories	**215**	
Calories from Fat	55	
Total Fat	**6.0**	**g**
Saturated Fat	1.1	g
Trans Fat	0.0	g
Polyunsaturated Fat	1.7	g
Monounsaturated Fat	3.1	g
Cholesterol	**0**	**mg**
Sodium	**195**	**mg**
Total Carbohydrate	**35**	**g**
Dietary Fiber	6	g
Sugars	17	g
Protein	**4**	**g**

BAKED PEACH CRISP

Serves 2; 1 cup per serving
Preparation time: 5 minutes

It takes very little time to get this dessert ready to pop in the oven. With crunchy, highly flavorful gingersnaps for topping, you don't need the usual dabs of butter.

2 cups frozen unsweetened sliced peaches
Cooking spray
1 tablespoon all-purpose flour
1 tablespoon sugar
1/2 teaspoon ground cinnamon
4 low-fat gingersnaps, crushed

1. Let the peaches stand at room temperature for 30 minutes in a shallow dish, reserving the liquid.

2. Preheat the oven to 375°F. Lightly spray two 8-ounce ramekins (4-inch diameter) with cooking spray.

3. In a medium bowl, gently stir together the peaches with reserved juice, flour, sugar, and cinnamon. Spoon into the ramekins. Sprinkle with the crushed gingersnaps. Transfer to a baking sheet.

4. Bake for 30 to 35 minutes, or until the peaches are tender and the mixture is bubbly.

Exchanges/Choices
2 1/2 Carbohydrate

Calories	160	
Calories from Fat	15	
Total Fat	1.5	g
Saturated Fat	0.4	g
Trans Fat	0.4	g
Polyunsaturated Fat	0.3	g
Monounsaturated Fat	0.5	g
Cholesterol	0	mg
Sodium	50	mg
Total Carbohydrate	37	g
Dietary Fiber	3	g
Sugars	24	g
Protein	2	g

TIRAMISÙ *Tiramisù*

Serves 2; 1/2 cup tiramisù and 1/4 cup strawberries per serving
Preparation time: 10 minutes

Reserve some of your morning coffee to use later for this tasty treat. Replacing the usual ladyfingers or sponge cake with animal crackers adds a dash of whimsy to the dessert.

- 2 tablespoons fat-free cream cheese
- 1/4 cup fat-free ricotta cheese
- 1 1/2 tablespoons light brown sugar
- 1/2 teaspoon vanilla extract
- 2 tablespoons fat-free frozen whipped topping, thawed
- 16 animal crackers, broken in half (32 pieces)
- 1/4 cup plus 2 tablespoons strong coffee, warm or chilled
- 2 teaspoons unsweetened cocoa powder
- 2 ounces strawberries, sliced

1. In a medium microwaveable bowl, microwave the cream cheese on 100% power (high) for 10 to 15 seconds, or until slightly softened. Whisk in the ricotta, brown sugar, and vanilla. Gently whisk in the whipped topping (the mixture will be slightly fluffy).

2. Put 8 animal cracker pieces in each of two martini or dessert-style glasses. Spoon 1 1/2 tablespoons coffee into each glass. Spoon 2 tablespoons cream cheese mixture into each. Using a small sifter, sift 1/2 teaspoon cocoa powder over each. Repeat. Top with the strawberries. Serve immediately, or cover and refrigerate for up to 24 hours.

Exchanges/Choices		
2 Carbohydrate		
1 Lean Meat		
Calories	190	
Calories from Fat	25	
Total Fat	3.0	g
Saturated Fat	0.8	g
Trans Fat	0.0	g
Polyunsaturated Fat	0.4	g
Monounsaturated Fat	1.6	g
Cholesterol	10	mg
Sodium	230	mg
Total Carbohydrate	32	g
Dietary Fiber	1	g
Sugars	16	g
Protein	8	g

Chai Panna Cotta

Serves 2; 1/2 cup per serving
Preparation time: 5 minutes

You can make this silky, spicy, and satisfying dessert up to one day before serving. Once the mixture is set, place plastic wrap directly on the surface. Refrigerate until needed.

1 teaspoon canola or corn oil
2 tablespoons and 3/4 cup plus 2 tablespoons fat-free half-and-half, divided use
2 tablespoons cold water
1/2 tablespoon unflavored gelatin
1 teaspoon sugar
2 bags chai spice tea
1/2 teaspoon vanilla extract

1. Pour the oil into a small bowl. Dip the tip of a paper towel in the oil. Lightly rub over the bottoms and sides of two 6-ounce custard cups.

2. Put 2 tablespoons half-and-half and the water in a small bowl. Sprinkle with the gelatin (no need to stir in). Set aside to soften.

3. In a small saucepan, heat the remaining 3/4 cup plus 2 tablespoons half-and-half and sugar over medium heat for about 5 minutes, or until the mixture begins to bubble around the edge. Remove from the heat.

4. Add the tea bags. Dunk several times. Let steep for 5 minutes. Dunk again several times. Squeeze the bags firmly against the side of the saucepan with the back of a spoon to extract more flavor. Discard the tea bags.

5. Stir in the gelatin until dissolved, about 2 minutes. Stir in the vanilla. Pour into the custard cups. Refrigerate until set, about 4 hours. Unmold onto small plates.

Exchanges/Choices		
1 Fat-Free Milk		
Calories	95	
Calories from Fat	20	
Total Fat	2.5	g
Saturated Fat	1.1	g
Trans Fat	0.0	g
Polyunsaturated Fat	0.2	g
Monounsaturated Fat	0.8	g
Cholesterol	5	mg
Sodium	125	mg
Total Carbohydrate	13	g
Dietary Fiber	0	g
Sugars	8	g
Protein	5	g

BASMATI OR JASMINE RICE PUDDING

Serves 2; heaping 1/2 cup per serving
Preparation time: 5 minutes

Here's a rice pudding with an exotic flair. Start with basmati or jasmine rice and add fresh fruit juice, mandarin oranges, and honey to transport the homey comfort food to another level.

1/4 cup uncooked basmati or jasmine rice
1 teaspoon grated orange zest
1/4 cup fresh orange juice
3/4 cup fat-free evaporated milk
2 tablespoons fat-free half-and-half
1 tablespoon honey
1/2 teaspoon vanilla extract
1/4 cup canned mandarin oranges or sliced peaches in juice or light syrup, chopped,
    1/4 cup juice reserved

1. In a small saucepan, prepare the rice using the package directions, omitting the salt and margarine.

2. Stir in the orange zest and juice, evaporated milk, half-and-half, honey, vanilla, and 1/4 cup reserved juice. Increase the heat to medium low and cook, uncovered, for 15 to 20 minutes, or until the pudding has a creamy consistency, stirring frequently. Stir in the mandarin oranges. Pour into two 8-ounce ramekins (4-inch diameter) or custard cups. Cover with plastic wrap touching the surface to avoid forming a skin. Let cool for 30 to 35 minutes, or to room temperature, and serve, or refrigerate to serve chilled. The pudding will continue to absorb the liquid and become firm as it cools.

Exchanges/Choices		
1 Starch		
1 Fruit		
1 Fat-Free Milk		
Calories	230	
Calories from Fat	5	
Total Fat	0.5	g
Saturated Fat	0.3	g
Trans Fat	0.0	g
Polyunsaturated Fat	0.1	g
Monounsaturated Fat	0.2	g
Cholesterol	5	mg
Sodium	130	mg
Total Carbohydrate	46	g
Dietary Fiber	1	g
Sugars	29	g
Protein	10	g

Poached Pears
with Pomegranate Sauce

Serves 2; 1 pear half and 1 tablespoon sauce per serving
Preparation time: 10 minutes

Serve this multipurpose dish warm, at room temperature, or cold as a dessert, salad, or side.

1/3 cup pomegranate juice
2 teaspoons sugar
1 medium pear, peeled, halved, and cored
1/4 teaspoon cornstarch
1 teaspoon water
1/4 teaspoon grated lemon zest
1/4 teaspoon vanilla extract
2 tablespoons sliced almonds, dry-roasted, crumbled

1. In a small saucepan, stir together the pomegranate juice and sugar. Add the pear halves with the cut side down. Bring to a boil over high heat. Reduce the heat and simmer, covered, for 5 minutes, or until tender, turning occasionally. Remove from the heat. Leaving the liquid in the pan, transfer the pear halves with the cut side down to dessert plates.

2. Put the cornstarch in a small bowl. Add the water, stirring to dissolve. Pour into the same pan. Bring to a boil over medium-high heat, whisking constantly. Boil for 1 minute. Remove from the heat. Stir in the lemon zest and vanilla. Spoon over the pears. Sprinkle with the almonds.

> **COOK'S TIP:** *Be sure to use a ripe pear for peak texture and flavor. Using a firm pear not only will require at least twice as much cooking time but also will not be as tender, sweet, and flavorful.*

Exchanges/Choices
1 1/2 Fruit
1/2 Fat

Calories	120	
Calories from Fat	25	
Total Fat	3.0	g
Saturated Fat	0.2	g
Trans Fat	0.0	g
Polyunsaturated Fat	0.7	g
Monounsaturated Fat	1.9	g
Cholesterol	0	mg
Sodium	0	mg
Total Carbohydrate	23	g
Dietary Fiber	3	g
Sugars	17	g
Protein	1	g

SKILLET BANANAS AND ICE CREAM WITH CHOCOLATE SYRUP

Skillet Bananas

Serves 2; 1/2 cup banana, 1/2 cup ice cream, and 1 teaspoon syrup per serving
Preparation time: 5 minutes

Can't decide whether to have a banana split or bananas Foster? This delectable dessert is a cross between the two.

1 tablespoon light tub margarine
1 medium banana, diced
1 teaspoon firmly packed dark brown sugar
1/4 teaspoon ground cinnamon
1/4 teaspoon vanilla extract
1 cup fat-free vanilla ice cream
2 teaspoons light chocolate syrup

1. In a medium nonstick skillet, melt the margarine over medium-high heat, swirling to coat the bottom. Cook the banana, brown sugar, and cinnamon for 2 minutes, or until the banana is soft and glossy, stirring gently and constantly. Remove from the heat. Stir in the vanilla.

2. Put 1/2 cup ice cream in each bowl. Spoon the banana mixture over the ice cream. Drizzle the syrup over all.

Exchanges/Choices
2 1/2 Carbohydrate
1/2 Fat

Calories	190	
Calories from Fat	20	
Total Fat	2.5	g
Saturated Fat	0.8	g
Trans Fat	0.0	g
Polyunsaturated Fat	0.8	g
Monounsaturated Fat	1.0	g
Cholesterol	0	mg
Sodium	105	mg
Total Carbohydrate	41	g
Dietary Fiber	6	g
Sugars	25	g
Protein	4	g

Grilled Peach Halves

GRILLED PEACH HALVES
WITH FRESH BLUEBERRY COMPOTE

Serves 2; 1/2 peach and 2 1/2 tablespoons blueberry compote per serving
Preparation time: 5 minutes

Grilling concentrates the flavor of the peach and caramelizes its natural sugars. The warm peach combines beautifully with bright berries in this appealing dessert.

Cooking spray
1 teaspoon light tub margarine, melted
1/2 tablespoon firmly packed light or dark brown sugar
1 teaspoon fresh orange juice and 2 tablespoons fresh orange juice, divided use
1/8 teaspoon ground nutmeg and 1/8 teaspoon ground nutmeg, divided use
1 firm but ripe freestone peach, halved
1 teaspoon honey
1/4 teaspoon cornstarch
1/3 cup fresh blueberries

1. Lightly spray a grill rack with cooking spray. Preheat the grill on medium high.

2. In a small bowl, stir together the margarine and brown sugar. Stir in 1 teaspoon orange juice and 1/8 teaspoon nutmeg.

3. Put the peach halves with the cut side up on the grill rack. Brush generously with the brown sugar mixture. Grill for 4 minutes, or until golden brown on the bottom. Turn the peach halves over. Brush generously with the brown sugar mixture. Grill for 4 to 5 minutes, or until the peach halves are heated through and golden brown.

4. Meanwhile, in a small saucepan, stir together the remaining 2 tablespoons orange juice, honey, and cornstarch. Cook over medium heat for 2 minutes, or until thickened and smooth, stirring constantly. Remove from heat. Stir in the blueberries and remaining 1/8 teaspoon nutmeg. Serve over the peach halves.

COOK'S TIP: *If fresh peaches aren't in season, you can use 3 ounces of frozen unsweetened thick peach slices. Thaw, drain, and dry the slices, then skewer them together closely before grilling. Reduce the grilling time to 2 to 3 minutes on each side, or until golden brown.*

Exchanges/Choices

1 Fruit

Calories	75	
Calories from Fat	10	
Total Fat	1.0	**g**
Saturated Fat	0.2	g
Trans Fat	0.0	g
Polyunsaturated Fat	0.3	g
Monounsaturated Fat	0.3	g
Cholesterol	0	**mg**
Sodium	10	**mg**
Total Carbohydrate	18	**g**
Dietary Fiber	2	g
Sugars	15	g
Protein	1	**g**

Ice Cream

DARK CHERRY AND CHOCOLATE CRUMB ICE CREAM

Serves 2; 1/2 cup per serving
Preparation time: 5 minutes

Enjoy this refreshing mixture for a trip to the ice cream parlor without leaving home.

> 3/4 cup fat-free chocolate ice cream
> 1/3 cup frozen dark cherries, halved
> 1 (1-ounce) packet baked chocolate wafer snacks, coarsely crushed
> 1/8 teaspoon almond extract (optional)

1. Put the ice cream in a small bowl and let it slightly soften, about 10 minutes. Fold in the remaining ingredients until just blended. Serve immediately for soft-serve ice cream, or cover with plastic wrap and freeze for 1 to 2 hours to serve firm.

COOK'S TIP: *You can find the chocolate cookies for this dessert in the snacks and cookie aisle.*

Exchanges/Choices
2 1/2 Carbohydrate

Calories	165	
Calories from Fat	20	
Total Fat	2.0	g
Saturated Fat	0.7	g
Trans Fat	0.0	g
Polyunsaturated Fat	0.7	g
Monounsaturated Fat	0.5	g
Cholesterol	0	mg
Sodium	145	mg
Total Carbohydrate	36	g
Dietary Fiber	4	g
Sugars	20	g
Protein	4	g

TROPICAL GRANITA

Tropical Granita

Serves 2; 1/2 cup per serving
Preparation time: 5 minutes

Granitas, with their crystalline texture, are sorbet's icy cousins. Mango adds lots of body for a coolly satisfying dessert.

1 medium mango, cut into 1-inch chunks
1/4 cup frozen unsweetened apple juice concentrate, thawed
1 teaspoon fresh lime juice

1. In a food processor, process the mango for 1 to 2 minutes, or until smooth. Add the apple juice and lime juice. Process until blended. Spoon into ice cube trays. Freeze until solid, about 3 hours. Meanwhile, put two small bowls in the refrigerator to chill.

2. To serve, flip the ice cube tray over and run the bottom under cold water to loosen the cubes. Place the cubes in the food processor and process until finely chopped (almost pebbly). Scoop the mixture into the chilled bowls.

COOK'S TIP: *If you don't have ice cube trays, put the mixture in four small freezer-proof containers, such as glass custard cups. Frozen portions that are too large will be difficult for your food processor to handle.*

Exchanges/Choices
2 Fruit

Calories	135	
Calories from Fat	0	
Total Fat	0.0	g
Saturated Fat	0.0	g
Trans Fat	0.0	g
Polyunsaturated Fat	0.0	g
Monounsaturated Fat	0.0	g
Cholesterol	0	mg
Sodium	10	mg
Total Carbohydrate	35	g
Dietary Fiber	2	g
Sugars	32	g
Protein	1	g

Strawberry-Orange Parfaits

STRAWBERRY-ORANGE YOGURT PARFAITS

Serves 2; scant 1 cup per serving
Preparation time: 15 minutes

The secret to this unbelievably creamy dessert lies in draining the excess liquid from the yogurt. The thickened yogurt then serves as a pillowy base for the fruit and nuts.

2 (6-ounce) containers fat-free plain yogurt
1 small orange
4 medium strawberries
2 teaspoons orange liqueur
2 teaspoons sugar
1/4 cup coarsely chopped dry-roasted pecans

1. Line a rustproof colander or large strainer with two layers of cheesecloth or an unused paper coffee filter. Pour the yogurt into the colander. Place the colander in a deep bowl, making sure the bottom of the colander doesn't touch the bowl. Cover the colander with plastic wrap. Refrigerate for 2 hours, or until a scant 1/2 cup whey (yellowish liquid) has drained off and the yogurt has thickened. Discard the whey.

2. Meanwhile, peel the orange and divide into segments. Cut each segment into thirds. Quarter the strawberries.

3. In a small bowl, stir together the orange pieces, strawberries, and liqueur. Let stand at room temperature, stirring occasionally, until the yogurt has drained.

4. Transfer the drained yogurt to a medium bowl. Stir in the sugar. Drain the fruit mixture in a colander.

5. Spoon 1/4 of the yogurt into each parfait glass. Spoon 1/4 of the fruit mixture over the yogurt. Sprinkle with 1/4 of the pecans. Repeat. Serve immediately.

Exchanges/Choices
1 Fat-Free Milk
1 Carbohydrate
1 1/2 Fat

Calories	230	
Calories from Fat	90	
Total Fat	10.0	g
Saturated Fat	0.9	g
Trans Fat	0.0	g
Polyunsaturated Fat	2.9	g
Monounsaturated Fat	6.1	g
Cholesterol	10	mg
Sodium	80	mg
Total Carbohydrate	25	g
Dietary Fiber	3	g
Sugars	21	g
Protein	10	g

INDEX

RECIPES BY SUBJECT